ATMOSPHERIC LANDSCAPES

USING OILS AND COLD WAX

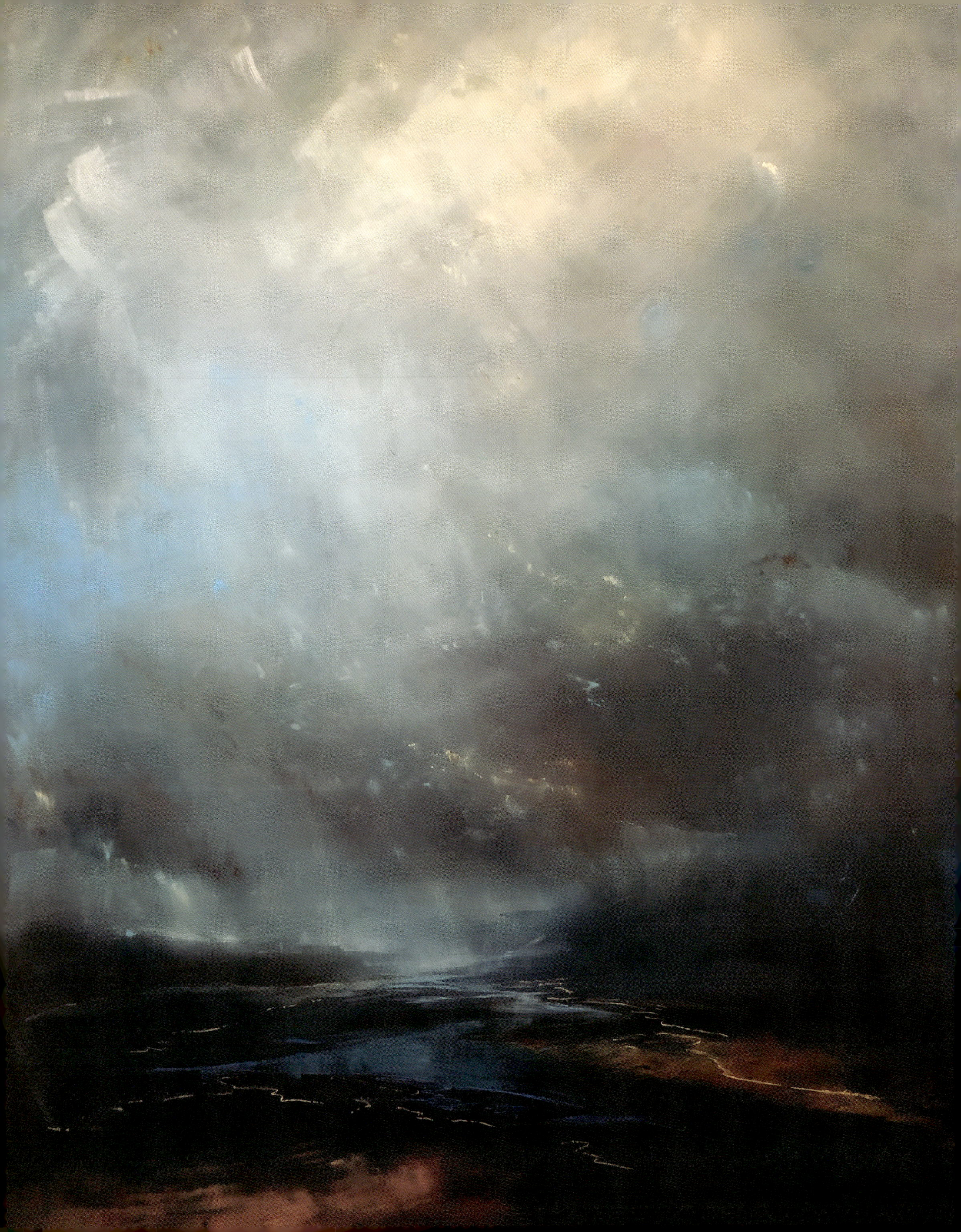

ATMOSPHERIC LANDSCAPES

USING OILS AND COLD WAX

Paula Dunn

THE CROWOOD PRESS

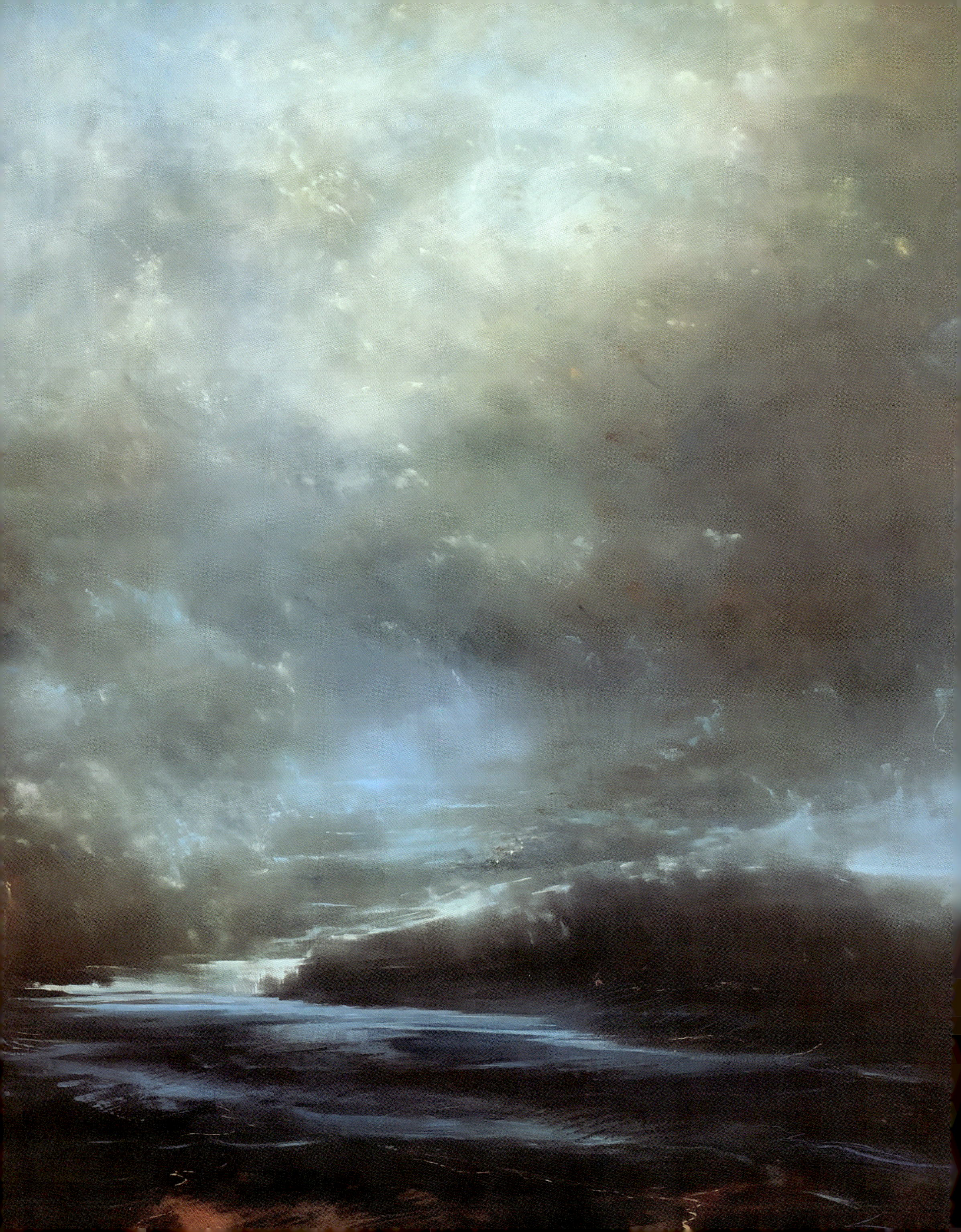

Contents

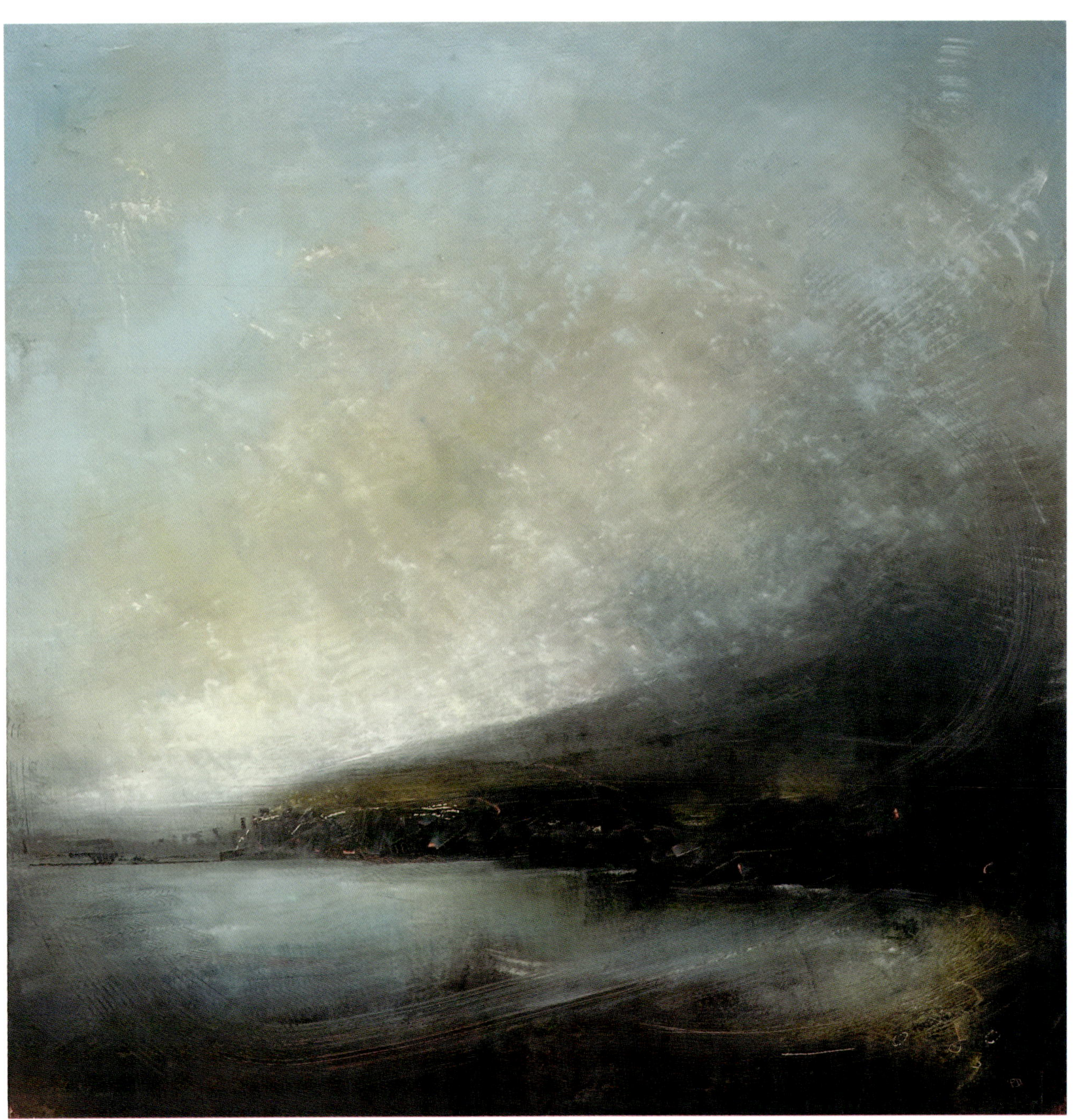

INTRODUCTION

The work of an artist – any artist – should be an evolutionary process, as they deepen their understanding of the artform(s) they practise, the materials they use, their personal style, the subjects that inspire them and how their approach to all these facets combines to produce the 'things' they are creating. All of this is underpinned by exploration, experimentation, and refinement, as well as being shaped by personal experiences and a strengthening connection to the subject matter. Over the years, I have moved away from creating large-scale representational landscapes, defined by thick, textural impasto, to embracing a more experimental and abstract approach with thin, delicate layers of transparent and opaque paint. Although my style – and my practice – have developed, some constants have remained: the influence of the weather, the environment, and the ever-changing light on the landscape, continue to inspire me.

My introduction to cold wax began during a transformative residency in Ireland with the American abstract artist Rebecca Crowell. I found that this medium, which was new to me, allowed me to loosen my approach to painting and explore new possibilities in my work. Cold wax provided a thickness to my paint that I favoured, while also opening doors to a bolder use of colour and texture. This shift encouraged me to move away from using sketches and photographs for reference, instead drawing on memories, emotions, and what I found to be the essence of a place.

Cold wax is a versatile medium that enables artists to explore textures and layering techniques which are distinct from traditional oil painting methods. It has been a revelation for my practice, encouraging experimentation with embedding materials such as marble dust, pigments, and gold leaf, dissolving paints with solvents, and embracing colour in my work. As a result, I have found that the boundaries between abstraction and representation in my art are becoming increasingly blurred.

Historically, the use of wax in painting has its roots in ancient practices, particularly the encaustic, which involved fusing wax and pigment onto the surface of the painting using heat (Doerner, 1921). In the mid-twentieth century, artists began to explore cold wax to create texture and depth without the need for heat, making it more accessible than traditional encaustic methods (Crowell & McLaughlin, 2016). Its recent resurgence owes much to contemporary artists such as Rebecca Crowell, whose encouragement has inspired artists like me to push boundaries, challenge conventional approaches to oil painting, and discover new ways to express ourselves.

Cold wax provides artists at any stage of their practice with the opportunity to work with oils without the daunting complexities often associated with traditional methods. It encourages freer experimentation, allowing for spontaneous techniques that foster innovation and creativity. Throughout the book, I will explore the techniques, possibilities, sharing insights from my own practice with the aim of encouraging you to experiment, take risks, and embrace the joy of creative exploration in your work. Whether you are a seasoned practitioner or just starting out, a landscape painter or an abstract artist, I hope that this book will demonstrate that cold wax offers an exciting and dynamic new dimension to explore when painting in oils.

OPPOSITE: *Where the Curlew Calls*, 60 × 60cm (23½ × 23½in), oils, cold wax and gold leaf on a wooden panel.

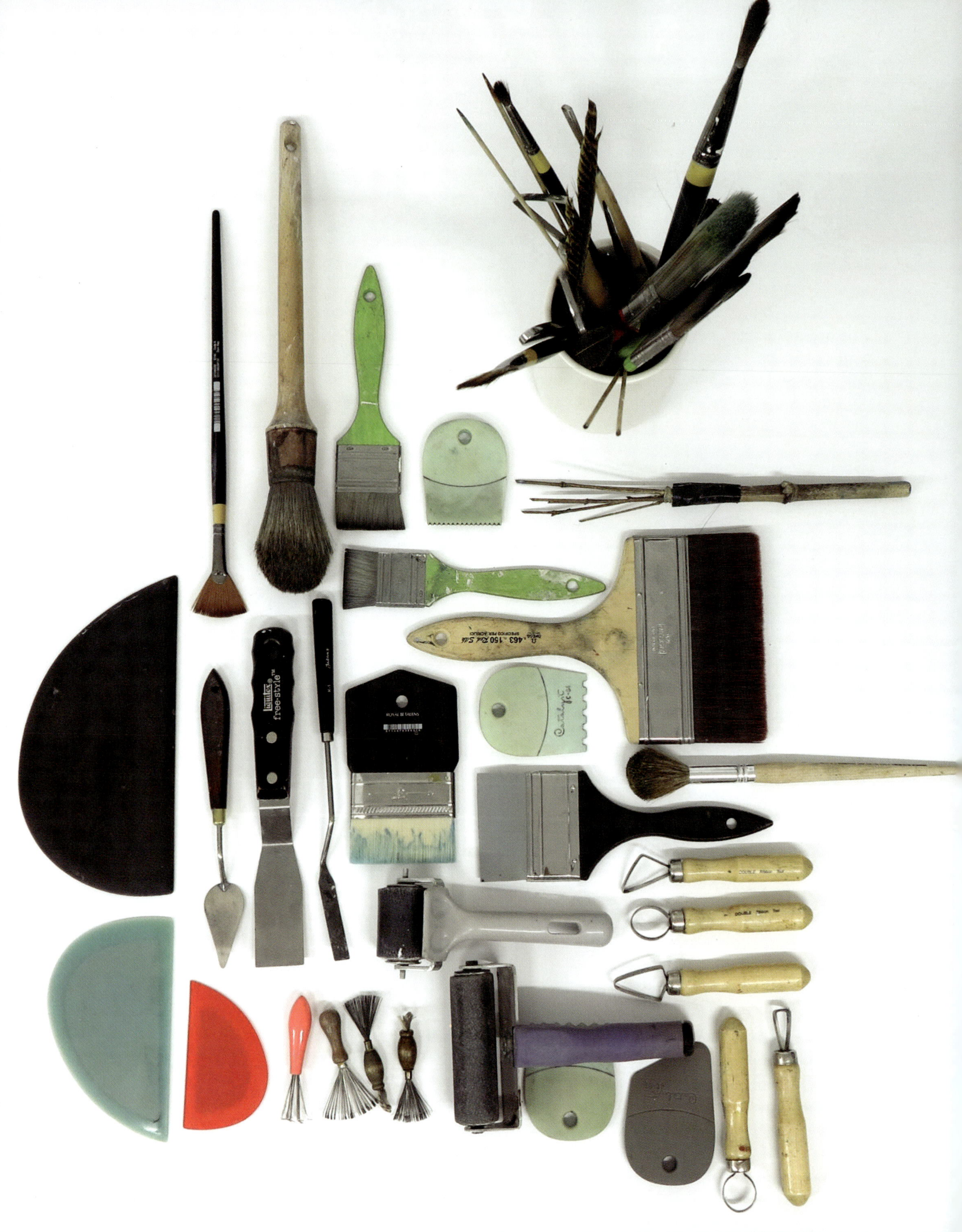
liquitex
free-style™
Catalyst

CHAPTER 1

MATERIALS AND TOOLS

Whether you are looking to create thick, textured surfaces, enhance transparency, or incorporate mixed-media elements such as collage, cold wax offers a versatile medium for experimentation. In this chapter, we explore its benefits, which include preserving marks, speeding up drying times, and adding depth through layering. We will also discuss the various types of cold wax, their ingredients, and how to make your own. Additionally, this chapter will provide practical advice on essential tools and materials, oil colours, solvents, and best practices for maintaining a safe and organised workspace.

WHAT IS COLD WAX?

Cold wax is a versatile medium used with oil paints to alter their texture, consistency, and drying time, offering a wide range of creative possibilities for artists. Like other oil painting mediums, it can change the behaviour of your paints depending on the effects you want to achieve, such as making paint more fluid, thickening it, or adjusting drying speed. It can even be used as a varnish for oil, acrylic, and watercolour paintings.

Cold wax is typically a blend of beeswax, solvent, and resin. The solvent softens the beeswax, creating a paste that can be easily mixed with oil paints. Unlike encaustic painting, which requires heat to melt the wax, cold wax does not. Instead, the paint dries as the solvent evaporates, and the resin helps to harden the paint surface.

Benefits of using cold wax

One of the most exciting aspects of cold wax is the freedom it provides for experimentation and playfulness in your work. Cold wax opens up a world of creative possibilities, from building thick textures to embedding collage materials, found objects, or pigments. It also facilitates the layering of both opaque and transparent colours, helping to add atmospheric depth in your paintings.

Textural effects: Before using cold wax, my approach was often impasto, creating thick, textured paintings. However, when I scratched into wet oil paint, the paint would seep back into the marks, softening the lines. Cold wax, on the other hand, thickens the paint, allowing you to work with wet-on-wet layers while maintaining the sharpness of your marks. This means you can preserve the detail of scratches and create additional texture through sgraffito or impasto techniques. You can even incorporate materials such as sand or marble dust to enhance the texture further.

Matt finish: Mixing cold wax into your oils will reduce the inherent glossiness of the paint, giving it a more matt finish that persists throughout the painting process. If you prefer a silk sheen or gloss, this can be achieved later during the varnishing stage (*see* Chapter 10).

OPPOSITE: From baking tools to fan brushes, and from brush combs to barbecue sticks, the essential tools for working with oils and cold wax are crucial to the painting process. Each tool serves a specific purpose, offering versatility in mixing, applying, and mark-making. Together, they enable you to create a wide range of textures and effects in your paintings.

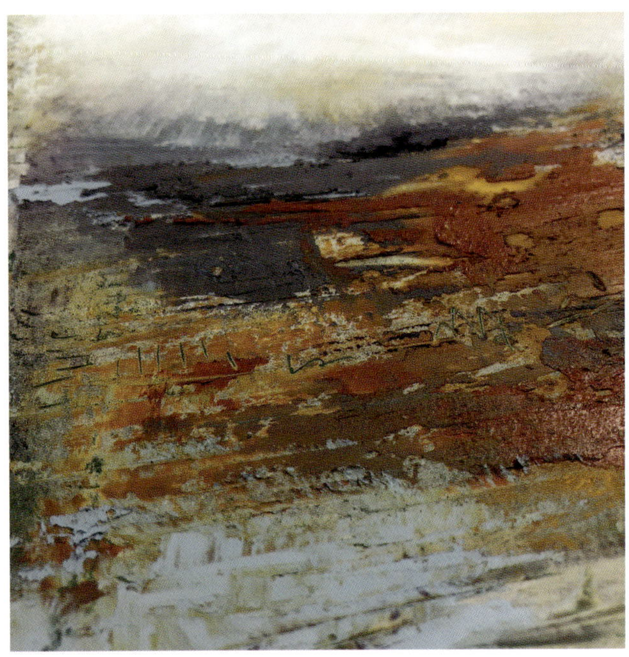

You can use oils and cold wax to create impasto effects, which can produce engaging and visually dynamic surfaces. In this example, a variety of colours were applied with a palette knife, layering them on top of one another to build thick textures and depth.

Transparency and depth: Cold wax increases the transparency of oil paints, making it easier to build depth and luminosity. This allows you to experiment with layers of transparent and opaque colours, creating beautiful glowing effects and subtle tonal shifts.

Faster drying time: Cold wax can speed up the drying process of oil paints, but its effect is somewhat variable. While oils generally take longer to dry, the addition of cold wax can help them become touch-dry within a day and fully dry within a couple of weeks, depending on factors such as the thickness of your paint, air flow, temperature, and the specific pigments used. However, it is important to note that cold wax does not speed up drying as dramatically as acrylic paints, which dry much faster, but it still offers a noticeable reduction in drying time compared to traditional oils without any medium.

Mixed media opportunities: Cold wax can behave like an adhesive, making it ideal for embedding dry pigments, thin collage papers, metallic leaf, and other materials into your paintings. This opens up exciting opportunities for multimedia work, allowing you to combine different textures, materials, and pigments. I often incorporate marble dust, pigments, and metallic leaf into my work, adding another dimension to my paintings.

Is it fat or is it lean? There is a rule associated with oil painting referred to as 'fat over lean': in basic terms, this means you should avoid applying thinned down (lean) paint over thicker (fat) undiluted paint. The thicker your paint, the more slowly it will dry, which can result in the thin paint cracking and flaking. Some say that using cold wax eliminates the need to consider this, whereas others suggest that adding cold wax is diluting your paints and therefore creating a 'lean' paint. I have introduced so many people to oils over the years who had previously avoided them because they were seen as complex with too many rules, taking the joy out of painting. My experience with using cold wax is that it enables you to be more playful and experimental in your work. While understanding your materials and how they behave is important, experimentation and pushing boundaries is equally, if not more important, both in terms of the work you create and the process of getting there.

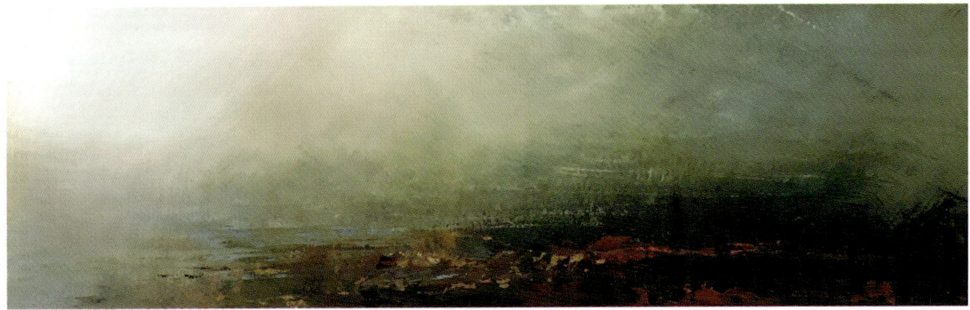

Gloaming, 37 × 12cm (14½ × 4¾in), oil and cold wax on Arches Huile paper. This piece was created using a squeegee for blending and a palette knife to apply impasto, adding texture and depth. Metallic pigments were carefully embedded into the surface with a brush, imparting a subtle flash of light that enhances the autumnal atmosphere of the painting.

TYPES OF COLD WAX

There are various brands of cold wax available, each with its unique formula and characteristics. If you are new to cold wax, it is worth experimenting with a few different brands to find the one that best suits your painting style and studio environment. Key factors to consider when choosing a cold wax medium include the solvent used (some have a strong smell), and the overall consistency of the wax. It is also important to check ingredient compatibility, as some plant-based resins may not work well with synthetic resins. If you are uncertain, it is safest to stick with one brand to avoid any potential issues with incompatibility.

Below is an overview of some of the most popular cold wax brands, focusing on their unique qualities, consistency, and performance with some of the techniques covered in this book. To evaluate these brands, I conducted experiments using Arches Huile paper and a limited palette of ultramarine blue, alizarin crimson, and titanium white. I tested each cold wax for its effectiveness in layering wet-on-wet, ease of blending, effective mark-making, solvent reduction, and glazing to unify the surface.

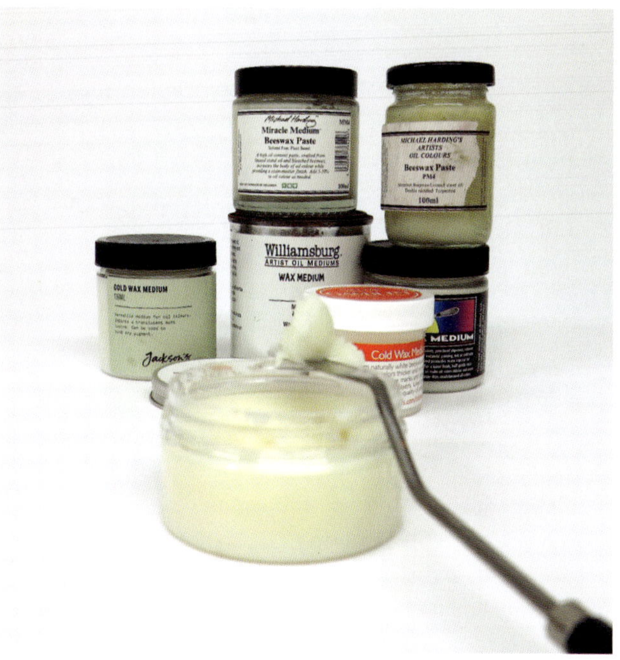

There are several cold wax brands available, each offering unique formulas and characteristics. Experimenting with different brands can help you find the one that best suits your painting style and studio environment. When choosing, consider factors such as the solvent used, the consistency of the wax, and ingredient compatibility to ensure optimal results.

Gamblin cold wax medium

Made from: Pure beeswax, alkyd resin, and Gamsol odourless solvent
Availability: Gamblin is a US-based company and its cold wax is widely available internationally
Smell: Slight waxy odour
Colour: White, transparent
Mix used: 50:50

Observations
This is the medium I use in my own work, and I have developed and refined my own techniques based on its performance. It has a short, grainy texture that produces peaks when mixed with oil paints and instantly turns the oils matt. The thick consistency allows for easy layering of colours wet-on-wet, while staying wet enough to enable smooth colour blending without overmixing, preserving the vibrancy of individual hues. It creates well-defined marks when scratched into, as well as when using solvent reduction techniques. A final unifying layer was easily applied wet-on-wet, and the paintings were touch-dry within 24 hours.

Dorlands cold wax medium

Made from: A blend of waxes, damar resin, and odourless mineral spirits
Availability: Dorlands is made by Jacquard, a US-based company, and is widely available internationally
Smell: Slight waxy odour
Colour: White, transparent
Mix used: 50:50

Observations
This cold wax has the shortest consistency of those tested in this experiment. It creates peaks when mixed with oil paints and instantly turns the oils matt. Its slightly thicker texture makes layering colours wet-on-wet effortless, while remaining wet enough to allow for effective colour blending. The added thickness also enhances the definition of marks when scratched into and performs particularly well with solvent reduction techniques. However, applying a final unifying layer wet-on-wet felt slightly stiff, resulting in a thicker layer of colour. The paintings were touch-dry within 24 hours.

Jackson's cold wax medium

Made from: A blend of different waxes and resins, including damar resin
Availability: UK-based art supplier which ships worldwide.
Smell: No detectable odour
Colour: White, transparent
Mix used: 50:50

Observations
This cold wax has a smooth consistency which is easily mixed with oil paints. It is not as short as Gamblin or Dorlands, and leaves the oil mixture with a soft sheen. The first layer of paint was easy to apply; however, the second layer working wet-on-wet was a little slippery and care was needed to retain the individual layers of colour. It creates well-defined marks when scratched into, as well as when using solvent reduction techniques. A final unifying layer was applied wet-on-wet, which did lead to a little colour mixing. The paintings were touch-dry within 24 hours.

Zest-it cold wax medium

Made from: A blend of waxes, linseed, aliphatic hydrocarbon, damar, citrus oil
Availability: UK-based company with availability primarily in the UK and Ireland
Smell: Strong citrus odour which can be overwhelming, especially when working with it for extended periods
Colour: Yellow, transparent
Mix used: 50:50

Observations
The medium has a short, sticky, grainy texture that creates a satin sheen when mixed with oils. This sticky consistency makes it challenging to pull across thin layers wet-on-wet, though the colour blending proves very effective. While it produces well-defined marks when scratched into, the medium is initially less responsive to solvent reduction techniques, particularly when attempting to cut back to lower layers or create precise marks. These effects can be achieved through repeated use of solvent or by allowing the solvent to sit longer on the surface. The final unifying layer felt stiff, which resulted in some unintended colour mixing. The paintings were dry to the touch within 24 hours.

Michael Harding beeswax paste

Made from: Pure bleached beeswax, linseed stand oil and turpentine. As this medium does not contain resin, it will not achieve the same hardening characteristics of true cold wax mediums
Availability: UK-based company and product is widely available internationally
Smell: Strong smell of turpentine and linseed
Colour: Yellow, transparent
Mix used: 10 per cent

Observations
This medium adds some body to the oil paints while maintaining a slick, glossy consistency, unlike cold wax mediums which notably stiffen and thicken the paint. Its wet nature makes it challenging to apply thin layers wet-on-wet while preserving colour integrity, though it excels at producing beautiful, vibrant colour blends. When scratched into, the paint tends to creep back into the marks rather than maintaining crisp definitions, though it responds well to solvent reduction techniques.

The slick quality of the medium led to unwanted blending with the unifying layer. Paintings remained wet for a lengthy period of time, so the medium did not speed up the drying process. Users should note its strong odour, which can become overwhelming during extended use. While the medium creates striking colour blends that may prove valuable in other applications, it lacks the thick consistency needed for the techniques presented in this book.

Michael Harding Miracle Medium™ beeswax paste

Made from: Miracle Medium™, bleached beeswax, linseed stand oil
Availability: UK-based company and product is widely available internationally
Smell: Odourless
Colour: White, transparent
Mix used: 10 per cent

Observations:
Michael Harding's new product replaces traditional solvents with their plant-based Miracle Medium™

offering a safer and more environmentally friendly alternative to their standard beeswax paste. In this experiment, it largely mirrors the properties of their traditional beeswax paste, with one notable difference: during the unifying layer stage, the medium not only tends to over-blend, but also develops a sticky, stringy consistency. Like its predecessor, however, this medium lacks the thick body necessary for executing the techniques presented in this book.

Williamsburg® wax medium

Made from: Bleached beeswax, linseed stand oil, damar resin
Availability: Owned by Golden, a US-based company and is widely available internationally
Smell: Smells of linseed oil
Colour: Yellow, transparent
Mix used: 20 per cent

Observations:
This medium adds body to oil paints and has a slick, glossy, and grainy texture. While it allows for easy application of thin layers of paint, it presents challenges with over-blending, which leads to the reduction in light and dark tones. The medium's consistency fails to maintain defined marks when scratched into, and solvent reduction techniques removed too much paint and failed to create the crisp marks usually associated with solvent splashes. Its slick properties caused further issues during the unifying layer stage, resulting in uncontrolled blending. Paintings remained wet for a significant period. Given these characteristics, the medium lacks the necessary consistency for successfully executing the techniques presented in this book.

The stiffer cold wax mediums proved to be the most effective for layering wet-on-wet, blending, mark-making, solvent reduction, and glazing techniques discussed in this book. The top row (left to right) features Gamblin, Jackson's, and Dorland's, while the bottom row (left to right) includes Zest-it, Michael Harding Miracle Medium beeswax, and Williamsburg.

MAKING YOUR OWN COLD WAX MEDIUM

If you are feeling adventurous and want to create your own cold wax medium, the process is relatively simple, though it does require some basic equipment, such as an electric hotplate. Making your own cold wax can be both fun and rewarding, offering the opportunity to customise the medium to suit your specific needs. My preferred recipe is adapted from *Cold Wax Medium: Techniques, Concepts & Conversations* (Crowell & McLaughlin, 2016, page 46). To create your own cold wax medium, you will need the following materials:

- 11-parts bleached or unbleached beeswax – I recommend buying beeswax pellets rather than the blocks, as this is much easier to measure and melts more quickly.
- 1-part damar resin crystals – To help with measuring and to speed up melting, put your damar resin in a plastic bag and use a hammer to crush the crystals into smaller chunks.

- 12-parts odourless solvent – Be careful when handling solvents; use gloves and be sure to wipe up spills immediately.

As with the original recipe, I have found that the easiest way to measure these ingredients is by using a small, clean tin or ramekin, filling it according to the specified measurement. This method ensures accurate measurements, while keeping things simple and, in my experience, reduces mess compared to using scales. You will also need the following:

- a hotplate
- a metal pan preferably with a pouring lip
- a clean tin or ramekin for measurement
- wooden spoons
- funnels
- clean metal tins or jars for storage
- cheesecloth for filtering
- a flat work surface covered with oilcloth to prevent damage.

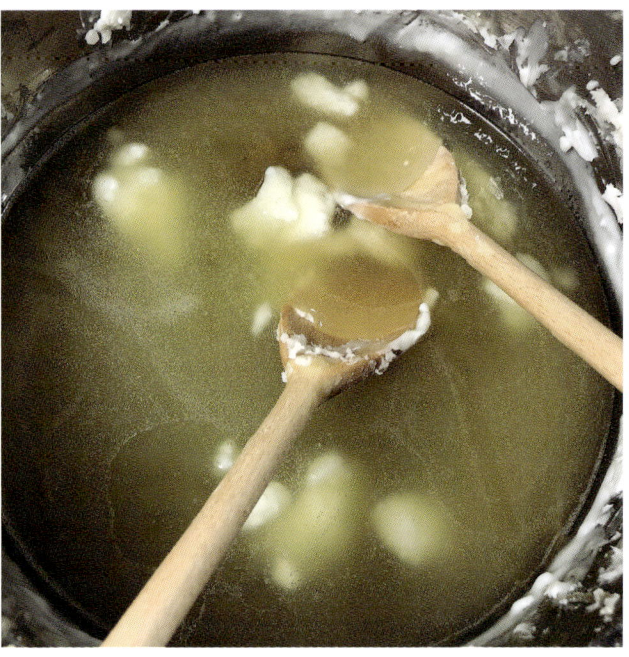

Be patient, as beeswax can take a little time to fully melt. Stir the resin and beeswax mixture continuously with a wooden spoon to ensure it melts evenly. If the mixture begins to smoke, immediately remove it from the heat and lower the temperature. Always work in a well-ventilated area to maintain proper airflow and minimise any health risks.

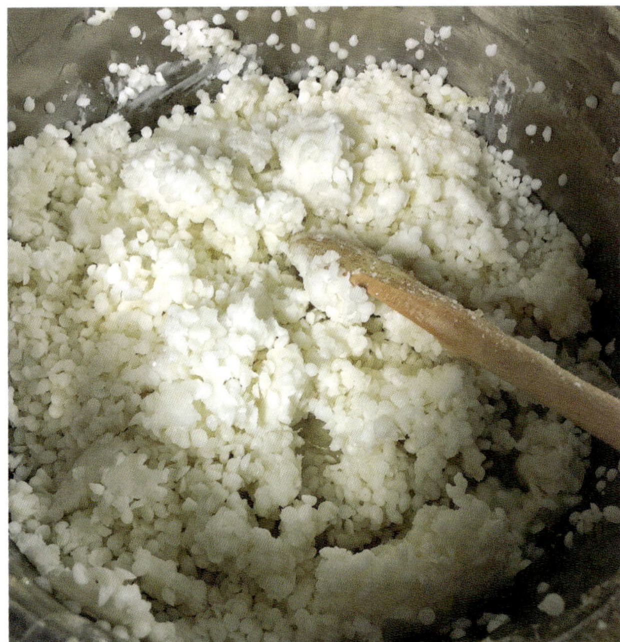

Buy beeswax pellets instead of blocks, as they are easier to measure and melt more quickly. Using pellets also saves you the time and effort of cutting or grating blocks. Once you have melted the damar resin, add the pellets to the mixture and stir continuously. This will help the beeswax dissolve evenly and mix in with the resin.

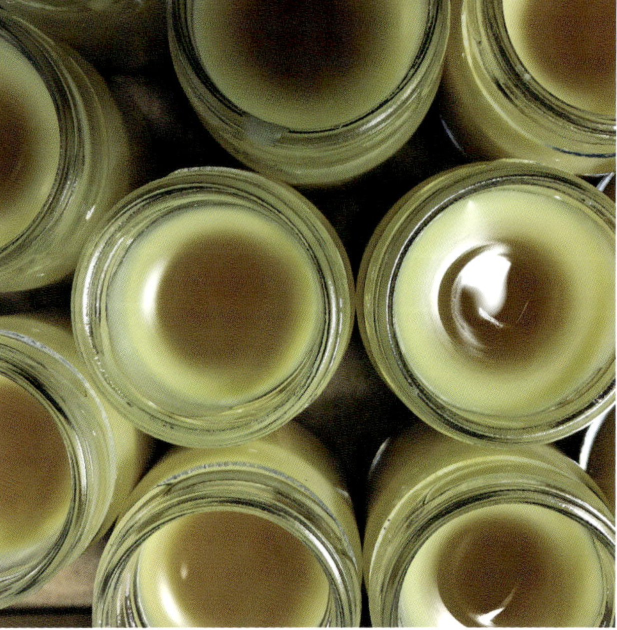

While the mixture is still liquid, carefully pour it into clean metal tins or glass jars for storage, using a funnel to avoid spills. Allow the cold wax to cool completely before sealing the containers with lids. Make sure to label each jar or tin with the ingredients and date of preparation for future reference, ensuring easy identification when needed.

Instructions

1. **Heat the damar resin**: Begin by placing the crushed damar resin crystals into a metal pan on the hotplate. Damar resin requires a higher temperature to melt than beeswax, so once it has liquefied, reduce the heat slightly.
2. **Filter the resin**: Damar is a plant-based resin and unfiltered crystals may contain plant or insect residue. You can melt the resin and filter it using cheesecloth before adding the beeswax to avoid any impurities in your wax mixture. You will need to work quickly as the resin will become sticky and will quickly harden as soon as you take it off the heat.
3. **Add the beeswax**: Once the damar has melted, add the beeswax, and continue to heat until it fully liquefies. If at any point the mixture begins to smoke, remove it from the heat and lower the temperature. Ensure your workspace is well ventilated.
4. **Add the solvent**: Once the beeswax and resin have melted, remove the pan from the hotplate and turn off the heat. Slowly pour in the solvent, stirring constantly to combine.
5. **Decant the mixture**: Whilst the mixture is still liquid, carefully (as it will be hot) decant it into metal tins or glass jars for storage. A funnel can help with this. Allow the cold wax to cool completely before sealing the containers with lids and labelling them with the ingredients for future reference.
6. **Clean tools**: Be sure to clean your pan and utensils with solvent before the wax hardens, as it can be difficult to remove once set.

PAINTING TOOLS

In this section, we cover the essential tools for working with oils and cold wax, each playing a vital role in the painting process. These tools offer versatility in mixing, applying, and manipulating paint, helping you achieve a wide range of textures and effects.

Silicon squeegee (also known as a blade)

The squeegee originated as a baking utensil for scraping mixture out of a bowl and has now become the go-to tool for artists who use oils and cold wax. It is used to apply thin layers of paint, for blending, as well as for mark-making and comes in a range of sizes. I find that the 6-inch squeegee is just the right size and does not place too much strain on my hands. I will also use a smaller squeegee when I am working on details as it allows me to blend in more intricate areas without disturbing paint in the surrounding area. There are a range of tools available made from silicon, both art tools and cookery tools, some being more flexible than others so it is worth experimenting to see what effects you can achieve with these tools.

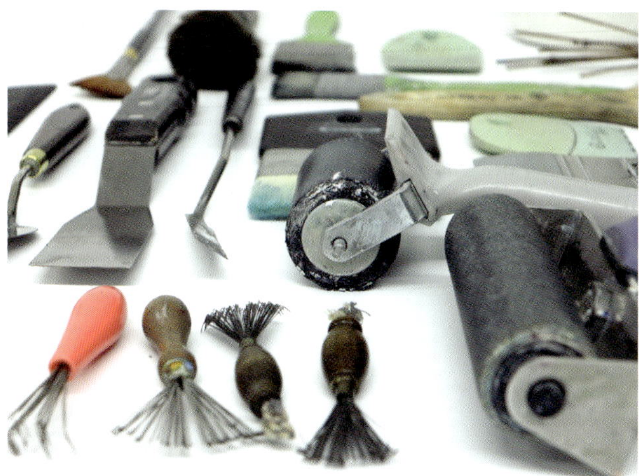

These tools provide flexibility for mixing, applying, and manipulating paint, allowing you to achieve diverse textures and effects. From baking tools and fan brushes to brush combs and barbecue sticks, each plays a vital role in the oil and cold wax painting process. Designed for specific tasks, they enhance mark-making and application techniques, expanding the creative possibilities in your work.

Brushes

My approach to mark-making, solvent application, and blending relies primarily on brushes, each selected for its specific qualities and purpose. For broad strokes and solvent application, a basic household paintbrush serves well, while a large mottler or mop brush excels at bold, sweeping marks across expansive areas. The varying bristle qualities, from soft to stiff, produce a range of textural effects, from feathery strokes to bold, dramatic marks.

Blending demands more specialised tools: a soft synthetic fan brush is ideal for subtle colour transitions, while a synthetic flat brush handles larger areas effectively. For detailed work, fine brushes such as riggers or long-haired liners create flowing, delicate lines that add movement and fluidity to the composition. A medium flat brush offers a contrasting option, producing squared or angular edges that complement the softer lines, creating dynamic visual tension in a painting.

Palette knives

Palette knives are incredibly versatile tools used not only for mixing and applying paint, but also for creating a wide variety of marks and textures. Their primary function is to mix paint, but they can also be used directly on the surface to apply the paint, scrape away areas of the painting, or create impasto effects. Having a selection of palette knives in different shapes and sizes is essential for achieving a broad range of marks in your work.

Brayers and rollers

Brayers and rollers are invaluable for various painting techniques, from blending and paint application to mark-making and for embedding materials. The choice between soft and hard rollers significantly impacts their effectiveness: soft brayers are good for working paint into scratched and textured areas, conforming to surface irregularities to ensure even coverage. In contrast, hard rubber brayers tend to skip over these textured areas, though they can create interesting effects.

These tools come in a range of sizes, from small handheld rollers perfect for detailed work to larger versions ideal for covering expansive areas. The width of the roller affects not only the scale of marks possible, but also the pressure distribution across the surface. Smaller brayers offer more precise control for intricate patterns and textures, while larger ones facilitate uniform blending across broader areas. When selecting a brayer, consider both the scale of your work and the specific techniques you plan to use them for, as the right size can significantly impact the effectiveness of your process.

Other mark-making tools

There are many tools available for creating a wide range of mark-making possibilities, some of which you can easily find in your kitchen. Barbecue sticks and forks are all readily accessible and perfect for making unique marks. If you are looking to expand your tool collection, one of my earlier discoveries was a brush comb, which now features regularly in my work. Another valuable addition are the Princeton Catalyst contour tools, available in various shapes and edges. These tools are rigid enough to scratch back into your painting or scrape off layers of paint, offering great versatility for texture and detail.

Palettes

When it comes to mixing paints, having the right surface is essential. While traditional wooden palettes have long been favoured by artists, today there are many alternatives to choose from. Disposable paper palettes, often made from wax-coated paper, offer the convenience of easy clean-up. Alternatively, freezer paper or greaseproof paper can serve as an affordable and accessible option. Glass palettes have become increasingly popular due to their smooth surface and ease of cleaning. Although you can purchase dedicated glass palettes from art suppliers, a more budget-friendly alternative is to use a glass place mat, available at most kitchenware stores. For artists who need a larger mixing surface, a glass table protector can make an excellent, cost-effective choice.

COLOURS

Oil paints are renowned for their rich, buttery texture and come in an extensive range of colours. With so many options available, the selection can quickly become overwhelming and expensive. To simplify things, I recommend starting with a few essential colours before deciding on whether to expand your range. These include both warm and cool versions of the primary colours, some opaque and some transparent, providing versatility for mixing and creating a wide range of colours. They are:

- Titanium white
- Cerulean blue
- Ultramarine blue
- Alizarin crimson
- Cadmium red (or Scarlet)
- Cadmium yellow deep (or Indian yellow)
- Lemon yellow

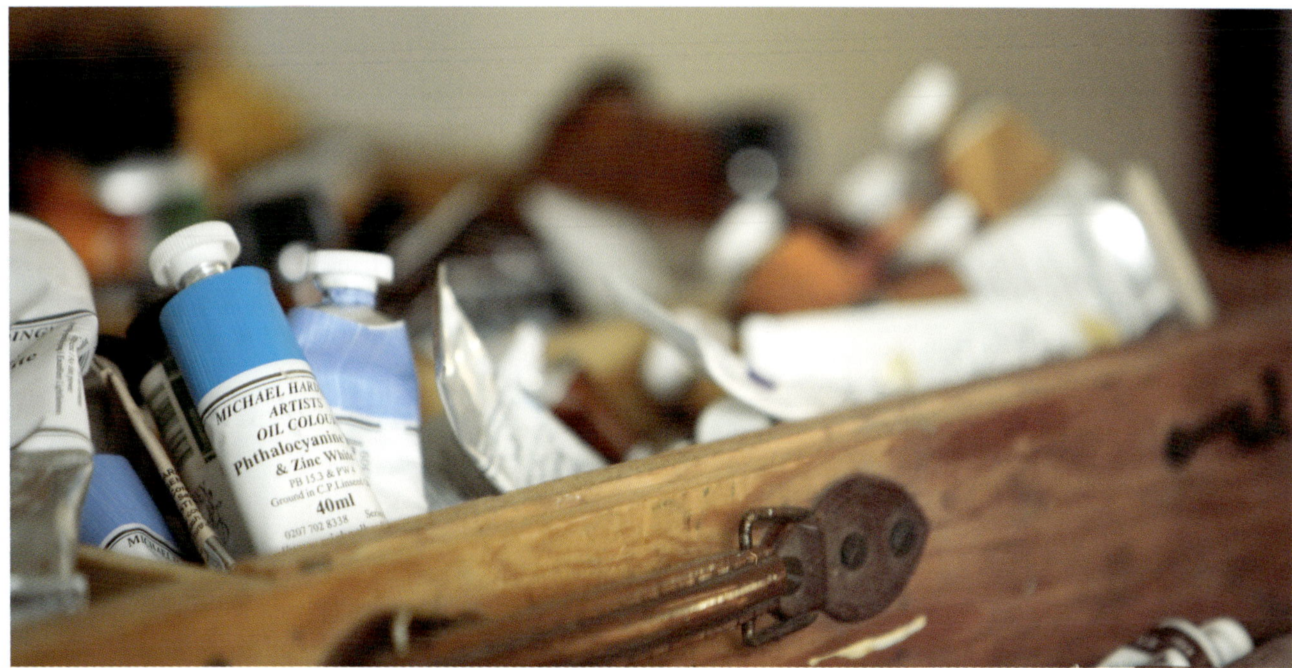

When selecting oils, opt for artist-quality paints such as Michael Harding, Sennelier, Wallace Seymour, Jackson's, and Gamblin. These paints have a higher pigment concentration, meaning you need less to achieve the desired intensity and coverage. While the initial cost is higher, they yield more vibrant, lasting results and require less paint compared to student-grade options.

Whenever possible, opt for artist-quality paints over student-grade ones. Artist-quality paints contain a higher concentration of pigment, meaning you will need less paint to achieve the desired intensity and coverage. While the initial cost is higher, this investment pays off in the long run by achieving more vibrant, lasting results while generally using less paint overall.

Water-mixable oils

Water-mixable oils are a type of oil paint that have been modified to allow the use of water instead of traditional solvents for both thinning the paint and cleaning brushes. Many artists prefer these paints, especially those who are sensitive to solvents. However, when incorporating cold wax into your painting process, the benefits of using water-mixable oils are diminished. This is because cold wax contains solvents, and the wax itself is not water-soluble. As a result, cleaning your tools becomes more challenging, requiring solvents or an excessive amount of soap. If you already use water-mixable oils, there is no reason for you not to use them with cold wax, but keep in mind that you will not be able to thin your paint with water as you typically would.

Oil sticks, oil bars and Pigment Sticks®

Oil sticks, oil bars and Pigment Sticks® are oil paints in a solid form, offering a unique way to apply pigment directly to the surface of your painting. I find them particularly useful for making initial marks and for adding colour to the dry surface of a painting, as they provide the freedom to create bold, expressive strokes. They can also be used creatively for making transfer papers, which are discussed in Chapter 7.

I am especially fond of R&F Pigment Sticks®, which come in a wide range of colours and levels of transparency. R&F describe them as 'lipstick soft', which is a fitting description, as they do glide effortlessly over the surface of a painting. These sticks differ from other

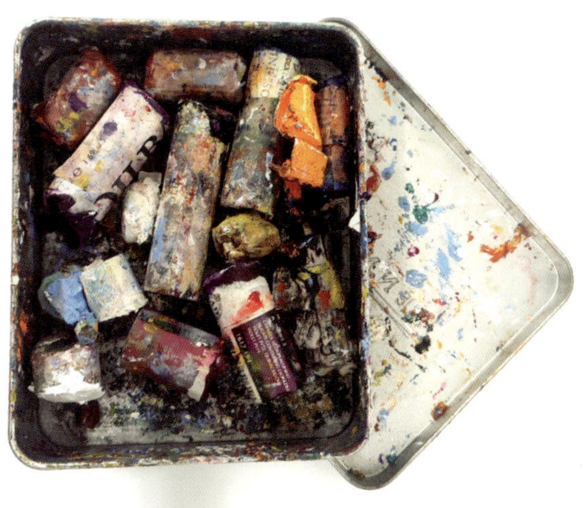

The primary difference between these products is their composition. Sennelier and Winsor & Newton oil bars contain mineral wax mixed with oil, while R&F Pigment Sticks® use beeswax, resulting in a softer, more malleable consistency. These sticks typically form a thick skin as they dry, which must be peeled away to access the softer paint underneath.

brands such as Winsor & Newton or Sennelier, which are stiffer and have more of a crayon-like texture. If you are new to these products, I recommend trying sample packs first, as this allows you to experiment and decide if they suit your practice before making an investment.

Dry pigments

Dry pigments are the colours which form the foundation of all paints and offer artists opportunities to incorporate colour in their work beyond pre-mixed paints. While traditionally used by artists who created their own paints, dry pigments have found a place in mixed-media work.

When building your pigment collection, start with a few vibrant colours which complement your palette. These concentrated colours can be sprinkled directly into a wet painting for brilliant pops of colour, mixed with cold wax to create a coloured paste, or used to create transfer papers (*see* Chapter 7). While pigments offer extraordinary creative potential, they do require careful handling. Store them in secure containers, work in a well-ventilated space, and consider wearing a mask when handling loose pigments.

TAPES

If you are working on paper, artist-quality masking tape is essential. It not only secures your paper to a surface for easier handling and painting, but it also creates crisp white borders which frame your work beautifully. Masking tapes vary in price, with some unnecessarily packaged in plastic containers. Good masking tape should be tacky enough to prevent oil paint seepage, but not so sticky that it damages your paper. If you find that your tape is too sticky, you can press it onto your jeans first to reduce tackiness.

SOLVENTS

Solvents are essential to my studio practice, serving not only as a tool for cleaning, but also as a key element in my painting process. I often use them for reduction techniques – brushing, pouring, or splashing solvent – which allows me to manipulate the paint dynamically, pushing and pulling it across the surface until the composition naturally reveals its direction. This process enables me to experiment with textures and layers, bringing depth and movement to my paintings.

When selecting a solvent, it is important to consider factors such as odour, flashpoints, and chemical composition. Odourless solvents are a popular choice for minimising unpleasant smells, but even these can release harmful vapours. Proper ventilation is essential, regardless of the solvent used. Additionally, while some solvents are marketed as environmentally friendly, they may still cause adverse reactions in certain individuals. Testing different options is key to finding what works best for you and your environment.

For my studio and workshops, I use Gamblin's odourless solvent, Gamsol, which is one of the safest options available. Another effective choice is Shellsol T, a low-odour solvent with a slight earthy smell. Both work well for the solvent reduction techniques described in this book. For those seeking natural alternatives, lavender spike serves as a substitute for turpentine and mineral spirits, although its scent can be overpowering, especially for artists using it frequently. An odourless, plant-based alternative to solvent is Michael Harding's Miracle

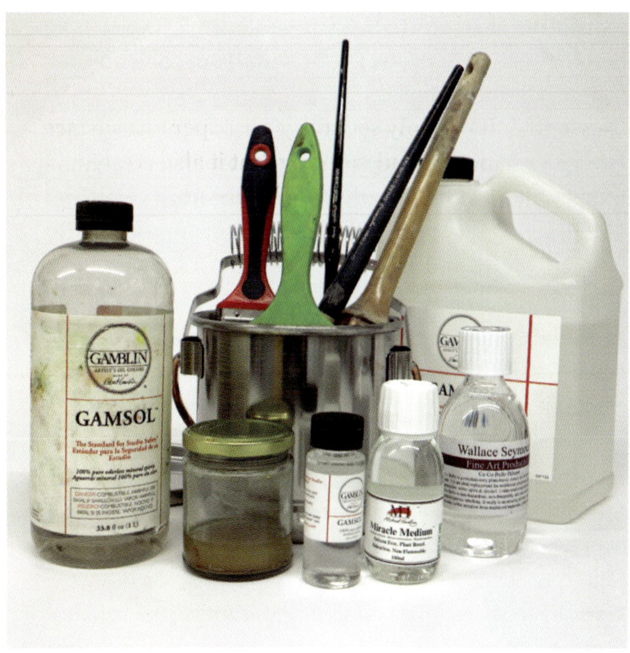

In my workshops and studio, I use Gamblin's Gamsol. For a solvent-free option, Michael Harding's *Miracle Medium* offers a low-toxic, plant-based alternative. To clean my brushes, I use a brush washer, which allows you to suspend brushes without damage and features a lid to minimise fumes when not in use.

Medium™, which provides a safer, eco-friendly option for studio use.

Ultimately, the best solvent depends on your personal needs, studio environment, and health considerations. Always prioritise safety by ensuring good ventilation and using protective equipment when necessary.

OTHER MEDIUMS

Incorporating additional mediums into your oil paints alongside cold wax can help create a more fluid mixture, which is beneficial for certain techniques in this book. A more fluid consistency allows for organic marks and a dynamic flow across the surface.

One option is to add solvent, which will thin your paint by dissolving it. While this will increase the flow of your paint significantly it can also lead to a less flexible paint which could lead to cracking. Alternatively, adding linseed oil can enhance the fluidity of your paint while still retaining some viscosity. This option creates a softer, more spreadable consistency, making blending easier, especially if you find the cold wax too stiff for achieving smooth transitions. Linseed oil will also add a satin sheen and will increase the drying time of your oils.

Liquin is another popular medium for increasing flow. It has a more fluid texture than linseed oil, dries faster, and also adds a slight sheen to your paints. You might also consider using Gamblin's Galkyd, Galkyd Lite, or Solvent-Free Fluid to achieve a more fluid mix than linseed oil or Liquin can provide. These mediums will provide you with a brushable consistency, will further increase transparency, and will also add a sheen to your paints.

If you are working on flexible surfaces, such as stretched canvas, or using high amounts of cold wax (that is, 75 per cent or more in your mix), adding Gamblin's Solvent-Free Gel, Galkyd Gel, or Galkyd Lite Gel can help maintain the body of your wax while providing the flexibility you need.

WHERE TO WORK

You can paint on a flat surface, an easel, or even against a wall, with each option offering its own advantages depending on the size and style of your work. For smaller paintings on paper, I prefer working on a flat surface, which I cover with oilcloth to make it easier to clean up while protecting the underlying surface of my workbench. When I work on larger paintings, I typically use a cradled panel placed against a wall in my studio, often utilising the grid system I have installed, which allows me to adjust the position of the painting vertically as I work. Having the painting upright also helps me check the perspective, which can become distorted with larger paintings when they are laid flat. If you do not have access to wall space, an easel is a great alternative, offering flexibility for standing or sitting while painting.

I am fortunate to have a studio space where I can alternate between working flat on my workbench and moving my pieces to the wall for larger-scale projects. However, if you do not have a dedicated studio, any clean, flat surface will work. When I first started painting, I worked from my kitchen table, eventually moving into my basement, which was a big improvement as it gave me the freedom to leave my work set up without needing to pack

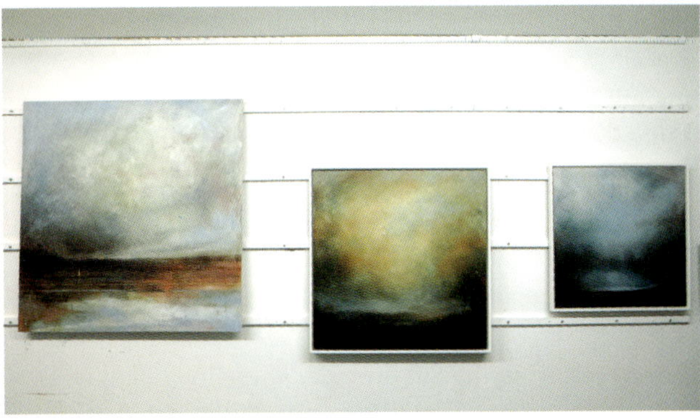

I installed a grid system in my studio to maximise space and easily adjust the position of paintings on the wall while working. This simple DIY project involved attaching wooden battens to the wall and adding screws that protrude just enough to hang paintings securely. The spacing aligns with the dimensions of my most-used cradled wooden panels.

everything away at the end of the day. I worked from that basement studio for ten years before I was ready to rent a separate studio space away from home. If you are just starting out and do not have a dedicated workspace, my advice is not to wait for the perfect setup to come along. Find a table, cover it with something protective, and start painting!

GOOD STUDIO PRACTICE

Working with oils and cold wax is generally safe, but it is essential to understand the materials you are using and adopt safe practices in your workspace to minimise any risks to your health and the environment. Below are some key practices to follow to ensure a safe and efficient working environment.

Safety guidelines for your workspace

Wear protective clothing: To avoid damaging clothing consider wearing old clothes or a protective apron.

Minimise skin contact with solvents: Use gloves or barrier creams to protect your skin from solvents and other harsh chemicals.

Cover any cuts or abrasions: Use a plaster or bandage to prevent dirt and chemicals from entering any open wounds.

Wash your hands regularly: Always wash your hands thoroughly at the end of each session, and especially before eating or touching your face. Remove protective clothing before eating to avoid cross-contamination.

Avoid eating or drinking in the workspace: Keep food and drink away from your work area to prevent accidental ingestion of harmful materials.

Use solvents safely: Solvents can irritate the respiratory system and are flammable. Always keep your workspace well ventilated when using solvents and wear protective masks where necessary.

Control solvent exposure: Limit your exposure to solvents, as prolonged inhalation can lead to dizziness or nausea. Ensure that solvent containers are sealed when not in use.

Handle pigments with care: Some dry pigments may contain hazardous substances. Wear a mask and gloves as necessary and use a damp cloth for cleaning up any pigment spills.

Ventilation and breaks: Ensure your workspace is well ventilated and take regular breaks to step outside and get fresh air.

Clean up spills immediately: Promptly clean up any spills to reduce hazards.

Store materials safely: Always store paints, solvents, and other materials in properly labelled, secure containers.

Cleaning up

Cleaning your tools regularly is essential when working with cold wax, as the wax can harden quickly, making removal much more difficult. I make it a habit of cleaning my tools at the end of each session to ensure they are ready for my next time in the studio. It is equally important to dispose of waste responsibly. Never pour oil paints or solvents down the sink, as they are toxic and can pollute the water supply.

Here are some suggestions for how to clean up effectively and responsibly:

Remove excess paint: Wipe or scrape excess paint off your palette and tools before cleaning. Use old rags, scrim, or paper towels to remove as much paint as possible. Use palette knives to scrape off any hardened oils and cold wax from your palette.

Clean brushes properly: After rinsing brushes in solvent, I then give them a thorough clean with Co-Co-Bella soap from Wallace Seymour, as it helps to condition and restore the brush hairs. I also use it for hand cleaning, as it is more effective than other soaps, gentler on the skin, and more eco-friendly than baby wipes.

Recycling solvents: After using solvent to clean brushes, pour the leftover solvent into a lidded glass or metal container. Allow the pigment to settle at the bottom, then decant the clear solvent for reuse. Dispose of the pigment sludge responsibly, or repurpose it as a ground for your next painting.

Dispose of rags safely: Rags, scrim or paper towels soaked in oil paint and solvents can be a fire hazard due to the risk of spontaneous combustion. Store these materials in a metal container with a lid, away from direct sunlight, to reduce the risk. Regularly remove waste from your workspace to avoid any build-up of fumes or odours.

Dispose of hazardous waste responsibly: Never throw solvent-soaked rags in general household waste or landfill, as they can contaminate the environment. Instead, take them to a local recycling centre or hazardous waste disposal site. Check with your local council for guidelines on disposing of hazardous materials.

Tube disposal: Empty paint tubes can be disposed of in regular waste, but first, ensure any residual paint is dried out. Squeeze out as much paint as possible by cutting the bottom of the tube to remove any remaining pigment.

By following these good studio practices, you will not only protect yourself and the environment, but also maintain a more efficient, organised workspace.

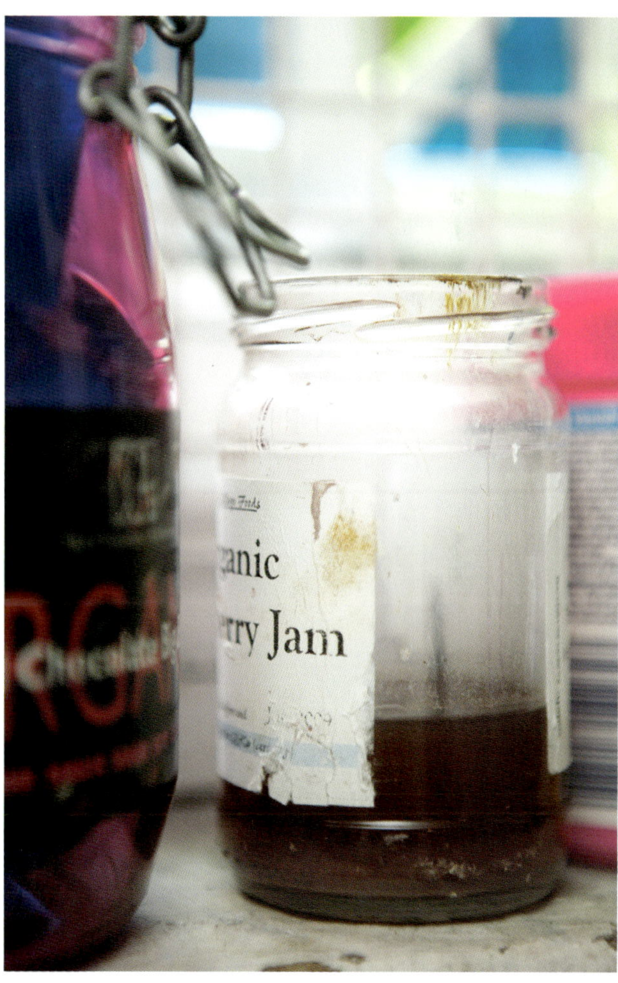

After rinsing your brushes, allow your solvent to sit undisturbed for a few days. During this time, the pigment will settle at the bottom of the container, leaving a clear layer of solvent on top. This clear solvent can then be reused for cleaning your brushes or thinning paints, extending the life of your materials.

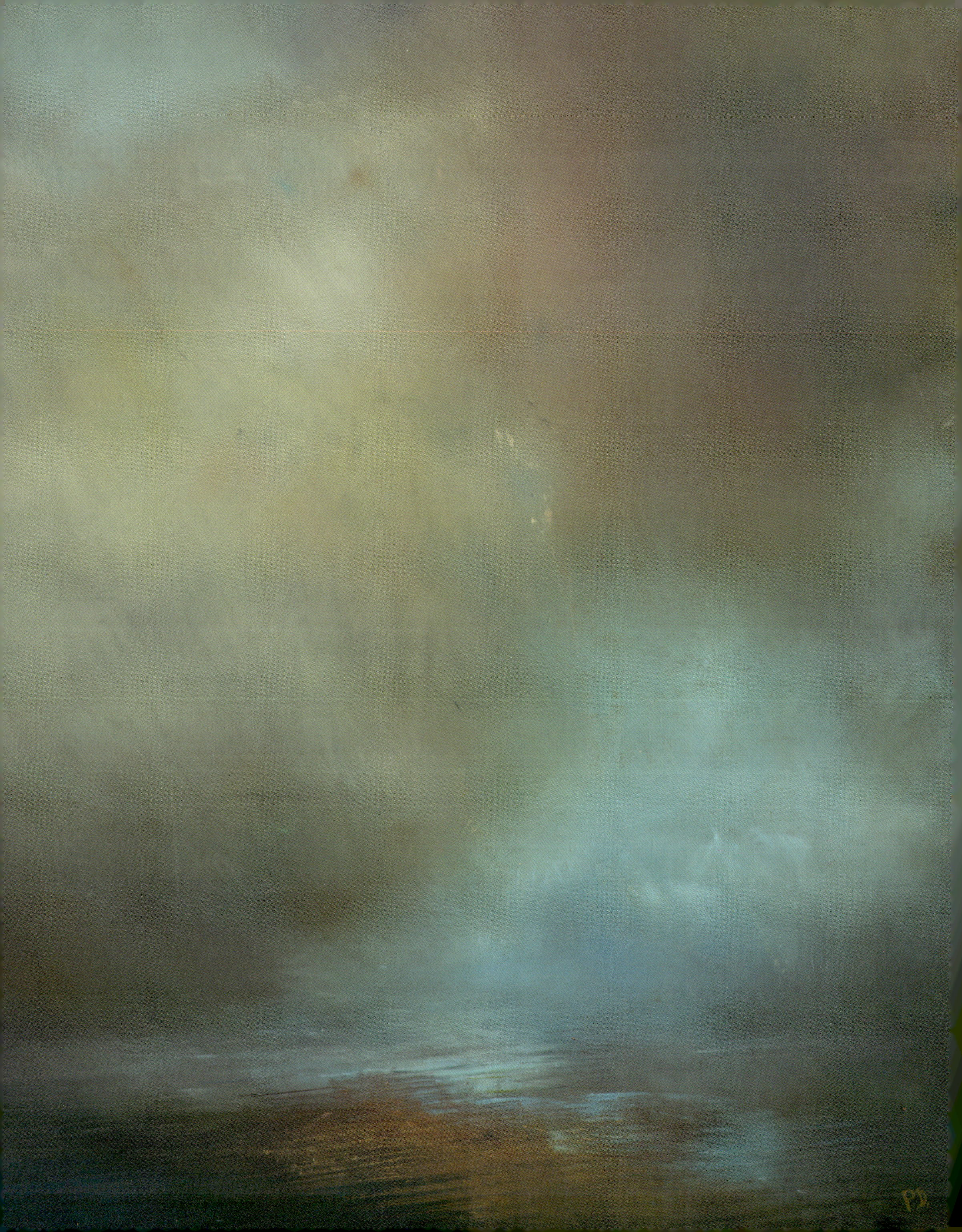

CHAPTER 2

CHOOSING YOUR SURFACE

This chapter explores the various surfaces (substrates) available for painting with oils and cold wax, highlighting their opportunities and limitations. When working with cold wax, carefully considering your surface is crucial, as the medium reduces the flexibility of your oil paints. This means that your support, that is, the surface you paint on, needs to be relatively rigid. The more wax you use, the greater the risk of cracking if the painting is on a flexible support, such as stretched canvas.

Understanding the characteristics of different substrates is key to making the best choice for your work. For instance, paper is ideal for smaller-scale pieces, allowing for experimentation and quick sketches. Canvas, with its textured surface, is better suited for larger works but requires additional precautions when used with cold wax due to its flexibility when stretched. Wooden panels, on the other hand, provide stability and a solid foundation, making them an excellent option for larger-scale works.

To help determine which substrate is best for your painting, a good starting point is to think about the size and format (landscape, portrait, square, circle) of the work you want to create and how you ultimately envisage the finished painting being displayed, that is, framed, behind glass or no frame at all. The size of your work and how you want to display it may reduce the options you have in terms of surfaces. By understanding the properties and limitations of each substrate, you can make informed decisions that enhance your process and help you achieve your creative vision.

PAPER

If you are looking to paint on a smaller scale, then working on paper is an ideal surface. Paper is lightweight and less expensive than stretched canvas or wooden panels, making it easier to store as well as being a great surface on which to experiment with techniques. There are some papers which come in glued pads, or in sheets and rolls, so you can cut it to the size you want. When working on paper, you also have the option to cut down your work if your composition could be improved with being cropped.

Working on paper also enables you to easily work across the edges of your surface, providing you with the opportunity to create more dynamic marks. You can paint on a flat work surface or vertically by bonding the paper to a panel, or taping it to a wall. If you tape the edges of your paper, you can create a crisp, clean border around your work. The downside of leaving a border around your work is that it will need to be framed behind glass to protect the unpainted paper from dirt, dust and changes in the atmosphere.

You may prefer to frame your painting behind glass, and this may have been a consideration when you were choosing paper as your substrate. The size of your painting is something you should also consider as the larger your work the more expensive it will be to frame. It will also be considerably heavier, requiring sturdy fixings which are able to take a heavier load. The larger the painting, the more likely a glazed frame will produce reflections, which

OPPOSITE: *Dreaming of the Sea (cropped),* measuring 40 × 40cm (15¾ × 15¾in), combines oils, cold wax, and gold leaf. The substrate was carefully prepared prior to painting by bonding Arches Huile paper to a bare-faced cradled wooden panel.

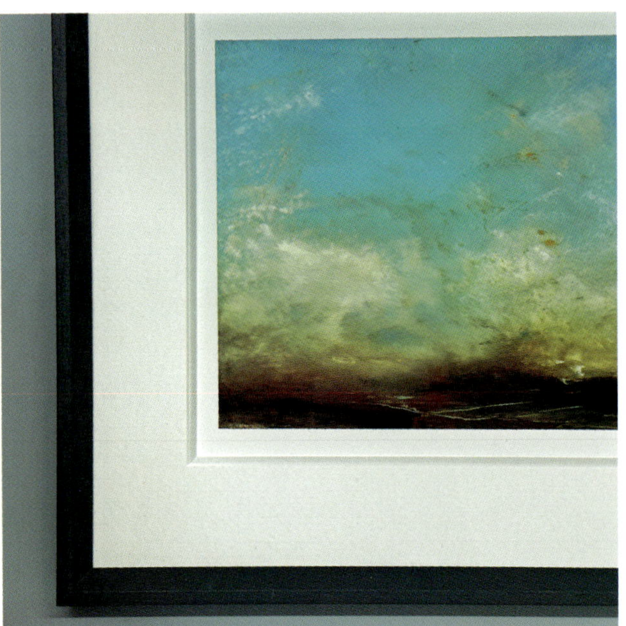

Haar, 71 × 23cm (28 × 9in), oil and cold wax on Arches Huile paper. Larger works on paper tend to be more expensive to frame and can become quite heavy, requiring sturdy fixings for safe display. Additionally, larger glazed surfaces are more prone to glare, which can detract from the viewing experience. To address this, opt for anti-reflective or museum-grade glass.

can hinder the viewer's ability to fully appreciate your work. If this is a concern, using anti-reflective or museum-grade glass can help to minimise reflections and provide UV protection. However, it is important to note that this option can increase the overall cost of framing.

If you are keen to create large-scale works on paper but want to avoid glazing, consider bonding your painting onto a wooden panel and applying varnish for protection (*see* Chapter 10). Alternatively, you can mount the paper to a panel before painting (instructions are provided at the end of this chapter). If this approach appeals to you, it is a good idea to source the panel in advance. This allows you to choose from readily available options, giving you greater flexibility and potentially avoiding the need for a custom-made panel, which can become expensive.

There is a variety of papers which are specially treated (sized) for working with oils; alternatively, you can prime watercolour paper for this purpose. Oil papers differ in composition, quality, weight, and cost, typically featuring an embossed texture on their surface. They are sized to prevent the absorption of the oil content in the paint, which can darken your colours and, in the long-term, damage the natural fibres of the paper. If the paper is not properly prepared for oil painting, it can absorb too much oil, leading to issues such as oil rings and the pigment from your paint becoming unbound. This can lead to the paint flaking off the surface over time (Jackson's, 2021).

Here are some examples of oil papers that I have experimented with over the years while working with oils and cold wax, along with insights into their suitability for the techniques discussed in this book. All of these papers are specifically designed and sized for oil painting, so priming is unnecessary unless you wish to modify their texture or absorbency. For a comprehensive list of oil papers and their characteristics, Jackson's (2021) offers an extensive overview.

Arches Huile (300gsm)

Arches Huile paper is made of 100 per cent cotton linters and is regarded as a professional-grade paper (Jackson's, 2021). The long cotton fibres add strength to the paper, enabling it to withstand rough handling, including repeated use of solvent reduction techniques, scratching, and scraping. This paper is made from cold-pressed watercolour paper that is both internally and externally sized. Cold pressing (also known as 'NOT', meaning 'not pressed with heat') involves pressing the paper through cold metal rollers, resulting in a slightly textured surface. You will notice that one side is slightly more textured than the other, but you can use either side for painting.

Arches Huile is available in a variety of formats, including glued pads, sheets, and rolls. The sheets and rolls have deckled edges created during the papermaking process when the wet pulp spills over the edges of the mould. Once seen as a flaw, deckled edges are now embraced by some artists and integrated into the overall design of their work (Jackson's, 2021). It is worth noting that Arches Huile is on the higher end of the price range and that the size used in its production contains gelatine.

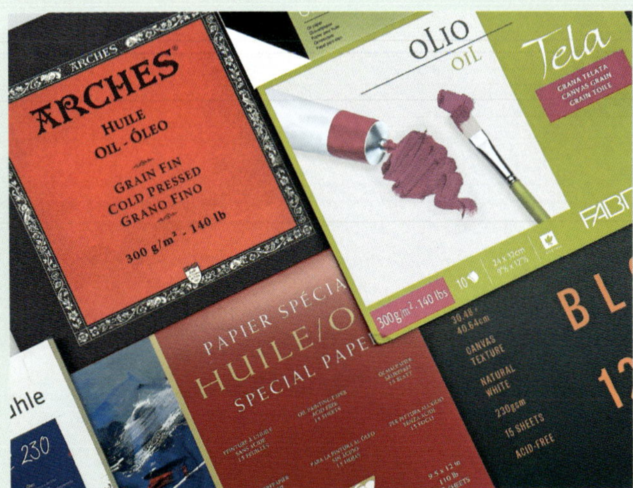

Opt for specially treated, acid-free oil painting papers to prevent oil absorption and to retain your colours and protect the paper fibres. Alternatively, heavyweight watercolour paper can be primed with gesso to protect the paper and also allow you to customise the texture and absorbency for painting with oils.

Made from: 100 per cent acid-free cotton linters
Sized: Internally and externally – contains gelatine
Texture: Slightly textured surface with one side being more textured than the other
Format: Pads, individual sheets, and rolls

Observations

- This paper is my preferred choice for its professional quality and cold-pressed surface, which offers a soft surface with greater staining possibilities.
- Among the papers tested (results shown in the image overleaf), Arches Huile stands out for producing the most vibrant base colour. Its surface allows the oil colour to stain the paper and creates a vibrant and uniform base layer, ideal for scratching back to.

Clairefontaine (240gsm)

Made from: Acid-free wood pulp
Sized: Internally
Texture: Linen
Format: Pads, blocks and individual sheets

Observations

- At 240gsm, this paper is relatively thin and may not stand up to repeated scratching, scraping and solvent reduction techniques.
- Paint tends to sit on the surface and moves freely, making it somewhat challenging to control blends. Achieving seamless transitions may require additional skill and practice.
- Being non-absorbent, the paper does not allow the paint to stain the surface. As a result, scratching back to the base layer reveals a less vibrant colour, with the white of the paper shining through in areas. While this creates an appealing textured effect, it lacks vibrancy and consistency.

Hahnemühle (230gsm)

Made from: Acid-free wood pulp
Sized: Internally
Texture: Linen, featured on one side only, with a noticeably prominent texture
Format: Blocks and individual sheets

Observations

- At 230gsm, this paper is relatively thin and may not stand up to repeated scratching, scraping and solvent reduction techniques.
- Paint stays on the surface, moving freely, which can make blending more difficult to control.
- Among the papers tested, this was the least effective at retaining the base colour. Scratching back resulted in a less vibrant colour, with more of the textured white of the paper showing through.

Fabriano Tela (300gsm)

Made from: Acid-free wood pulp
Sized: Internally and externally
Texture: Linen with a noticeably more prominent texture
Format: Blocks, individual sheets, and rolls

Observations

- At 300gsm this heavier paper, unlike Arches Huile paper, was somewhat difficult to fold and tear.
- The paper holds the base layer paint more effectively than Clairefontaine and Hahnemühle, with less of the white textured surface showing through.

Jackson's (230gsm)

Made from: Acid-free cotton and wood pulp
Sized: Internally and externally
Texture: Canvas
Format: Blocks

Observations

- A relatively thin paper with performance similar to Clairefontaine and Hahnemühle, showing the textured white surface through the paint.
- Despite being taped with the same low-tack masking tape as the other papers, the removal of the tape resulted in the paper tearing easily. As a result, this paper may not stand up to repeated scratching, scraping and solvent reduction techniques.

Royal Talens: Rembrandt (300gsm)

Made from: Acid-free cellulose
Sized: Internally and externally
Texture: Canvas with a noticeably more prominent texture
Format: Blocks

Observations

- This paper is one of the heavier options and effectively retains some of the base colour. While the results are not as vibrant and some of the textured white surface is still prominent, this paper comes closest to matching Arches Huile paper.

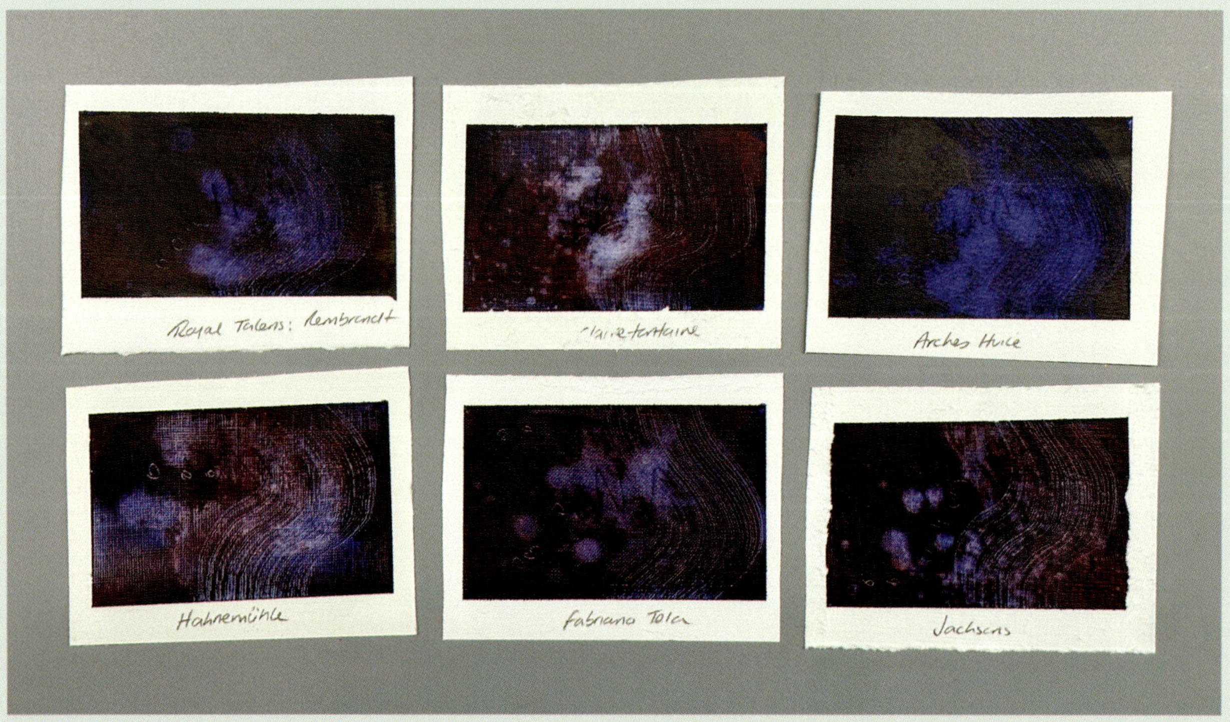

The oil papers in this chapter were tested for their ability to produce vibrant, consistent base colours. A thin layer of ultramarine blue was applied with a squeegee, followed by alizarin crimson. Marks were scratched back using various tools, and solvent reduction techniques were employed to evaluate how effectively the papers retained the base colour.

CANVAS

Working on canvas offers a textured surface that many artists prefer. It is a cost-effective, lightweight option that allows for versatility in size, including large-scale paintings. Canvas can come stretched over a frame or mounted on cardboard-backed boards. Like paper, canvas must be sized to prevent the oil from deteriorating the fibres over time. If you plan to use stretched canvas for oil and cold wax painting, it is advisable to reduce the cold wax content from 50 per cent to about 30 per cent or less. This reduction is important because cold wax decreases the flexibility of your paints and since stretched canvas can move with changes in temperature and humidity, there is a risk of cracking over time. Alternatively, you can incorporate Gamblin's Solvent-Free Gel, Galkyd Gel, or Galkyd Lite Gel to preserve the body of your oils and cold wax mix while adding the flexibility needed to work on canvas.

With stretched canvas you can work flat or vertically on an easel or wall. Being able to paint vertically for larger pieces makes it easier to work on, but also ensures the perspective of your painting is not distorted by painting flat. Stretched canvas comes in a range of pre-made sizes, primed or unprimed, and a range of shapes: square, portrait, landscape, or circular. They typically come in a range of standard depths:

- Shallow (16–21mm): This is the most common depth for stretched canvas, making it suitable for framing with a tray frame.
- Medium (25–28mm): This depth offers additional sturdiness, making it ideal for larger works, while still fitting comfortably in a tray frame.
- Deep (35–38mm): Often referred to as 'deep edge', these canvases are frequently used for larger artworks. The extra depth provides a more substantial feel, allowing the artwork to be displayed without a frame.

Similar to some of the oil papers discussed earlier, when painting on canvas, the paint mix has a tendency to sit on the surface and move freely, which can make controlling blends a bit challenging, especially when working wet-on-wet. Additionally, the inherent springiness of a stretched canvas adds to this complexity, while the texture of the canvas may not produce the smooth surface you are looking for.

WOODEN PANELS

Unlike canvas, wooden panels are solid and do not bounce, which makes this rigid surface ideal for paints, such as oils, that have the potential to crack. Wooden panels can be bought ready-made or made to your specifications. Panels need to be primed to create a suitable surface on which to paint and to protect the wood from the linseed oil in your paints. You can prepare panels yourself (see later in this chapter), or you can buy them ready primed depending on your budget and the time you have available.

Panels generally are made from plywood or MDF, both of which are more resistant to warping, although some MDF panels are not suitable for painting, as the glues used may not be pH neutral. MDF can also be susceptible to water damage and become very heavy and cumbersome when you scale up in size.

If you are working on a larger scale, then a cradled panel can be a more practical surface, as their construction allows for easy handling and hanging and offers a more stable surface while you work. A cradled panel is the equivalent of a deep-edged canvas in that the wooden panel is fitted with bracing bars to the back, increasing stability and resistance to warping. You can easily attach hanging hardware to cradled panels, enabling you to display your work without the need to frame. The standard depths for cradled panels typically fall into the following categories:

- **Shallow (20–22mm):** These are lightweight and ideal for tray framing and are commonly used for smaller works where a sleek profile is preferred.
- **Medium (25–32mm):** Provides more stability than shallow panels, making it more suitable for larger works. Can fit a tray frame or be displayed without a frame.
- **Deep (40–50mm or more):** Designed for a bold, contemporary look, often displayed without a frame. Ideal for larger works but can become heavy, requiring secure hanging solutions and careful framing considerations.

When choosing a depth, consider the scale, weight, and presentation style of your work. Shallower panels are practical and lightweight, while deeper panels can add a striking visual effect but may pose handling and framing challenges.

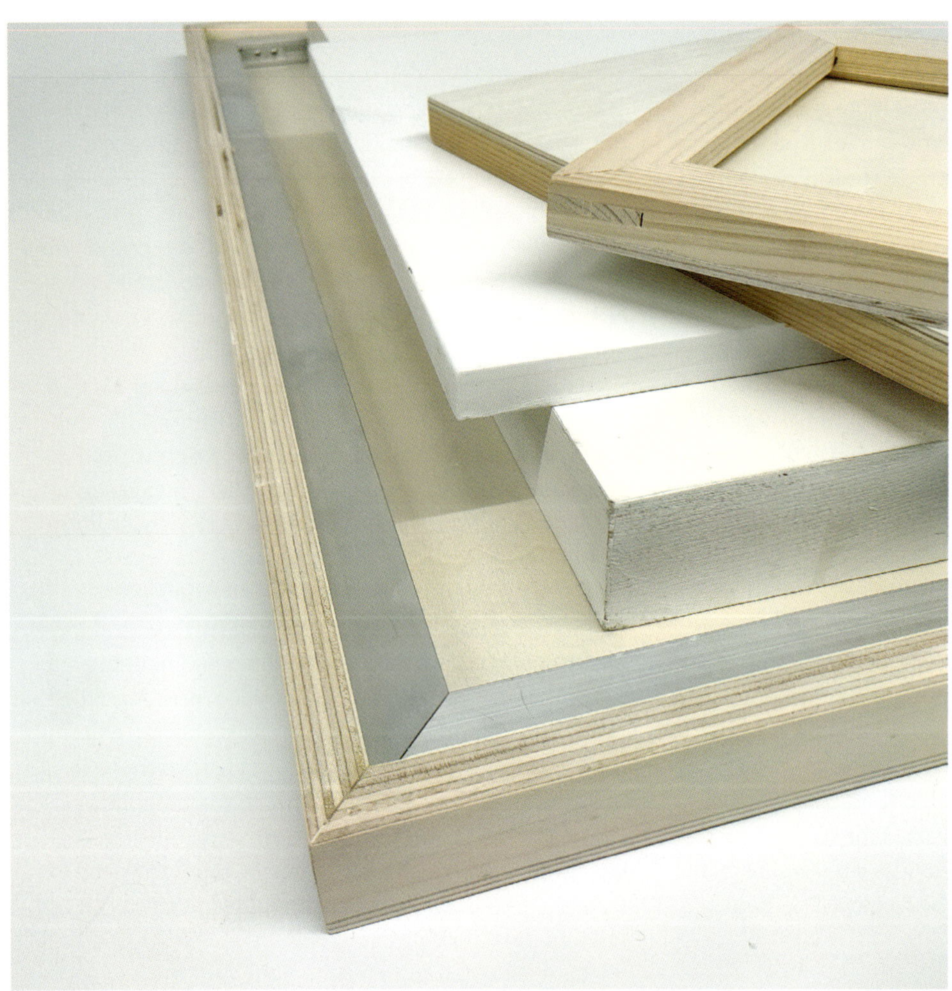

A cradled panel is similar to a deep-edged canvas, consisting of a sturdy wooden panel with bracing bars for added stability and reduced warping. These panels are ideal for larger projects and can be purchased ready-made, available in both primed and unprimed options. For specialised projects, you can also have custom-built panels made to your specifications, featuring aluminium bracing bars (as shown) for museum-standard anti-warping.

HANDLING SMALL PANELS

When working with small panels, you may find them challenging to handle without leaving fingerprints or smudging your painting. To make handling easier and to assist with storing your work while it dries, you can use a technique called a piano hinge, which involves attaching your panel to another surface such as print paper or cardboard. Here's how:

1. Take your panel, some masking tape and either some print paper or cardboard, depending on the size and weight of your panels.
2. Apply two horizontal strips of masking tape across the back of the panel and another two strips vertically.
3. Flip the panel over so the sticky edges of the tape are facing up, and place the panel on to your print paper or cardboard.
4. Secure the edges of the tape to your print paper or cardboard using masking tape.
5. Your panel should now be firmly fixed, allowing you to move and store it safely without the risk of leaving fingerprints in your painting.

This technique not only helps you handle the panel more easily, but also protects your artwork as it dries.

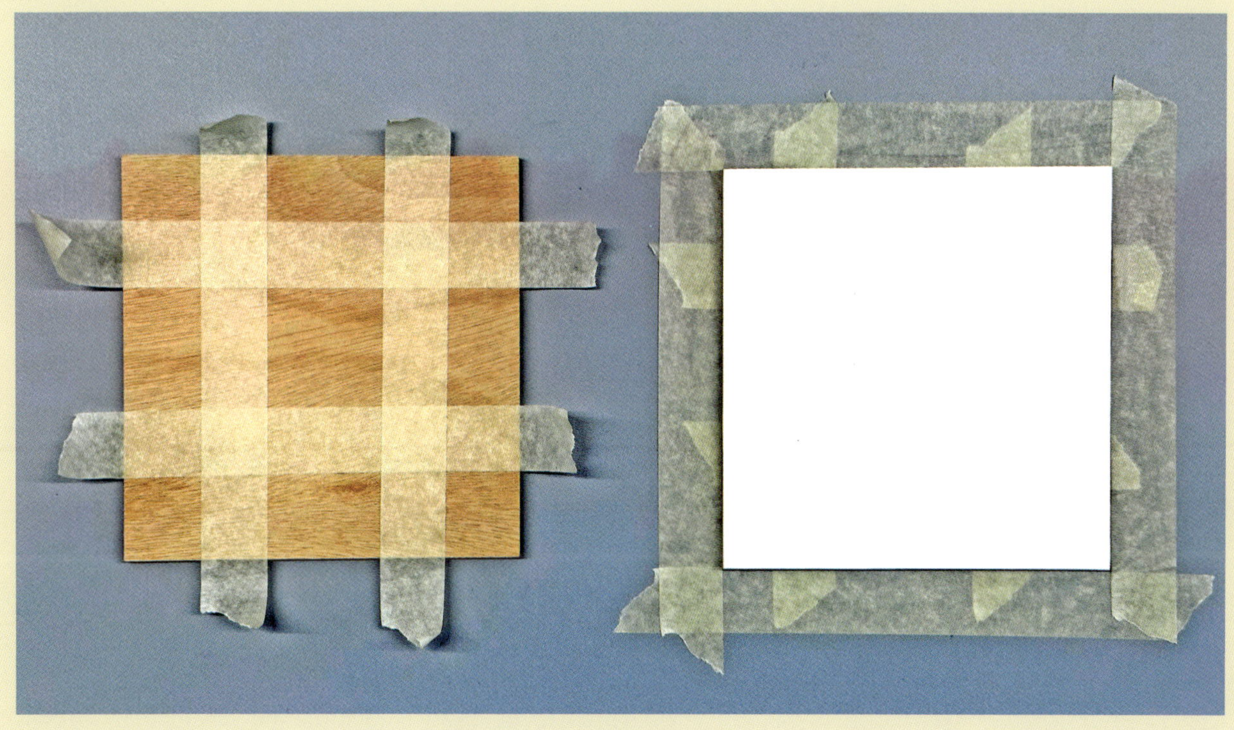

PREPARING YOUR SURFACES

Whichever surface you choose, it will need to be prepared to protect it from the linseed oil in your paints and to ensure proper adhesion of the paint. Sizing prevents the surface from absorbing colour like a sponge, while priming creates texture (tooth) and affects both absorbency and brightness. For ease, most people use an acrylic primer, which can serve as both a size and a primer.

If your surface is not already sized or primed, or if it is not designed for use with oils (for example, watercolour paper), it will require priming for protection. Depending on the surface, you may need only one coat of primer for paper. However, for canvas or wood, you may need three or four coats, ensuring that you allow 24 hours between each coat for full drying. With wooden panels, lightly sanding between layers can help achieve a smoother finish and more tooth. Additionally, when working on a large panel, applying acrylic primer to the reverse side can help prevent warping.

Bonding paper to a panel

As mentioned earlier, you can bond your paintings on paper to wooden panels after completing your artwork. Alternatively, you may wish to consider bonding the paper to the panels before painting. This method offers several advantages:

- Working vertically allows for better handling of larger pieces and helps maintain perspective, avoiding distortion that can occur when painting flat.
- By bonding the paper before you start painting, you reduce the risk of damaging a finished piece.
- Panels are easier to frame and offer a wider variety of framing options compared to loose sheets of paper.

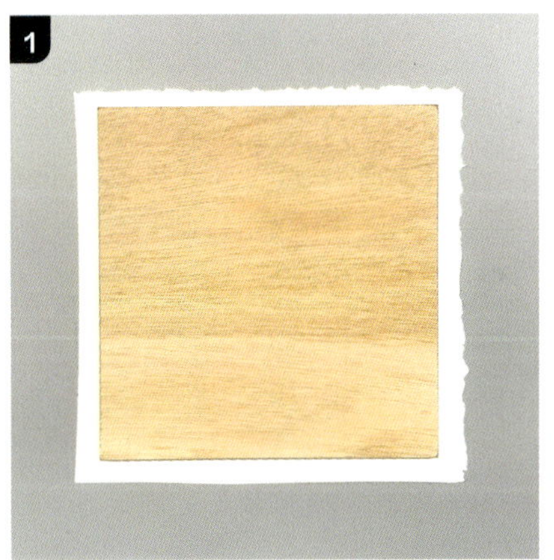
1

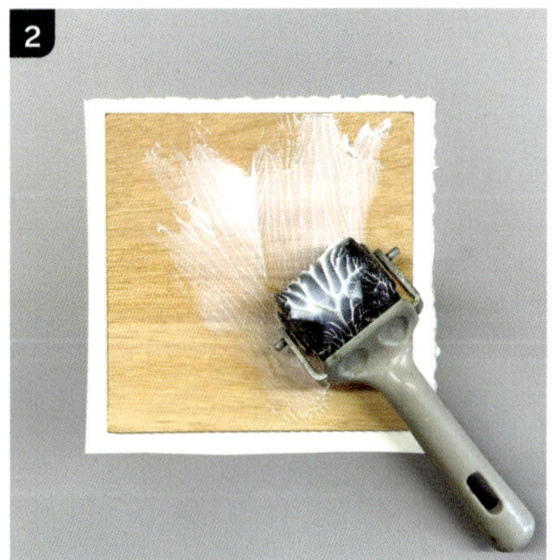
2

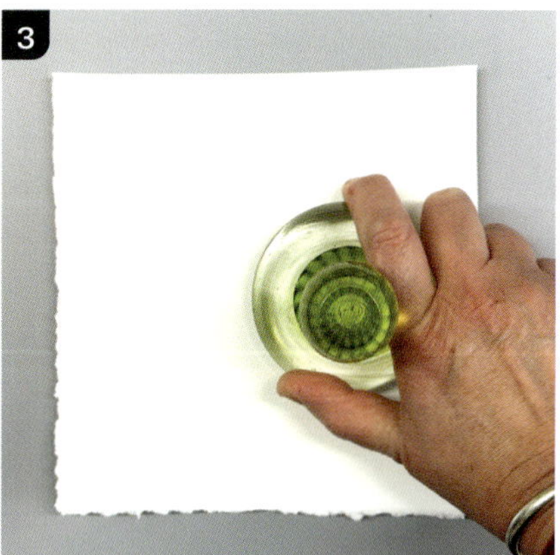
3

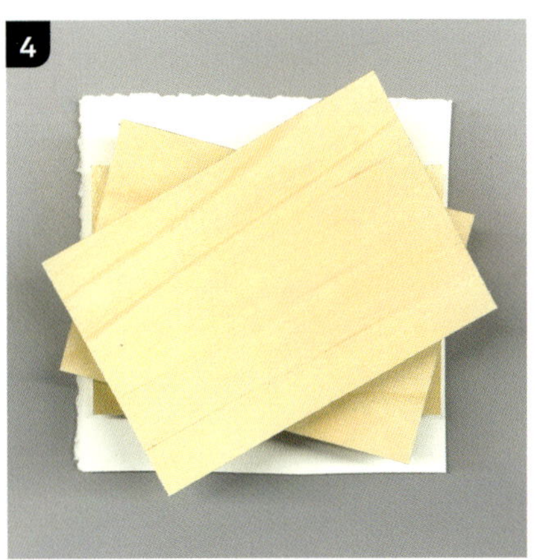
4

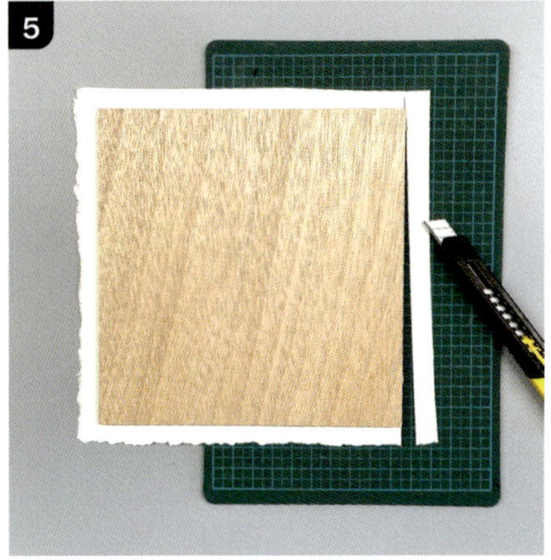
5

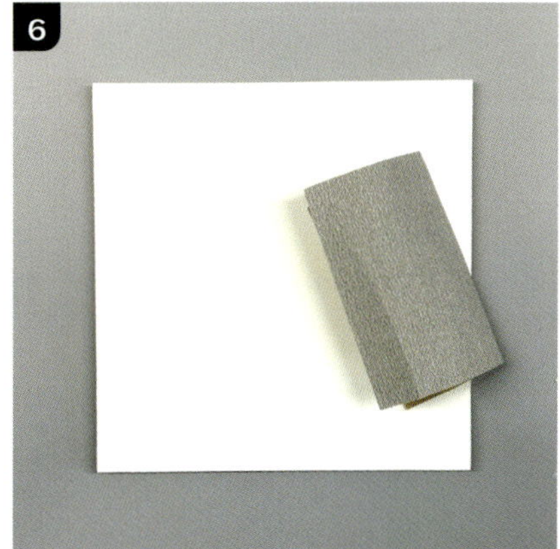
6

Depending on the size of your wooden panel, you can use either neutral pH PVA glue or a heavy or extra-heavy gel medium to adhere your paper. PVA glue works well for smaller paintings, but for pieces larger than 30 × 30cm (12 × 12in), as PVA is quite fluid, it may cause the paper to cockle as you use more adhesive. This is especially true when using heavyweight paper like Arches Huile, as more adhesive is required to ensure proper adhesion on larger surfaces.

Here is my step-by-step guide for bonding paper to panel prior to painting.

What you will need:

- Arches Huile paper (size determined by the size of the panel)
- A bare-faced wooden panel or a cradled panel (ensure the surface is not primed for proper adhesion)
- Sharp craft knife or scalpel
- Neutral pH PVA glue or heavy/extra-heavy gel medium (using pH neutral fixatives for this purpose ensures that it does not discolour or become brittle over time)
- Squeegee, blade, or roller
- For larger pieces, something to smooth out the paper (for example, a hard roller or a printer's baren)
- Palette knife
- Fine or extra-fine grade sandpaper and sanding block

Step 1: Prepare your paper

On a clean, flat surface, lay down your Arches Huile paper. The size of your panel will determine whether you purchase pre-cut pads, sheets, or rolls of paper. Place your panel on top of the paper and cut it using a sharp scalpel or craft knife, ensuring you cut wider than the actual panel.

Step 2: Apply adhesive

Take the pH neutral PVA or heavy/extra-heavy gel medium and generously coat the front of your panel, paying particular attention to the edges and corners. Use a squeegee or a roller to evenly spread the adhesive. With the paper flat on your work surface, carefully place the panel face-down onto the paper, ensuring it is fully covered.

Step 3: Bond the surface

Turn your panel over so it is face up. Gently smooth out the paper with your hands, working from the centre outwards, pushing any lumps of adhesive towards the edges of the panel. If you are having difficulty smoothing the surface, try using a clean rubber brayer or a baren (as shown) and apply an even pressure.

Step 4: Leave to dry

Once you are satisfied that you have smoothed out the surface and that your paper has adhered to the panel (including the edges and corners), place a layer of tissue on top along with some heavy weights such as books or other panels (as shown) to help the surfaces bond. Leave overnight to dry fully.

Step 5: Trim the edges

Flip the panel over so the paper side is face-down and, using a scalpel or craft knife, carefully trim the edges. Inspect the edges and corners of your panel to ensure the paper is securely fixed. If any edges lift, use a palette knife to push adhesive into the gaps, wiping off any excess.

Step 6: Finish the edges

Once the adhesive is dry, gently sand the edges of your panel using fine-grade sandpaper wrapped around a sanding block. Carefully remove any dried adhesive from the edges of the panel and smooth any ragged paper edges. After sanding, brush off any dust from the surface, and your panel will be ready for painting.

In this chapter, we have explored a variety of surfaces suitable for oil and cold wax paintings, emphasising their unique opportunities and limitations. Selecting the right surface is crucial, as it directly affects not only the longevity of your artwork, but also your ability to bring your creative ideas to life. By gaining a deeper understanding of the properties and constraints of each surface, you can make informed decisions that will help you achieve the results you are looking for.

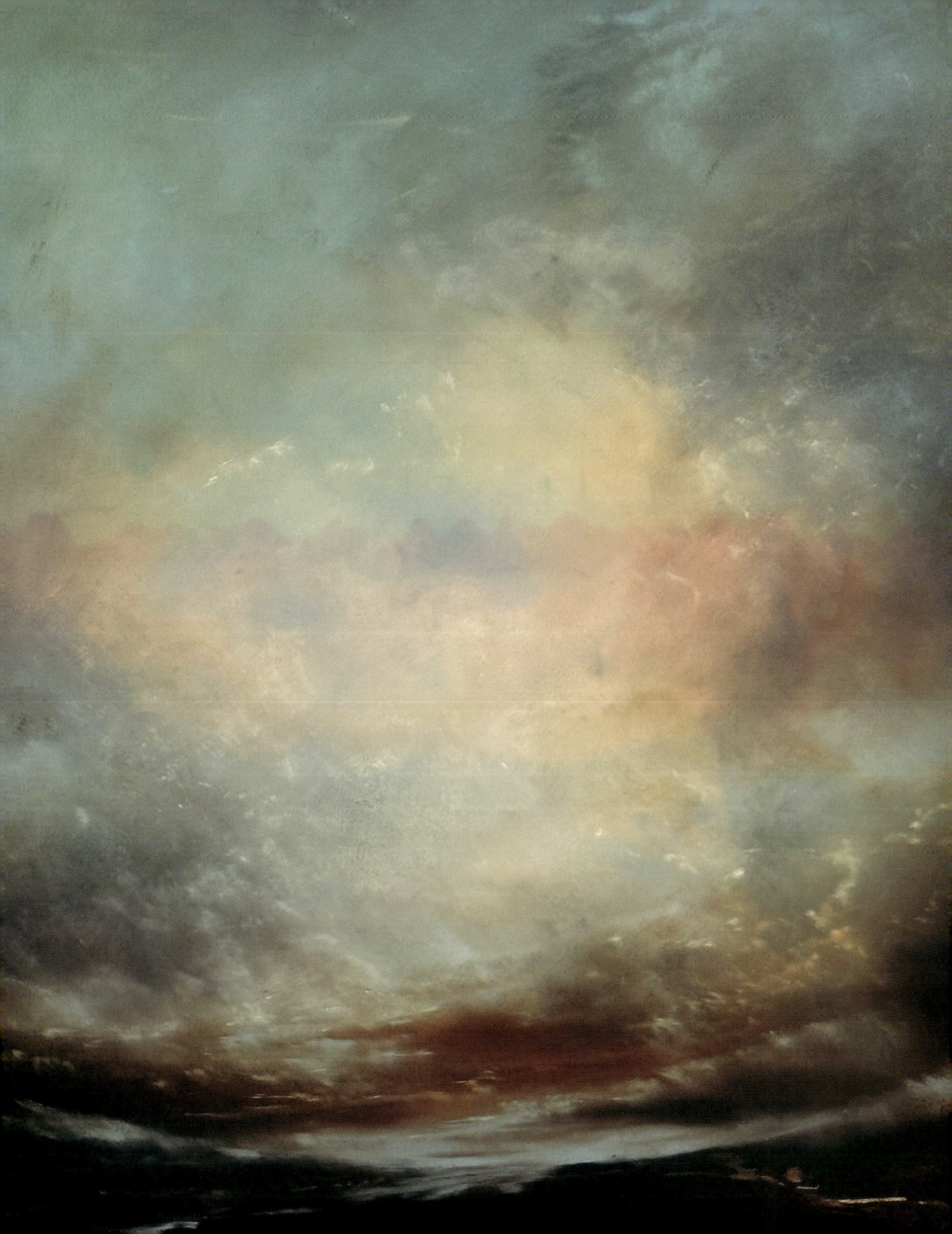

CHAPTER 3

METHODS AND TECHNIQUES

Painting with oils and cold wax offers myriad creative possibilities, inviting you to explore various techniques and approaches. Whether you choose to work on paper, panels, or canvas, each surface presents its own unique opportunities for exploration and experimentation. You can opt for a wet-on-wet application of paint, allowing the colours to blend seamlessly on the canvas, or you may prefer to let layers dry before reworking them, creating a more structured and deliberate composition. This versatile medium enables a range of techniques, from creating impasto textures that add a three-dimensional quality to your work, to employing sgraffito marks to reveal layers of colour beneath the surface.

As my painting style has developed, so too has my use of oils and cold wax, evolving alongside my changing interests and growing skills. My approach has transitioned from focusing on thick, impasto applications, where the emphasis was on maximising texture, to exploring thin, transparent layers of colour to create depth and luminosity.

In this chapter, I share some of the methods I use when working with oils and cold wax, with the aim of providing both instruction and inspiration. By experimenting with these techniques, you will gain a deeper understanding of how this medium behaves and discover ways to incorporate it into your own practice. Working with oils and cold wax requires an instinctive and intuitive approach, which develops through dedicated time spent in the studio. Embrace this opportunity to play, experiment, and uncover the possibilities that this medium offers for your own artistic practice.

MIXING OIL PAINT WITH COLD WAX

In my work I use equal amounts of oil paint to cold wax (50:50) which creates a good, thick consistency. If you are wanting to paint on stretched canvas then reduce

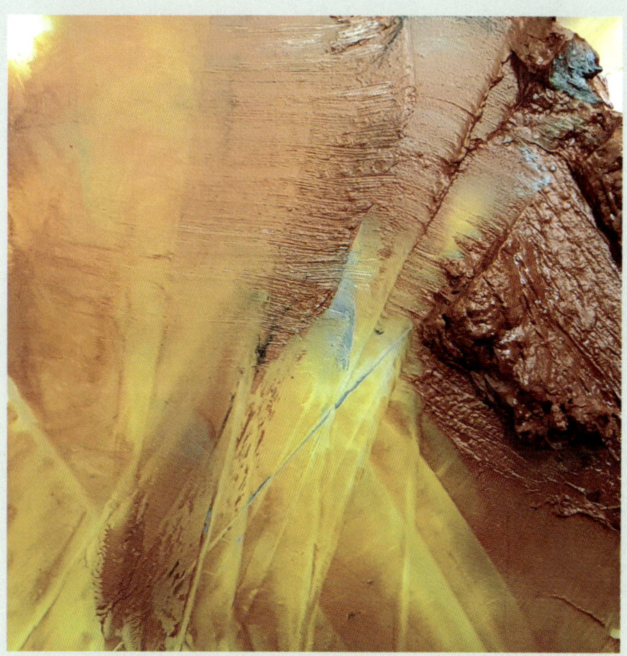

Mixing oils with cold wax creates a soft, thick, buttery consistency that is ideal for building texture, achieving impasto effects, and layering paint. It enables thin layers to be applied wet-on-wet, providing greater control and depth in your artwork. The addition of cold wax also transforms the finish of your oils from glossy to a beautifully rich matt surface.

OPPOSITE: *Tracing our way home (cropped)*, measuring 80 × 80cm (31½ × 31½in), combines oils, cold wax and gold leaf on a cradled wooden panel. Soft colour and tonal transitions are achieved, allowing hues to intermingle harmoniously while preserving their individual identities, creating a dynamic yet balanced composition.

the amount of cold wax to around 30 per cent and/or incorporate Solvent-Free Gel, Galkyd Gel, or Galkyd Lite Gel which will increase the flexibility of your paint mixture (*see* Chapter 2 for more information on surfaces).

Start by squeezing out some paint from the tube onto your palette and then take roughly the same amount of cold wax and give it a good mix together with a palette knife. Although the cold wax is an off white colour, it is transparent so when you mix it with your paint it will not alter its colour. The cold wax will transform your oils from glossy to matt, thicken up your paint and also bulk it out, so you end up with twice as much mixture to work with.

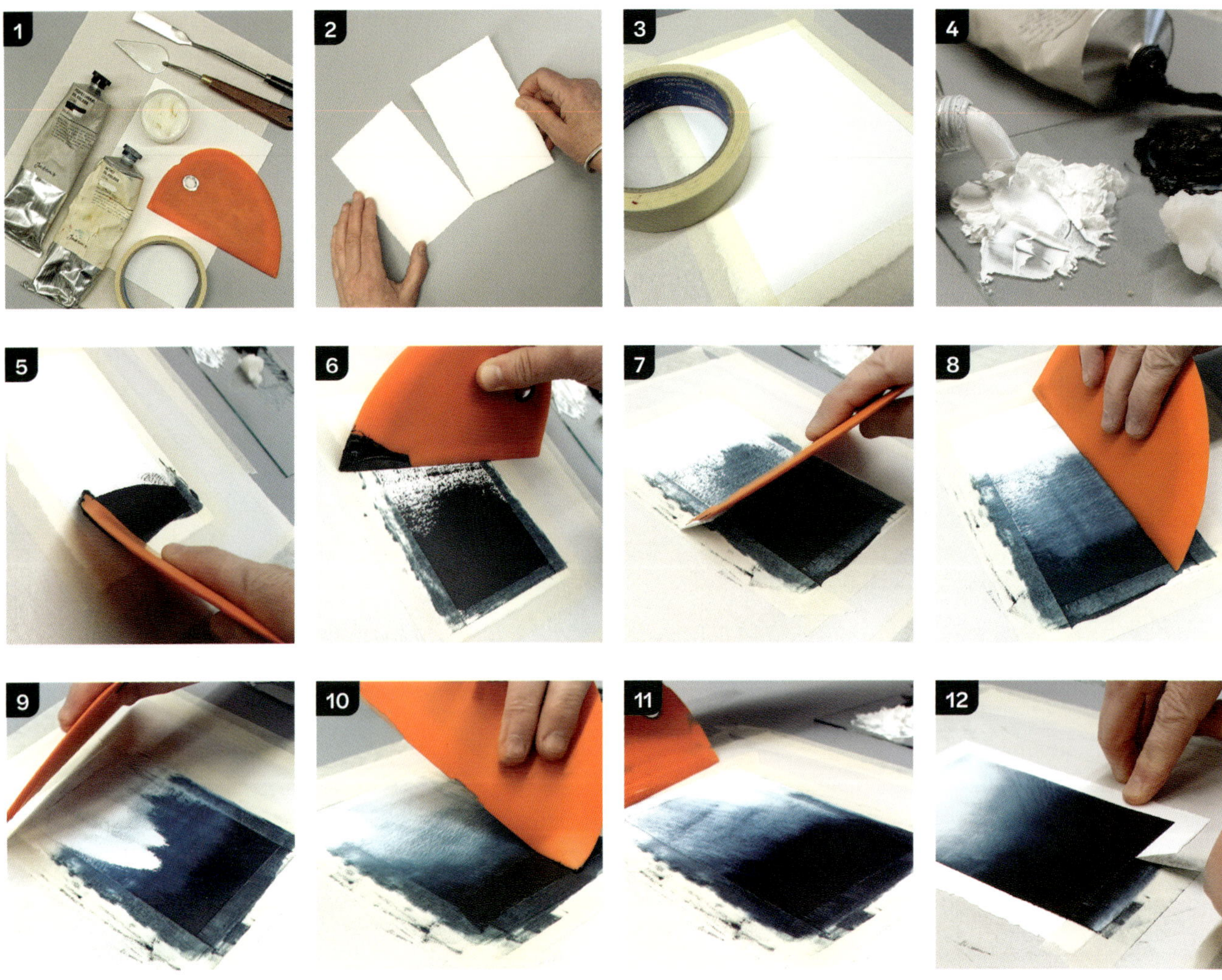

WORKING WITH A SQUEEGEE

The main go-to tool for artists who work with oils and cold wax is the squeegee, also known as a blade. It is an incredibly versatile tool that has been adopted by many artists who work with thick paint. It is excellent for skimming paint over wet areas, but it can be a little tricky to use to begin with, especially if you are used to working with brushes. The following exercise has been created for those who are new to working with a squeegee and cold wax. It has been designed to help you become more confident with using this tool to apply thin layers of paint, and for blending to create colour and tonal transitions.

Step 1: Tools and materials
What you will need:

- Arches Huile paper
- Some newsprint, newspaper, or scrap paper for taping the Arches paper to
- Oil paints – choose a light and a dark colour. In this exercise I have chosen titanium white as my light colour and indigo for my dark colour.
- Masking tape
- Cold wax medium
- Squeegee
- Palette knife
- Palette for mixing your paints and medium
- Paper roll, for cleaning your tools

Step 2: Prepare your paper
This only requires a small piece of paper, so cut down your large pieces by folding and tearing, so you do not waste too much paper on this exercise. As the paper is designed for painting with oils, there is no need to prepare the surface in advance and, although one side is slightly coarser than the other, there is no right or wrong side on which to paint.

Step 3: Fix your paper
Tape the paper to a sheet of newsprint or a clean surface using masking tape, ensuring even borders. Firmly press the tape down to prevent oil paint from seeping underneath.

Step 4: Mix your paints
Squeeze out some paint onto your palette. In this example I am using titanium white as my light colour and indigo as my dark colour. Using your palette knife, mix approximately 50:50 cold wax into your paint and give it a good mix. You will see, as you are mixing, that the paint turns matt. Also notice that, although the cold wax looks white, it has not changed the colour of your paint, that is, it has not changed the indigo to a pale blue colour. You will also see that you now have twice as much paint as you started out with; something to bear in mind when you next squeeze paint out of the tube.

Step 5: Apply your dark colour
Load some of your mixed dark coloured paint onto the long edge of your squeegee and spread the paint on to the bottom of your taped-up paper.

Step 6: Spread your dark colour
Using the long edge of the squeegee, hold it at a shallow angle to the surface of the paper and sweep upwards in one smooth motion, laying down a thin, even layer of paint.

Step 7: Apply your light colour
Wipe your squeegee clean with paper roll. Load it with the light-coloured mix and apply it to the top of the paper. Sweep downwards with the same smooth motion, allowing the light and dark paints to start mixing.

Step 8: Blend
Repeat the process with smaller amounts of paint, bearing in mind we are looking for thin layers. Once you have swept up with the dark paint and down with the light, wipe your squeegee clean before sweeping very gently from left to right and then right to left. Notice how this starts to create some subtle blends of colour and tones.

Step 9: Focus on contrast
This process will start to blend the dark and light colours to an extent the tonal values may start to look similar. If the paint is overly blended with your squeegee, you can end up with a painting of just one colour. Try adding a small amount of your light colour to the top of the

painting using your squeegee and see how much brighter this contrasts with the blended colours. Carefully blend this in with gentle sweeps of your squeegee.

Step 10: Create some depth
Do the same with your dark colour at the bottom of the paper and lightly sweep up. The darkness should provide a nice contrast to the mid tones and may start to suggest a foreground of an abstract landscape. Continue to keep your paint layers thin, as we are not aiming to create texture.

Step 11: Disrupt horizon lines
If you find that you are ending up with a hard, flat horizon line delineating your light and dark colours, then try sweeping diagonally and see if that disrupts it. Be very gentle. If you press too hard with your squeegee you will wipe off the paint you have just applied.

Step 12: Finalise and frame
Continue to sweep your squeegee across the painting surface until you are happy with the result and have a good mix of blends and tones. Remove the tape from your painting and see how the crisp white border nicely frames your work.

Repeat this process until you feel able to control the squeegee to create colour mixes and tones, and you are confident that you can lay paint down in smooth, thin layers. Experiment with different pressures with your squeegee from light sweeps to a firm pull across your paper to see what effects can be achieved.

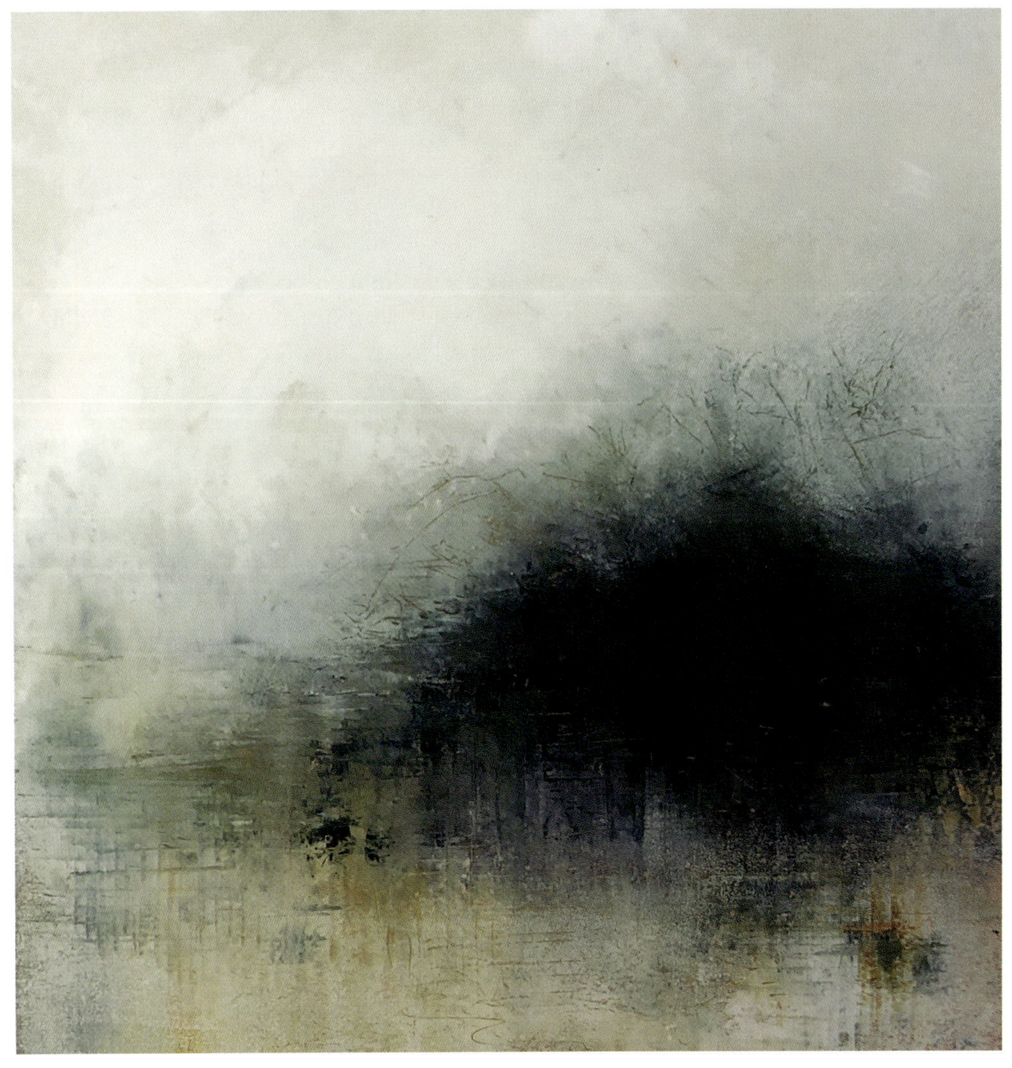

New Lands I, 30 x 30cm, oil and cold wax on Arches Huile paper.

WORKING WET-ON-WET

No matter the scale, whether it is a small warm-up exercise on paper or a 200 × 200cm panel, I begin a painting by working wet-on-wet, also known as *alla prima* or direct painting. This dynamic technique is exciting and fast-paced, challenging you to be bold and decisive. It involves applying freshly mixed wet paint onto layers of still-wet paint, allowing natural blending, and creating beautiful transitions between colours. This approach requires a readiness to work with accidents and not being precious about your work – something we can all struggle with at times.

For those accustomed to extensive research, sketching, and preparation before applying paint to canvas, this fluid approach may feel like a significant shift. Wet-on-wet painting demands a more generalised way of working, keeping the process fresh and spontaneous. It encourages you to allow colours to mix organically, move paint freely across the surface, and discover the emerging direction of the piece. Resolving the painting becomes an intuitive process, guided by those initial explorations.

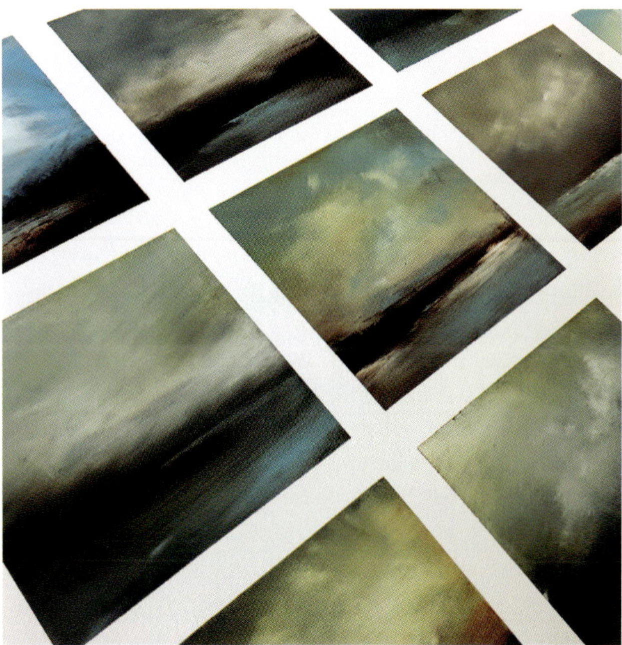

Try taping up a large sheet of paper and dividing it into smaller sections for your warm-up exercises. Dedicate a little time each day to create one small painting, using a consistent colour palette to develop a cohesive series. This method fosters exploration, builds creative momentum, and can serve as an inspiration for larger paintings.

Working on small pieces of paper, giving yourself a limited time to avoid the risk of overworking, is one way to practise wet-on-wet techniques using oils and cold wax. This is something that can easily be incorporated into your practice and a great way to set yourself up for a day in the studio. You can start with a fresh new palette to see what colour blends and tones you can create, or use paint left over at the end of the day. The immediacy of these paintings can create dynamic, expressive small works which can be used as inspiration for larger scale paintings.

LAYERING COLOUR

The buttery, thick consistency of cold wax makes it an ideal medium for layering paint wet-on-wet. When applied with a squeegee, it allows for beautiful colour mixes and blends that add richness and depth to your paintings. The initial colour mixing at the start of a painting can yield exciting results: the soft transitions as one colour merges into another, and the luminous effects achieved by layering transparent colours.

Incorporating this versatile medium in my practice has provided me with the opportunity to experiment with colour, resulting in my palette becoming bolder with more saturated hues making an appearance. I have introduced oranges, yellows, reds, and bright blues as base layers in my paintings, which I may then choose to reveal at a later stage in the painting process to create pops of colour. These colourful base layers greatly influence the direction of a painting; blues resulting in landscapes reminiscent of a Scottish landscape and its cool northern light; oranges and reds providing a warm contrast to a cool grey seascape.

Some colours have a higher tinting strength than others and will only require a small amount to be mixed before they start to dominate. They tend to be more vibrant and intense and will retain their colour for longer when mixed with white, whereas a paint with a low tinting strength will need a lot more paint to achieve the desired colour mix. Think carefully about your

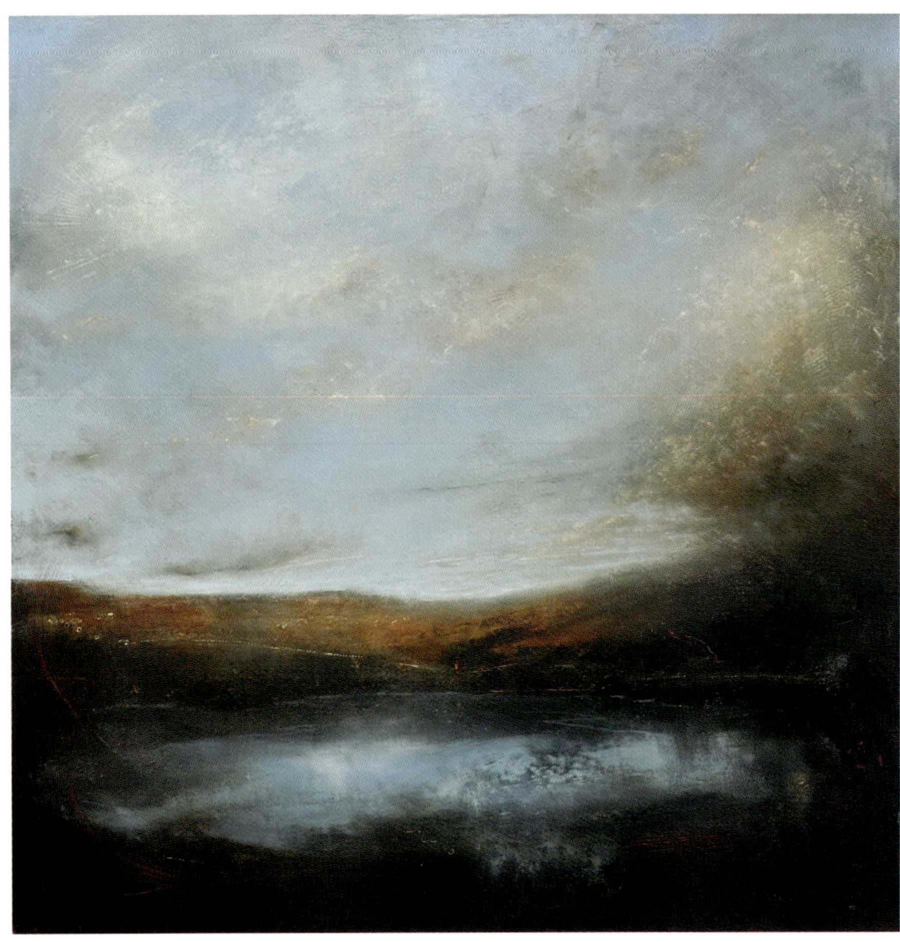

Drysnap of morning, 100 × 100cm (39½ × 39½in), oil, cold wax and gold leaf on board. This autumnal, Scottish-inspired landscape features Pyrrole Red by Michael Harding as the base layer. The vibrant pops of red, selectively revealed, guide the viewer's eye across the painting and link nicely with the soft tints of the same hue subtly present in the sky.

colours, the order in which they will appear, and how they will interact. Understand how they behave, what their tint strength is and whether they are transparent or opaque. Introducing cold wax into your oils enhances transparency, but the level of transparency will vary and is very much dependent on whether the colours are identified to start with as opaque, semi-opaque, transparent, or semi-transparent. More information about transparent and opaque colours can be found in Chapter 4.

Layering transparent and semi-transparent colours enables you to create beautiful glows and added depth to your paintings. They can also help to quieten down and unify surfaces, pushing back colours, marks, and patterns. With the right combination of transparent colours, you can create a colour mix where you produce the illusion of a third colour. For example, carefully applying a thin layer of the transparent alizarin crimson over a yellow such as lemon yellow, cadmium yellow or Indian yellow will result in a beautiful, glowing orange-red. Applying the same alizarin crimson over a blue such as cerulean blue or ultramarine blue will create the illusion of a dark purple colour. Experiment with different colours to see the illusionary colour mixes that can be achieved: the greater the contrast between the colours, the better the results.

Illusionary colour mixing works both with wet-on-wet and wet-on-dry techniques. There are limitations to how many layers can be applied wet-on-wet as the paint starts to blend, and it becomes increasingly difficult to retain separate layers of colour. If you do not control the extent of the mixing, there is the danger of creating what is referred to as 'a muddy mess'. By practising and mastering these techniques, you can achieve fantastic depth and atmosphere quickly in your painting, which can lead to beautiful colour and tonal blends.

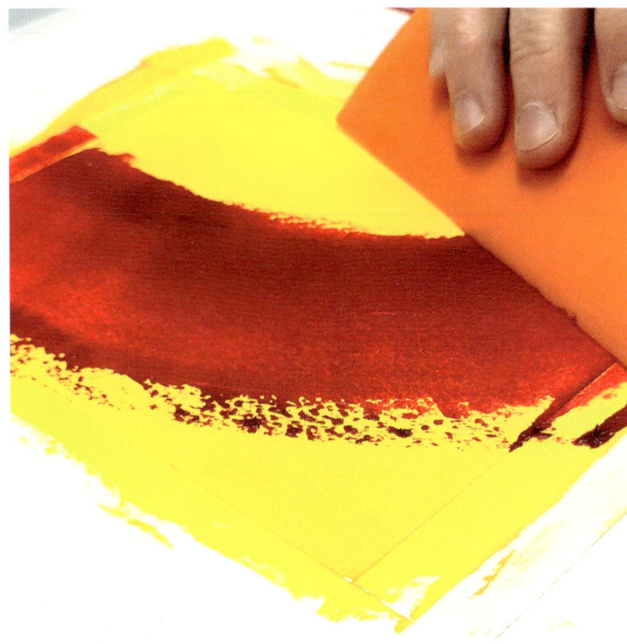

With the right combination of colours, you can create an illusionary mix where the eye perceives a third colour. In this example, a thin layer of transparent alizarin crimson was applied over cadmium yellow, creating an orange-red as the yellow shines through the red layer.

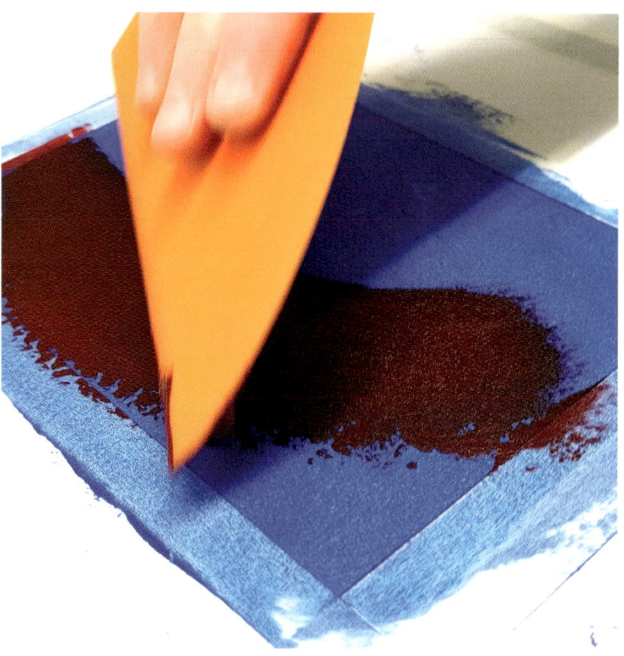

Notice how the underlying colour can significantly change the illusionary colour produced. In this second example, a thin, transparent layer of alizarin crimson is applied over an ultramarine blue base to create a deep, rich purple as the blue shines through the red.

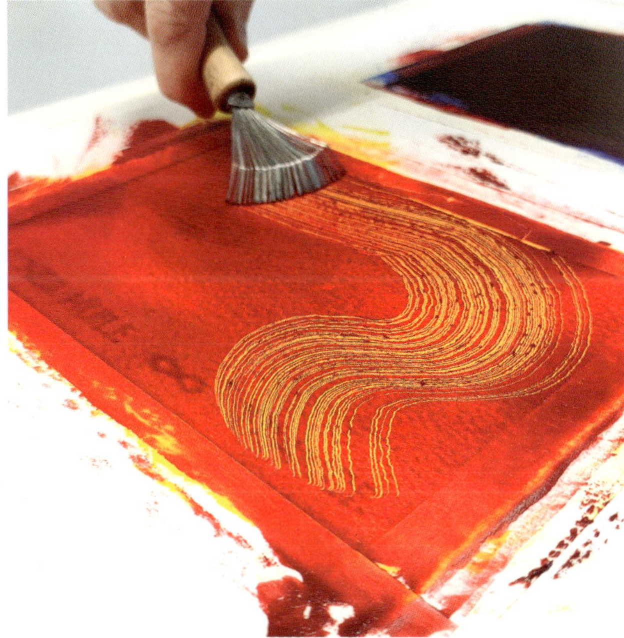

When you scratch back into the layers of colour, you will see that they have not mixed to create the orangey red. Instead, the yellow base remains intact, and can be revealed to create a vibrant pop of colour when scratched with a brush comb.

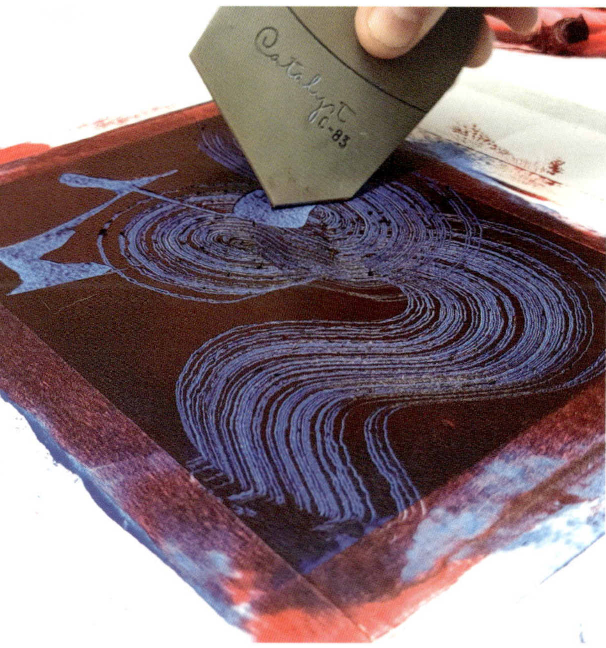

Experimenting with different tools allows you to create a variety of marks, from gestural to controlled. A brush comb creates fine lines, while scraping with a Catalyst tool can create bold marks, revealing as much or as little of the base layer as you want.

REMOVING PAINT

Removing paint is an integral part of my process, whether it involves delicately scratching back with a fine point in a sgraffito-like manner to reveal pops of the bright base colours, scraping off large areas with a palette knife, or dissolving layers with solvent. The goal is to expose unique marks, patterns, or shapes that add depth and character to the painting.

Cold wax increases the viscosity of oils, which results in any marks being scratched into the paint being sharper and more defined. If you attempt to do this with oils straight from the tube when the consistency is more fluid, your marks will become blurred as the oil paint starts to creep back into those marks. By using an array of tools, you can scratch back in a controlled, purposeful way, considering the types of marks you wish to make and where you wish to place them. It is possible to use any object that will allow you to scratch a line into your paint, whether it is the pointed end of a brush, palette knife, a fork, credit card or your squeegee. Experiment with a range of tools to see what opportunities there are for creating different types of marks: gestural, controlled, uncontrolled, Asemic writing – a wordless form of writing with no meaning.

A less controlled way to remove paint is imprinting tissue or papers onto the surface of your painting so that when it is removed it leaves behind a crackle effect, revealing flashes of colour from the lower layers. Depending on the effects you want to create, you can press down lightly on the tissue with your hand or use a brayer to roll over. The less pressure, the more delicate the marks tend to be. If your paint is touch-dry, then you may find that you need to apply more pressure to create any imprint. Do not be too disappointed if you do not get what you wanted to achieve. As is the way with the techniques used with cold wax, this can be a bit hit-and-miss and the results unpredictable.

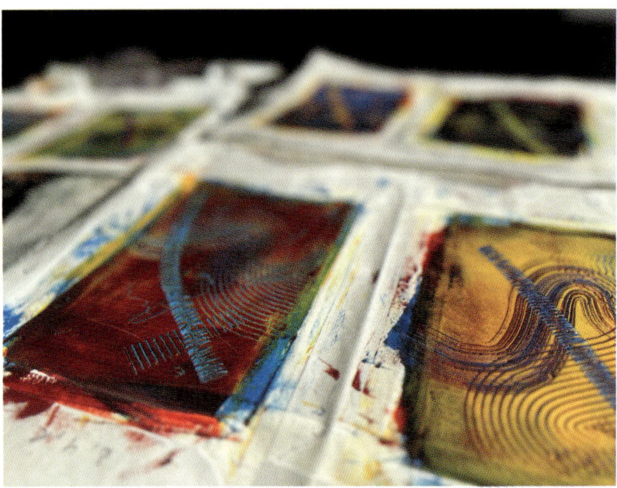

Experiment with layering different colours to create dynamic visual effects. The greater the contrast between layers, the more striking the result. Scratching back into these layers reveals the underlying colours, allowing them to interact in unexpected ways. When colours are placed side by side without blending, they merge optically from a distance, enhancing depth and vibrancy in your work.

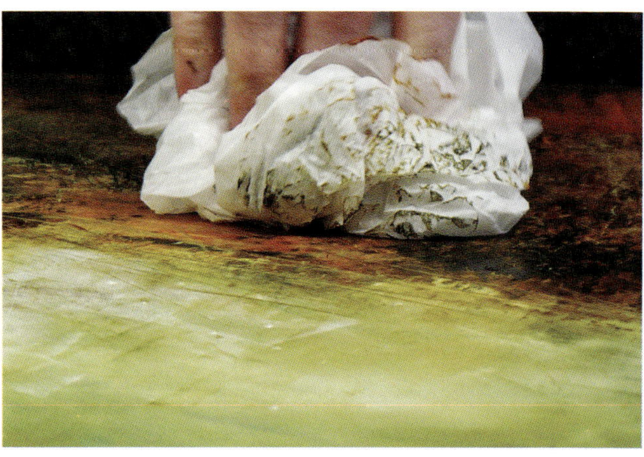

A slightly more controlled approach to using tissue for imprinting involves scrunching the tissue and gently dabbing it on to the area where you wish to reveal the underlying base colours. This allows for more deliberate marks, while still maintaining an element of unpredictability, as you may not know exactly how much paint will be removed.

Using solvents to dissolve paint offers an even more experimental approach. This technique produces organic marks and some colour mixing as the paint dissolves and softens. You can spray, pour, splash, or brush solvent onto the surface to create intriguing effects, pushing and pulling the paint until the piece begins to suggest a direction. For optimal results, work while the paint is still wet. Sprinkle, splash, or drip solvent onto the surface with a brush, then gently wipe it away with a squeegee for clean edges. Be mindful to not overwork the painting, as the surface can quickly become soft and very wet. If this happens, allow the painting to rest for a few hours and let the solvent evaporate before returning to it.

When working with solvents, always prioritise safety. Solvent splashes and fumes can be hazardous, as they may irritate the respiratory system and are flammable. Ensure your workspace is well ventilated, take regular breaks, and follow safety precautions to protect yourself.

BLENDING

The blending process carries an element of unpredictability; no matter how much control you exert while painting, you may find that colours mix too much or that your painting dries too quickly. Do not let this unpredictability discourage you. Embrace the experimental nature of your work, as it often leads to intriguing results that can take your painting in unexpected directions. Give yourself permission to play, experiment, and allow yourself to make a mess.

The initial blending on the surface involves using a squeegee, which is the perfect tool for applying thin layers of paint and for creating those first colour mixes. I find a medium-sized squeegee, no matter how large the surface I am painting on, fits comfortably in my hand. The larger the painting, the more dynamic my gestures will become, to a point where the application of paint and the blending becomes quite an energetic process.

Once a painting has a couple of thin layers of colour, I will introduce a light, opaque colour. Rather than covering the whole surface, I will introduce it to part of the painting using a sweeping motion with my squeegee, creating dynamic marks and allowing the paint to mix with the earlier layers of colour. Moving the squeegee across the painting, working intuitively and allowing the work to evolve. This approach can produce a beautiful array of colour mixes, and a range of mid-tones and muted colours. More complex colours can be achieved by introducing further layers of transparent colours across the whole painting, helping to unify the painting's surface and pushing back some of the lighter opaque colours. Additional mid-tones and muted colours can then be achieved when a pale opaque colour is reintroduced and allowed to mix.

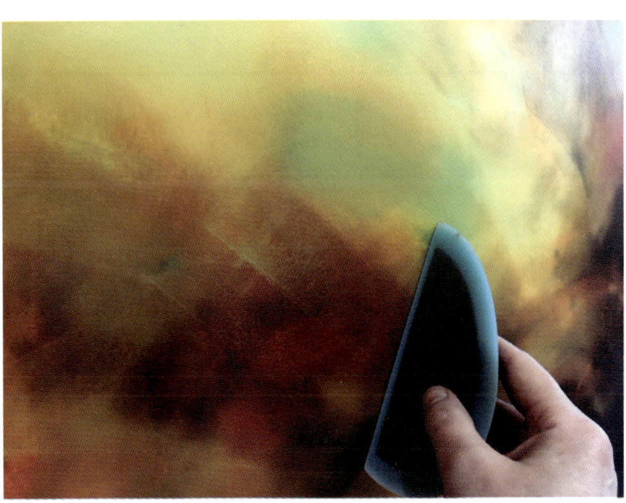

Adding a layer of transparent colour not only enriches the overall colour palette, but also helps unify the surface. As you build up these transparent layers, they work to push back some of the lighter opaque colours, allowing them to recede into the background and create depth to your work.

This spontaneous approach, embracing the uncertainty of the painting's direction and waiting for the right composition to emerge, is one of the most exciting aspects of the process. The only planning at this stage involves selecting colours for the base layers and determining the size and shape of the surface.

Since cold wax accelerates the drying process, paints mixed with the medium tend to stiffen after a few hours. While the paint remains workable, some blending techniques are best executed with a fresh mix of oils and cold wax. Alternatively, you can increase the fluidity of the mixture by incorporating mediums such as cold-pressed linseed oil, Liquin™, Galkyd, Galkyd Lite, or Solvent-Free Fluid. Each of these mediums provides varying levels of fluidity and drying times. Avoid using solvent to increase fluidity for blending as it will thin your paint too much, which will lead to overmixing your colours.

SFUMATO

Sfumato builds upon the earlier colour-blending process and is a technique that emphasises the creation of soft, seamless transitions between colours and tones, resulting in a hazy atmospheric effect that adds depth to a painting. By subtly blending edges and lines, eliminating hard boundaries, you can create a softness and ethereal quality to your work.

While blending focuses on the immediate mixing of colours to achieve smooth transitions, sfumato emphasises the gradual merging of tones and hues. This technique requires a delicate balance, involving not just the application of colour, but also the careful refinement of edges to maintain harmony while preserving the distinctiveness of each hue. By utilising tools such as synthetic fan brushes, flat brushes, squeegees, and even your fingertips, you can enhance the blending process, allowing colours to mingle seamlessly. The result is a cohesive union of colours that adds depth and transforms simple blends into complex, atmospheric layers which draw the viewer into the painting.

When blending with a fan brush, it is important to manage excess paint on the bristles. Start by wiping off the paint, then rinse the brush in solvent to ensure it is clean. After rinsing, dry the bristles thoroughly with a paper towel. This step is crucial as it prevents the bristles from separating, making them ineffective for blending.

The essence of sfumato lies in finding this balance, allowing colours to intermingle while retaining their individual identities. This meditative process aligns well with the wet-on-wet techniques using cold wax described in this book. It involves adjusting contrasts, refining details, and continuously blending and softening until the desired effect is achieved, where a light touch and patience are essential.

In *Dreaming of the Sea*, the blending and softening of colour transitions allows each hue to maintain its presence while contributing to an overall ethereal quality. I used a squeegee for colour blending, responding intuitively to cues from the painting as I refined the composition. My focus was on enhancing contrasts and improving the transitions between tones to evoke a soft, gentle feel in the clouds. After blending with the squeegee, I switched to working with brushes and palette knives to add highlights to further soften transitions and refine details.

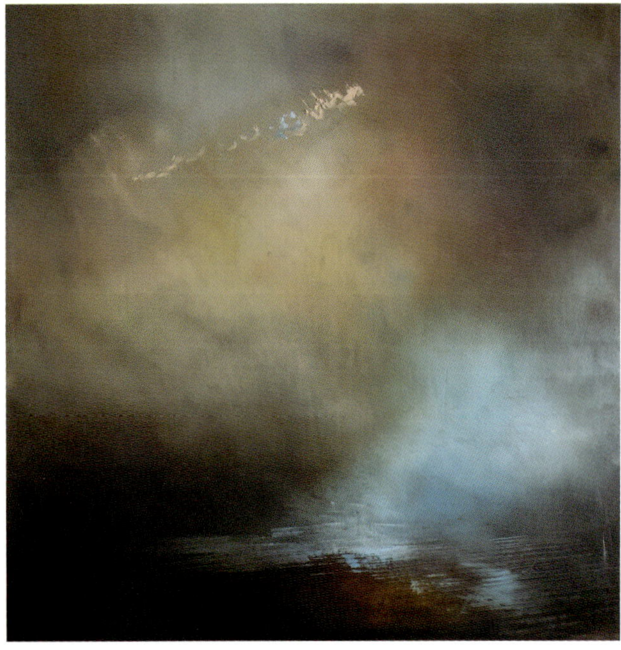

Dreaming of the sea, 50 × 50cm (19¾ × 19¾in), oils, cold wax and gold leaf). Blending wet-on-wet with a squeegee allowed for the creation of rich, complex colour transitions. As the colours merged, their tonal values became similar, so additional lights and darks were introduced throughout the process to enhance contrast, depth, and visual interest.

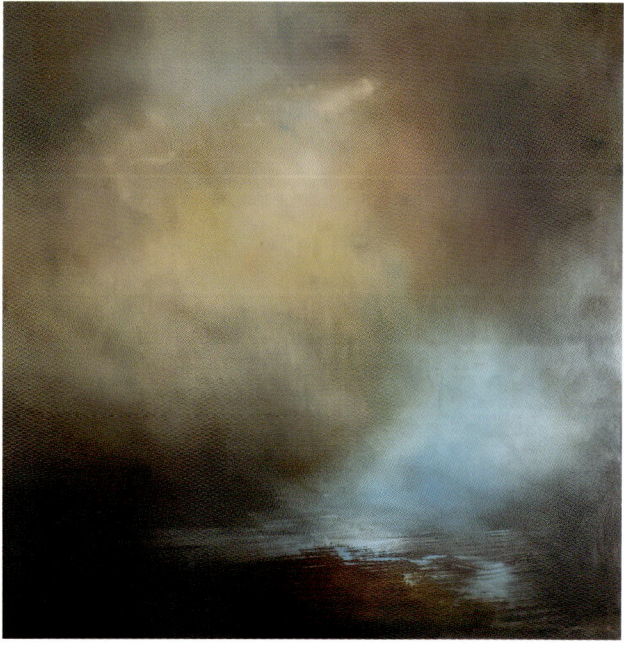

In the initial stages, colour mixing occurred directly on the painting's surface. Once the shapes and tones were established, colours were blended on the palette before being applied to create highlights. Small amounts of paint were carefully added, gradually building luminosity. Highlights were softened using a squeegee or smudged with a finger to achieve a more natural, seamless effect.

SCUMBLING

Scumbling is a technique that involves applying a thin layer of opaque paint over a dry layer, allowing the previous layers to show through in a soft, textured manner. To scumble effectively, use a stiff-bristled brush or a palette knife to apply a small amount of paint in a light, scrubbing motion. This technique works beautifully with both opaque and semi-opaque colours, providing a way to introduce new hues without overpowering the existing layers. Scumbling can enhance the atmospheric quality of your painting, much like sfumato, by softening edges and blending transitions.

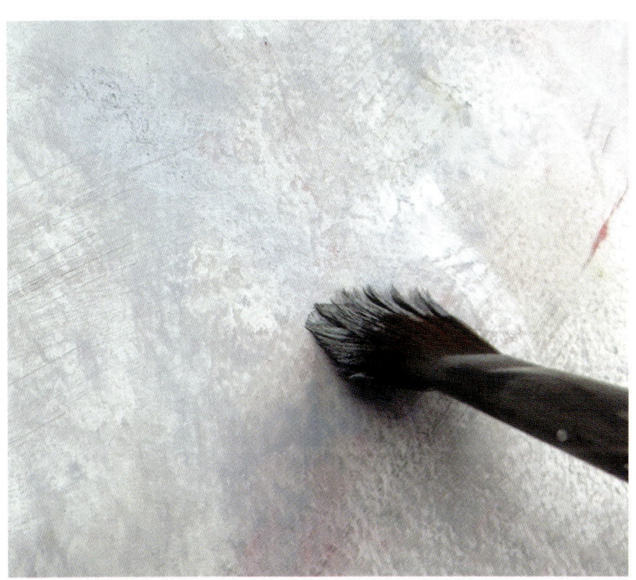

A stiff brush is used on the dry surface of this painting to apply a pale opaque colour, creating a soft transition between the clouds and the sky. This technique not only adds depth to the composition, but also fosters a luminous atmosphere, enhancing the overall sense of light and airiness in the painting.

IMPASTO

Impasto is characterised by thick applications of paint that create a textured effect on the surface. Cold wax serves as an excellent medium for achieving impasto textures, allowing you to build up areas of thick paint that maintain their shape and add a tactile quality to your work. To enhance the texture further, you can incorporate dry materials such as marble dust to create a gritty effect. This is particularly effective when applied with a palette knife in expressive strokes, allowing for layered, raised texture. The contrast between impasto areas and smoother passages can add dynamism and visual interest to your painting.

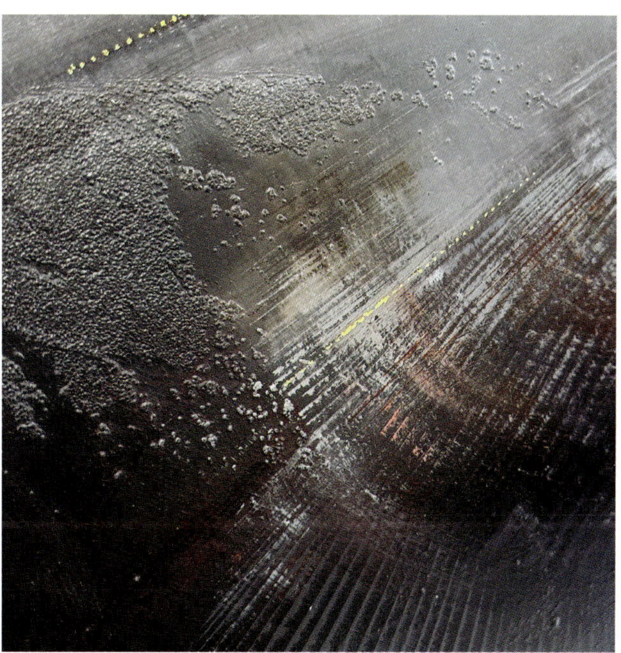

In this painting, oil and cold wax was mixed with marble dust to create added texture. This texture was further emphasised by pulling a pale colour across the surface, enhancing the textured appearance and creating a striking contrast against the adjacent smooth section. The interplay between rough and smooth elements adds depth and visual interest to the composition.

GLAZING

Glazing can play a critical role in pulling together a painting, especially when it feels disconnected or rough around the edges. Transparent glazes can harmonise the composition by integrating various elements, softening contrasts, and creating a sense of atmospheric depth. The right glaze not only brings balance, but also refines shapes, adjusts tones, and connects disparate parts of a painting. Effective glazing relies on good contrast between light and dark values, which provides a strong foundation for transparent layers, adding depth and complexity.

When a painting lacks direction, glazing acts as a transformative tool, forging new connections and introducing unexpected colour shifts. It offers an opportunity to recalibrate the artwork, shifting its energy and revitalising the creative process when it feels stagnant. By reconciling contrasting areas, enhancing depth, or enriching texture, glazing ties all elements together.

To achieve luminosity and depth, glazing involves applying thin, transparent layers of paint over dried layers. Cold wax can be used as the glazing medium, mixed with your chosen colour, and the amount of cold wax can be adjusted to achieve the desired transparency. Alternatively, you can mix your oil and cold wax blend with mediums such as Galkyd or a small amount of linseed oil to enhance transparency while maintaining the paint's body.

I often apply a glaze using a squeegee, which allows for a thin application. I will then use paper roll to wipe away the glaze in some areas or use a dry, stiff brush to fine-tune the glazing layers and achieve the desired tonal shifts. This technique allows underlying colours to shine through, creating a rich, layered effect while enabling you to adjust the glazing layers.

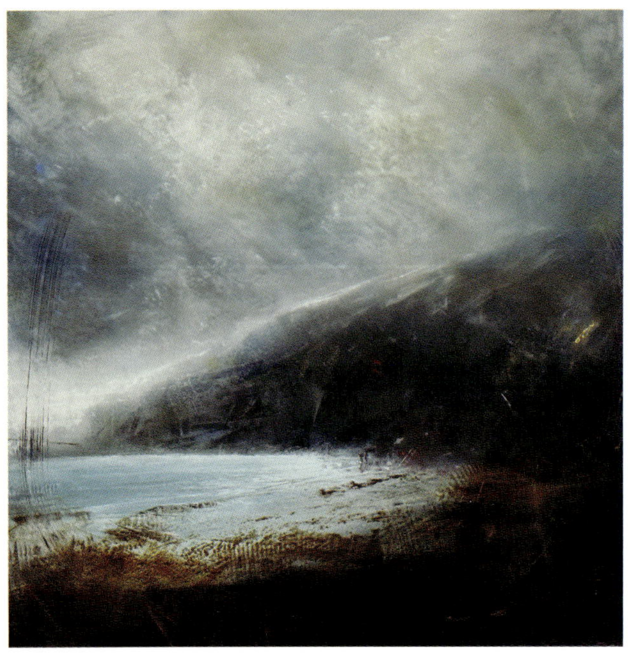

A thin layer of Transparent Red Oxide mixed with cold wax was applied to the bottom section of this painting using a squeegee. I then manipulated the surface by wiping off paint in some areas with paper roll and brushes, layering additional colours on top, and scratching back to expose the underlying colours and textures.

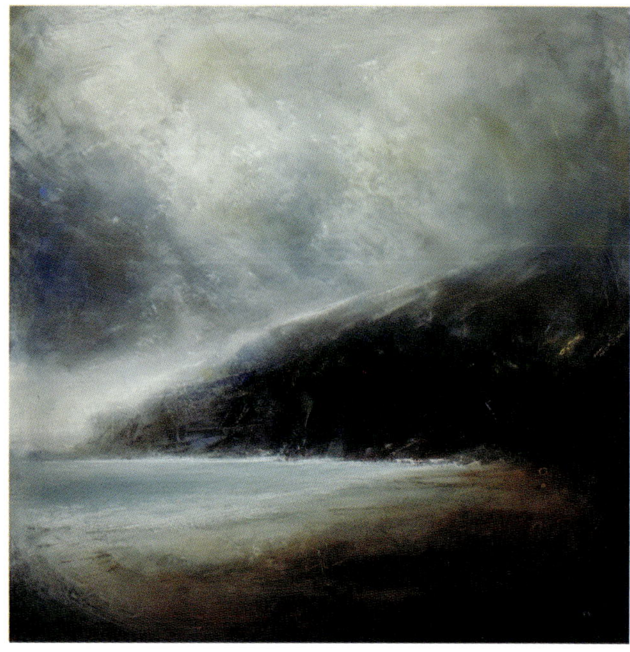

Wild Atlantic, 60 × 60cm (23½ × 23½in), oil, cold wax and gold leaf. Applying this transparent glaze enhanced the depth and complexity of the foreground, introducing a subtle warmth that contrasts beautifully with the predominantly grey-blue palette. It also enriched an area dominated by opaque colours, adding luminosity while creating a more dynamic and layered composition.

EXPLORING AND EXPERIMENTING

Painting with oils and cold wax opens up a world of creative possibilities, inviting artists to explore a diverse range of techniques and approaches. Whether you choose to work on paper, panel, or canvas, the versatility of this medium allows for various methods, from wet-on-wet applications to layering techniques that can produce rich textures and intricate patterns.

Painting with oils and cold wax is as much about the process as it is about the final artwork. Embracing the unpredictability of this medium can lead to unexpected and delightful results, transforming your approach to painting. Whether you find joy in the vibrant colour mixes achieved through layering or in the energetic application with a squeegee, each technique contributes to the development of your style.

As you continue to experiment with these techniques, you will gain a deeper understanding of how this medium can enhance your practice, encouraging you to embrace intuition and spontaneity in your work. Remember to give yourself permission to play and make mistakes – these moments often lead to the most rewarding discoveries.

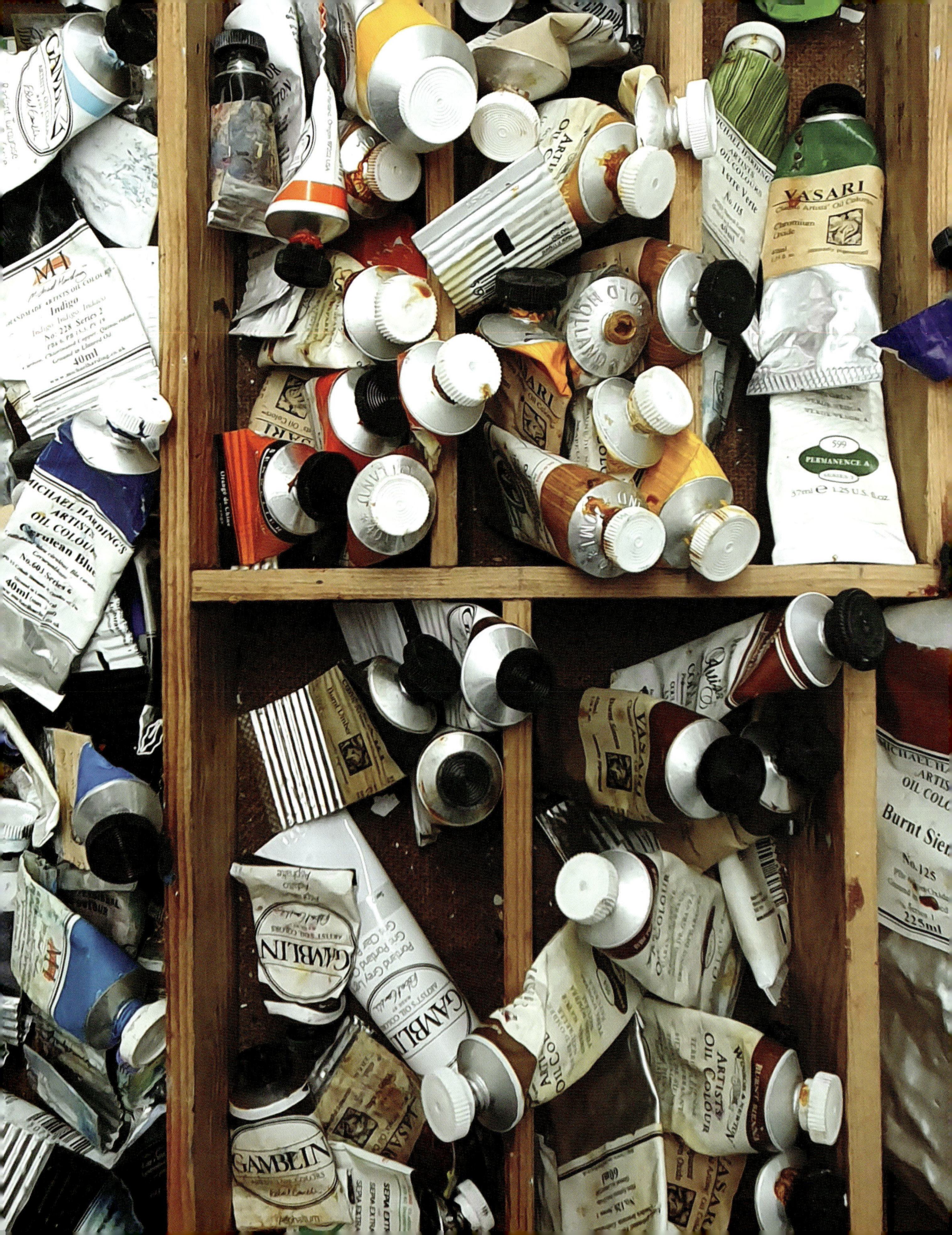

Indigo
No. 228 Series 2
40ml
VASARI
Chromium Oxide
PERMANENCE A
37ml 1.25 U.S. fl.oz
Terre Verte
No.115
MICHAEL HARDING'S
ARTISTS
OIL COLOURS
No.601 Series 6
40ml
GAMBLIN
No.125
225ml

CHAPTER 4

EXPLORING COLOUR

'If every colour was used at its maximum strength the picture would not become strong in colour as a consequence, but loud and gaudy.'

Max Doerner

Choosing the right colour combinations and mixes is essential, as overlooking this step at the start of a painting can lead to unnecessary challenges later on. But how do you decide which colours to use? For me, it often begins with a strong emotional response to a particular colour – a sense of excitement and inspiration that makes me eager to work with it. However, experience also plays a significant role. Over time, I have developed an understanding of how different colours behave on their own and with others, which helps guide my decisions.

That said, mistakes are inevitable. There have been times when I have purchased a new colour without realising it was transparent or had poor tinting strength, simply because I was drawn to the colour and overlooked its technical properties. One such example from early in my painting career was when I mistakenly bought zinc white, intending to use it for creating big, fluffy clouds. For a while, I could not understand why it did not provide good coverage. I later discovered the differences between opaque and transparent colours. Zinc white, for example, is far more transparent than titanium white, which I had previously used. Unlike zinc white, titanium white has the highest hiding power of all whites and can easily overpower other colours (Coles, 2018).

These experiences, while frustrating at the time, have been invaluable in developing my understanding of colour. Now, I actively seek out transparent colours to experiment with, balancing them with opaque options on my palette. This combination allows me to create the 'push backwards and pull forwards' effects that add depth and dimension to my work. Experimentation, including the occasional failure, is an essential part of building both knowledge and confidence.

In this chapter we look at how colour plays a pivotal role in creating depth, atmosphere, and mood in my paintings. It will guide you through identifying the differences between transparent and opaque colours, understanding how to use them effectively, and exploring methods for creating transparent tints and glazes. Additionally, the chapter includes techniques for colour mixing, harmonising colours, and the benefits of choosing a limited palette.

While this chapter is not intended as a comprehensive technical guide to colour theory, it introduces foundational principles to help you make informed decisions about colour mixing and composition. These principles aim to assist you in creating visual depth and developing atmosphere in your work. By understanding and applying these insights, you can gain more confidence in your use of colour and in experimenting with new combinations.

OPPOSITE: There are numerous brands and colours of oil paints available, but you only need a few to get started. A basic palette offers a solid foundation, providing the flexibility to mix and create a wide range of hues. With just a handful of essential colours, you can create bold, vibrant tones to soft, subtle nuances, unlocking endless colour-mixing possibilities.

COLOUR STRUCTURE

The colour wheel is a great reference tool for when you are beginning to explore colour mixing. It visually represents the hue continuum in a circular format, divided into twelve major hues: the primary, secondary, and tertiary colours. Additionally, the wheel is organised into four rings that illustrate hues, tints, tones, and shades.

The terms 'hue' and 'colour' are often used interchangeably, but not all colours are considered hues. Primary, secondary, and tertiary colours are classified as hues, while white, black, and grey, though commonly referred to as colours, do not qualify as hues. A hue refers specifically to the pure form of a colour as it appears on the colour wheel such as red, blue, green, or yellow, without considering lightness or saturation. In contrast, colour is a broader concept that includes hue, along with aspects of lightness (value) and saturation (intensity). For example, light blue and dark red are colours that have specific hues, but also include additional characteristics of lightness and saturation. Essentially, hue is a component of colour, while colour includes a broader range of variations, including tints (hues mixed with white), shades (hues mixed with black), and tones (hues mixed with grey) (Hornung, 2012).

Colours are arranged on the wheel based on their relationships and similarities. Colours adjacent to each other are closely related; for example, orange is most similar to yellow and red. Directly across from orange on the wheel is blue, its complementary colour. Complementary colours are positioned directly opposite each other, and there are three primary complementary relationships:

- Green is the complement of red.
- Orange is the complement of blue.
- Violet is the complement of yellow.

The primary colours (red, yellow, and blue) are foundational, as they cannot be created by mixing other colours. In theory, they can be combined to produce all other colours. Secondary colours (green, orange, and violet) are formed by mixing two primary colours. Tertiary colours (yellow-orange, red-orange, blue-green, yellow-green, blue-violet, and red-violet) are created by combining a primary and a secondary colour.

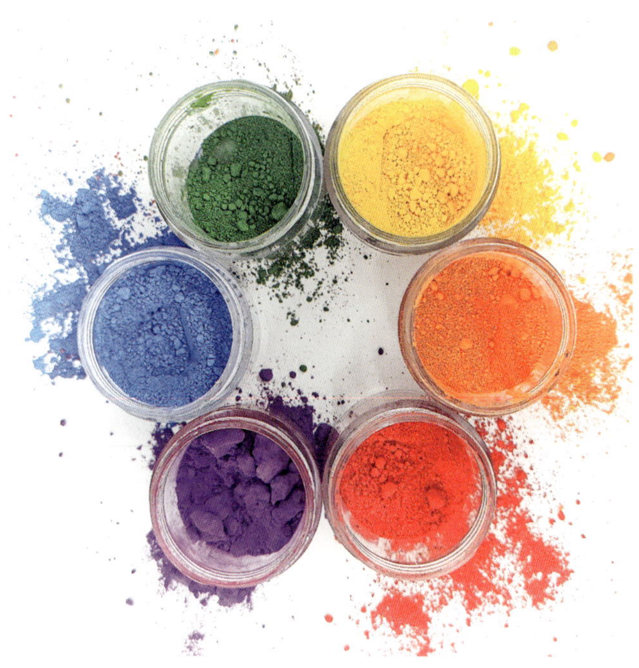

A colour wheel is a circular diagram that organises colours based on their relationships, featuring primary colours (red, yellow, and blue) and their secondary counterparts (green, orange, and violet). It illustrates how primary colours combine to form secondary colours and highlights colour schemes like analogous (neighbouring colours for harmony), and triadic (three evenly spaced colours for vibrant contrast and balance).

Temperature and colour bias

Temperature refers to the warmth or coolness of a colour, influenced by its hue. Generally, colours leaning toward orange are classified as warm, whereas those leaning toward blue and green are considered cool. However, this classification can be relative; for example, some oranges can be cooler than others, and certain blues can be warmer than others. The temperature of a colour is also referred to as colour bias, which I find to be a simpler way to describe a colour, as temperature does not always align with how people perceive colours. For instance, while reds are typically associated with warmth, Alizarin Crimson is classified as a cool colour due to its blue bias (Hornung, 2012).

Being able to recognise the colour bias is important if you want to mix clean, bright colours. If you mix colours that contain a pair of complementary colours within them, your colour mix is going to turn out muddier than you may have intended. For example, if you want a bright green, then choose a yellow and blue that do not have a red bias – for example, lemon yellow (blue bias) and

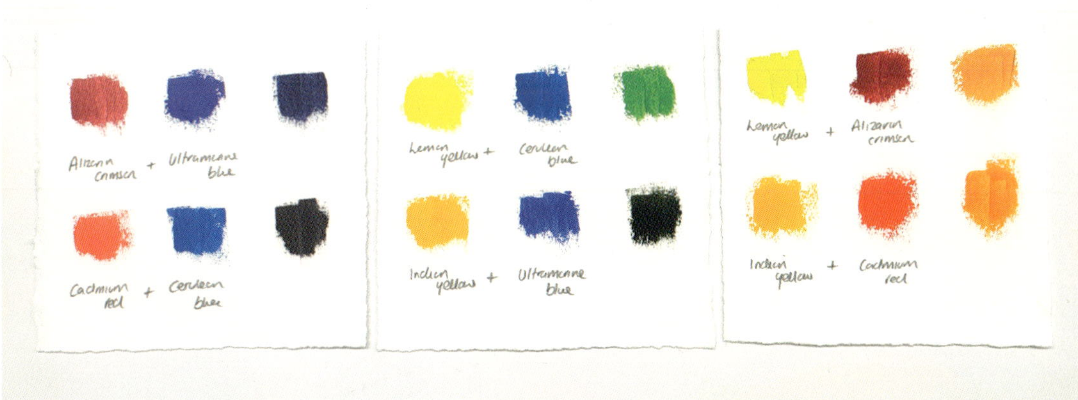

To achieve a bright, clean green, avoid red bias in the blue and yellow you choose to mix. For a bright clean violet, avoid yellow bias when mixing red and blue. To mix a bright, clean orange, avoid blue bias when mixing red and yellow.

cerulean blue (yellow bias). If you want a duller green, then you want the red to be present in the yellow and blue, for example, Indian yellow (red bias) and ultramarine blue (red bias). If you want a bright violet, then you choose a red and blue that do not have a yellow bias, for example, alizarin crimson (blue bias) and ultramarine blue (red bias). If you want a dull violet, then you want the yellow to be present in the red and blue, for example, cadmium red (yellow bias) and cerulean blue (yellow bias). To get a bright, clean orange, then choose a red and yellow that do not have a blue bias, for example, cadmium red (yellow bias) and Indian yellow (red bias). If you want a dull orange, then you want the blue to be present in the red and yellow, for example, alizarin crimson (blue bias) and lemon yellow (blue bias) (Hornung, 2012).

The table below shows some example oil colours for each temperature and colour bias (Casey, 2022).

Tonal value

The tonal value of a colour refers to its lightness and darkness or its luminosity. Primary and secondary colours exhibit varying degrees of tonal value, with yellow being the lightest and violet the darkest. This value range is often simplified into a graduated scale called a greyscale, which consists of ten steps ranging from black to white. A more straightforward way to envision tonal value is to categorise it into dark, medium, and light (Hornung, 2012).

Tonal value is a crucial aspect of colour, as the contrasts between colour values are often the first elements we perceive in a painting. Highly saturated colours, such as reds and oranges, can make it challenging to identify value because they shout more loudly than others, trying to convince you that they are the lightest (Albers, 2013). If you struggle to determine whether you have the right combination of lights, darks, and mid-tones, try taking a digital photograph of your work and converting it to black and white. This will help you assess whether you have a good range of values.

Experiment with your painting by adding lighter and darker value colours to see how they impact the overall composition. Notice how placing a colour with a lighter value next to one with a darker value draws the viewer's attention to that area, while colours that are close in value do not create the same visual stimulation.

Temperature	Bias	Oil colour
Cool reds	Blue bias	Alizarin crimson, quinacridone magenta
Warm reds	Yellow bias	Scarlet, cadmium red light
Cool yellow	Blue bias	Lemon yellow, cadmium lemon
Warm yellow	Red bias	Indian yellow, cadmium yellow deep
Cool blue	Yellow bias	Prussian blue, cerulean blue
Warm blue	Red bias	Ultramarine Blue, cobalt blue

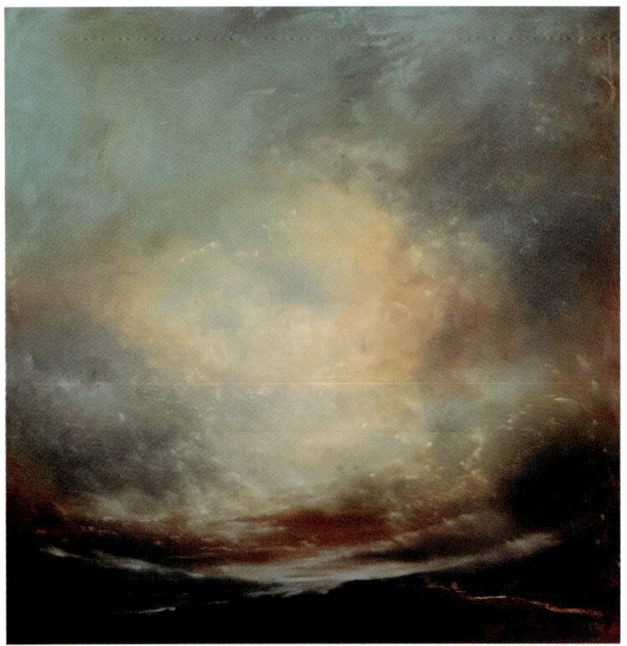

Tonal value refers to a colour's lightness or darkness and is often represented on a greyscale, typically ranging from black to white in ten steps. Highly saturated colours can sometimes mask their true tonal values, making them difficult to assess. A useful technique is to take a black and white photo of your work, which helps reveal the underlying values more clearly.

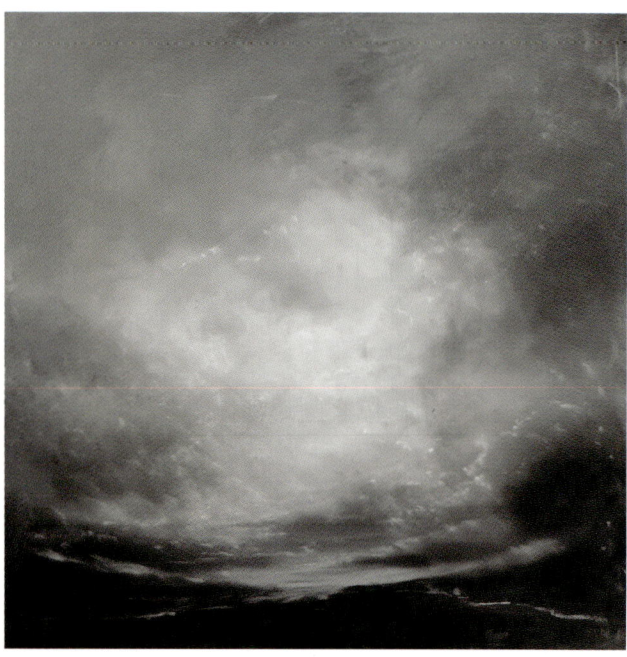

In *Tracing our way home* (80 × 80cm/31½ × 31½in, oil, cold wax, and gold leaf), the blue of the sky appears much brighter in the colour version than it does in greyscale. Similarly, the transparent red oxide used in the lower clouds, which may seem intense in colour, is revealed as a mid-tone when viewed in black and white.

Saturation

Saturation refers to the intensity of a colour. You will find the most saturated colours are those found on the outer rim of the colour wheel, including red, yellow, blue, orange, green and violet. As a colour moves closer to the centre of the colour wheel, where tints, tones, and shades are located, it becomes less saturated. This reduction in saturation occurs when other colours are added, particularly black and white, as well as complementary colours. Since black and white have zero saturation, adding them to a saturated colour reduces its intensity.

COLOUR HARMONY

Colour harmony is about creating relationships between colours. When colours work in harmony, they create structure, evoke a pleasing effect, and enhance the atmosphere of a painting. In contrast, a lack of harmony can make a composition feel chaotic or difficult to interpret (Casey, 2022).

For colours to harmonise, they need at least one shared element, though they often have more. Colours mixed from multiple hues tend to be richer and more cohesive. For example, mixing grey from black and white

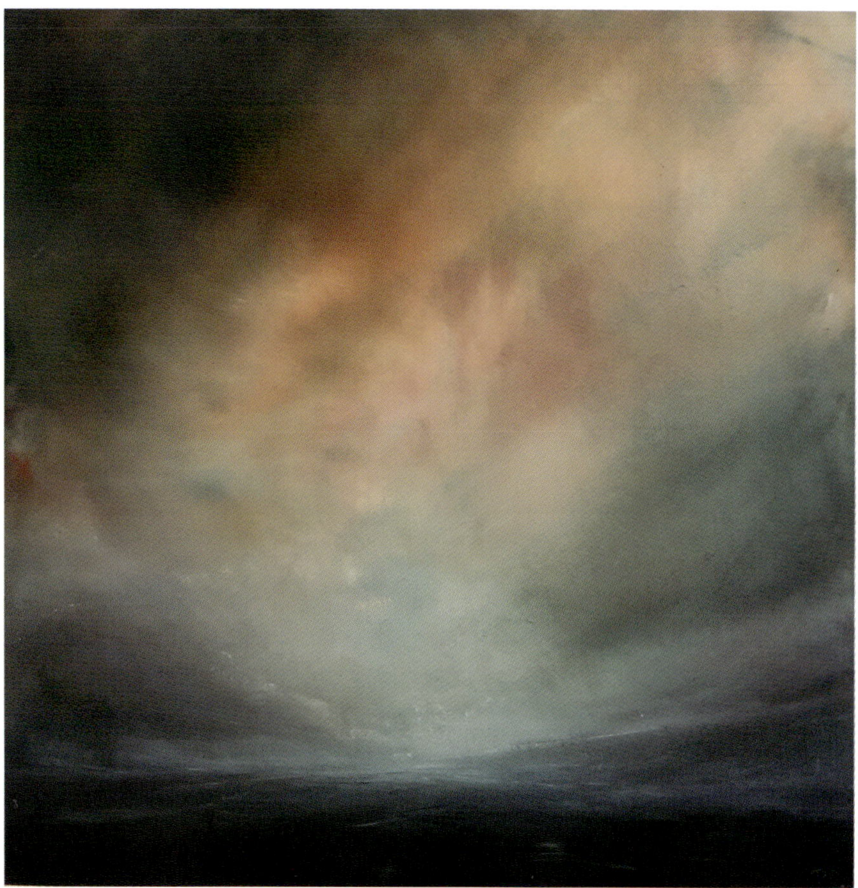

Mixing red with white creates pink, but adding a touch of yellow, blue, or another colour produces a more nuanced hue. These enriched pinks blend more naturally with surrounding colours by sharing subtle undertones. In *Shepherdess* (30 × 30cm/12 × 12in, oils, cold wax, and gold leaf), the pinks contain hints of blue and yellow, harmonising with the painting's cooler tones.

creates a basic colour, but adding a touch of yellow, red, blue, or another colour results in a more complex, nuanced grey. This richer grey naturally relates better to other colours in a painting because it contains subtle traces of them, enhancing overall harmony (Hornung, 2012).

Utilising complementary colours

Complementary colours are an excellent way to create more sophisticated colour palettes. When mixed, complementary pairs, such as green and red, neutralise each other, producing muted tones or even dark hues without relying on black, which can sometimes dull the vibrancy of a composition. This approach also enables the creation of chromatic blacks, rich in depth and subtlety (Doerner, 1921).

These colour pairings also allow for striking accents that add energy and contrast. For example, incorporating an orange base layer in a predominantly blue painting can create subtle warmth and depth. By strategically scratching back to expose the orange beneath, you can lift the composition, adding layers of visual intrigue and enhancing the overall effect.

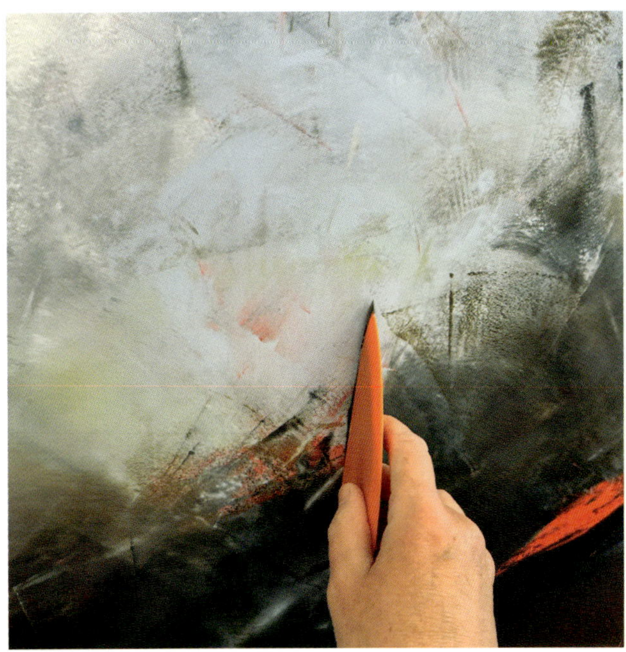

Passing storm – work in progress. A bright pink base layer, followed by a transparent orange, forms the foundation of this painting. Cooler tones are then layered over, shaping the composition and creating rich colour blends. Through scratching back, the vibrant base colours emerge, adding warmth and contrast that enhance the overall balance and guide the viewer's eye.

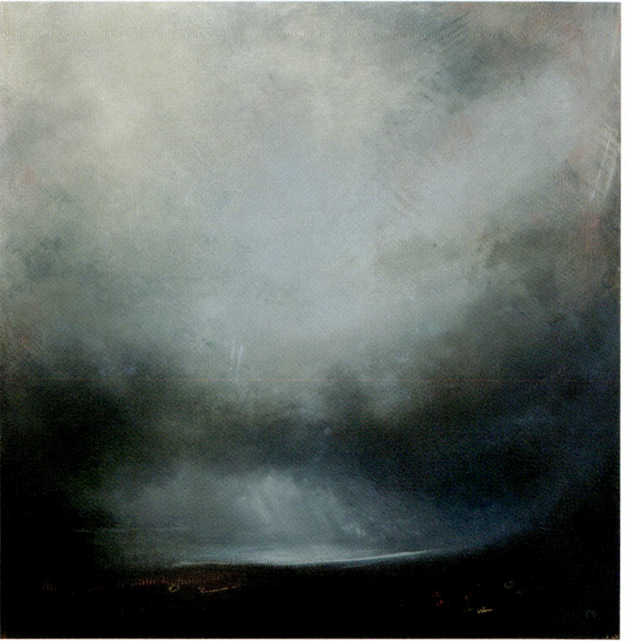

Passing Storm (60 × 60cm/23½ × 23½in, oil, cold wax, and gold leaf on board) features a predominantly cool blue and grey palette. Scratching back to reveal the pink and orange base layers introduces warmth to the sky, creating subtle contrast. This effect is further heightened by a few scratches in the foreground, where saturated orange-pink tones add depth and vibrancy.

Limiting your palette

Incorporating cold wax and its associated techniques can be liberating and encouraging of expressive and playful experimentation. However, sometimes it can be difficult to know where to stop, adding excessive texture or too many colours, which can lead to a chaotic composition where colours fail to relate. If your work feels disjointed or overwhelming, limiting your colours can be a helpful. Limiting your palette involves selecting just a few colours and using them to mix a broad range of hues, tints, and shades. This approach not only streamlines your process, but also encourages creative colour mixing.

A simple exercise in colour mixing

Start with a complementary colour pair, for example:

- Green (mixed from lemon yellow and cerulean blue) and paired with cadmium red or alizarin crimson
- Violet (mixed from alizarin crimson and ultramarine blue) and paired with Indian yellow or lemon yellow
- Orange (mixed from cadmium red and Indian yellow) and paired with cerulean blue or ultramarine blue

For this example, I have used violet (mixed from alizarin crimson and ultramarine blue) paired with Indian yellow. I have chosen titanium white to create my tints.

1. **Mix your colours**
    - Tape a sheet of Arches Huile paper to some print paper.
    - Mix your secondary colour (for example, violet) on your palette.
    - Squeeze out enough of your complementary colour (Indian yellow) and titanium white on your palette.

2. **Create a colour scale**
    - Take a palette knife and paint some Indian yellow at one end of your paper and the violet at the other.
    - Gradually mix a small amount of violet into the Indian yellow, adding each new mix with your palette knife next to the last. Repeat this for three or four steps.
    - Reverse the process by mixing small amounts of Indian yellow into violet, creating another three or four steps.
    - Finally, blend equal parts of both colours to create a neutral hue and place it in the centre of the scale.

3. **Experiment with tints**
    - Taking this a step further you can create a range of beautiful tints by adding a little titanium white to your colour mixes. Repeat this and add a little more white each time you move down the scale.

Through this process, you will discover how just two complementary colours can create a remarkably rich palette, from vibrant hues to subtle neutrals and deep tones, simply by dulling and neutralising each other. However, they do not have to be complementary – try pairing other colours together to explore the wide range of mixes and tints you can achieve.

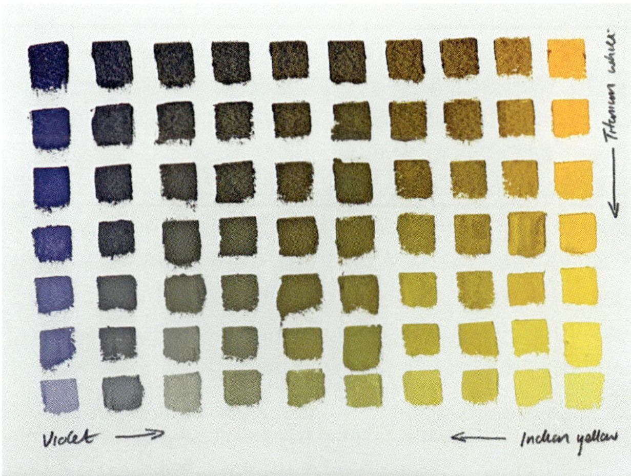

For this complementary colour scale I have used violet (mixed from alizarin crimson and ultramarine blue) paired with Indian yellow. Titanium white has been used to create the tints. While this exercise takes some time, it is invaluable for understanding the extensive range achievable with a limited selection of colours.

CREATING RICH MONOCHROMES

You can create monochromes by mixing white with a premixed black, but this often results in a flat and uninspiring range of greys. An alternative is to mix monochromes using ultramarine blue, burnt umber, and titanium white (Hornung, 2012). This combination produces a richer and more nuanced palette. For warmer monochromes, use more burnt umber; for cooler tones, emphasise ultramarine blue.

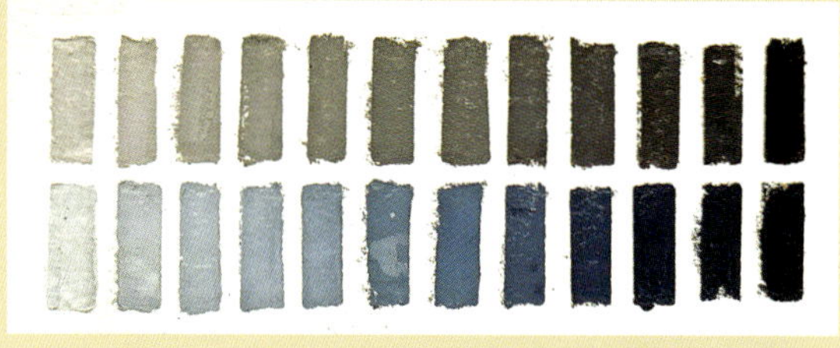

Harmonising your palette

Now that you have seen how many beautiful, rich colours you can mix from a limited palette try a selection of your go-to colours, limiting them to four, including white. It is worth making sure your selection has:

- a white for tints
- a dark colour for shades
- a transparent colour for depth
- a bright colour to add vibrancy.

To expand your palette, create a fifth colour by mixing small amounts of each colour on your palette to produce a neutral grey, beige, or brown. When mixing, reduce the quantity of high tinting strength colours to prevent them from dominating. Add a small touch of your neutral colour to each of the others. For lighter colours, use only a small amount to avoid dulling their brightness too much. You will find that your colours now have a relationship with each other and are in harmony.

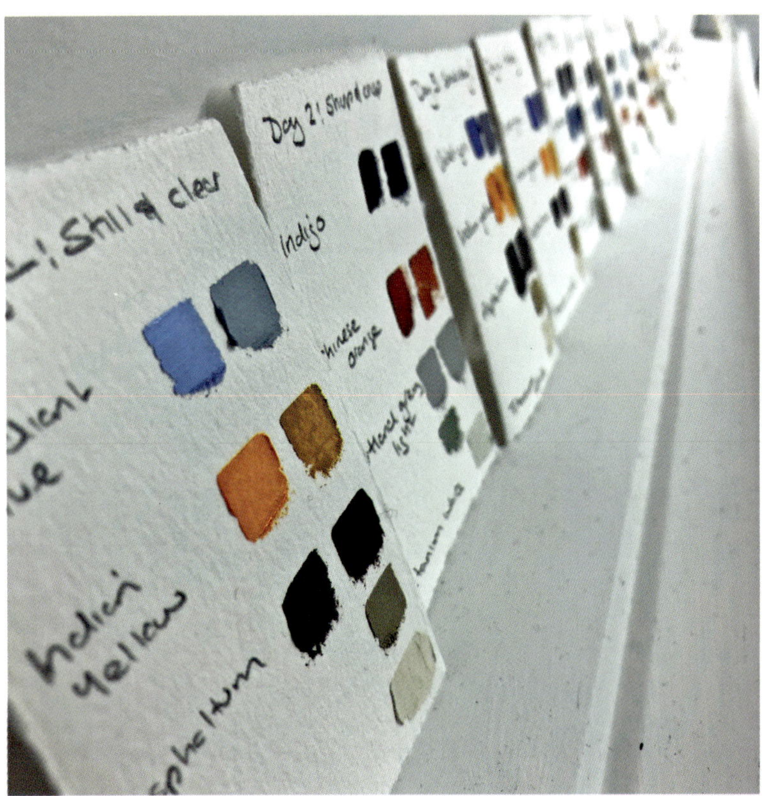

Harmonise your colours by blending each colour together to create a neutral mix. Add a touch of this neutral mix to each colour. Use a square-ended palette knife to apply a sample of the adjusted colour onto paper, alongside the colour straight from the tube. Compare to see how the colours now relate to one another.

Tinting strength and staining capacity

When mixing colours, it is important to consider the tinting strength and staining capacity of your paints, as stronger pigments can dominate the palette and shift the overall tone and feel of your work. The tinting strength of a colour is determined by several factors:

- Type of pigment: Some pigments, such as phthalo blue or quinacridone magenta, are naturally more intense and have stronger tinting power compared to others such as yellow ochre or raw umber.
- Amount of pigment: The concentration of pigment in the paint affects its tinting strength. Paints with a higher pigment load have more intense colouring power and require smaller amounts to influence a mix.
- Fineness of grinding: Finely ground pigments have a higher tinting strength because they disperse more evenly and thoroughly in the binder, increasing their ability to influence mixtures (Coles, 2018).

Paints with high tinting strength not only retain their vibrancy longer when blended, but also require careful control to avoid overpowering your mixtures. Before starting your painting, identify which colours in your palette have strong tinting strength, as this will help you achieve more accurate mixes and manage your paint usage more efficiently.

Staining capacity, like tinting strength, refers to a colour's ability to leave a mark or stain the painting surface when wiped. Colours with strong staining power also have a significant impact on mixtures. By understanding both the tinting strength and staining capacity of your paints, you can better control your colours.

Transparents and opaques

Colours can be classified as opaque, transparent, semi-transparent, or semi-opaque. Transparent colours allow light to pass through, revealing layers of colour beneath and enhancing luminosity on a white surface by enabling more light to reflect off it. In contrast, opaque colours absorb light and, unless heavily diluted, block

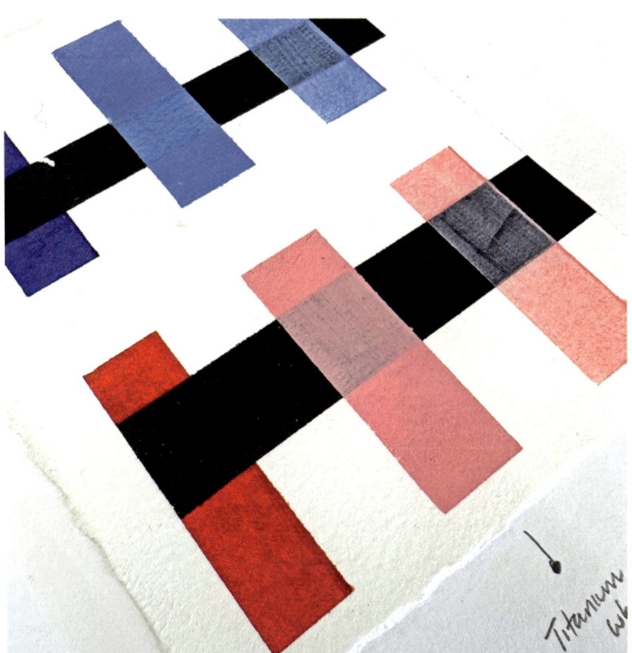

Adding titanium white to a colour creates an opaque tint, while zinc white maintains transparency. For example, alizarin crimson and ultramarine blue mixed with titanium white lose their transparency, as shown in the middle. The colour on the right is mixed using zinc white, which has preserved the colour's translucency, offering a softer, more luminous effect.

underlying layers from showing through. Opaque colours tend to have a more uniform appearance compared to transparent colours and are excellent for covering up.

If you are unsure whether a paint is transparent or opaque, check the tube label, as many manufacturers include this information. Online suppliers also typically list paint properties on their product pages. Look for a symbol on the tube, usually a square or circle, to determine transparency. An outlined symbol indicates transparency, a half-filled symbol represents semi-transparency or semi-opacity, and a fully filled symbol denotes opacity.

Over time you do become more familiar with which colours are opaque and transparent, but this simple exercise will also help. Paint a black line on a surface and let it dry. Then, using paint straight from the tube, brush a line across the black. If the black line remains visible, the paint is at least semi-transparent. If it is completely covered, the paint is opaque. Understanding these qualities helps you choose the right colours for layering, glazing, or achieving specific effects in your painting.

FINDING YOUR COLOURS

When selecting my colours, I start with the one that initially sparked my interest in painting with it. From there, I build a palette that includes a vibrant hue, along with some light and darks, and a transparent colour. One of these colours will serve as my base layer, a colour I am comfortable revealing as I scratch back through the layers. The base layer is crucial, as it influences the painting's progression and many decisions I make along the way. Additionally, it is important to consider the colours layered on top, as they can significantly impact the appearance of the base layer.

To familiarise myself with the range of colours produced by a new palette, I use a blending exercise on paper. This approach allows for a fluid exploration of colour mixes and is less structured than creating a colour scale, as described earlier in this chapter. Instead of mixing colours on the palette, I use the paints straight from the tube. Once mixed with cold wax, I apply the colours to the paper using a squeegee, and start blending. This method provides a quicker way to see potential colour mixes and helps me determine if my colour choices will work before committing.

Using a squeegee, I apply the brightest colour to my Arches Huile paper. I then slowly add the other colours, letting them blend together to see what mixes I can achieve. Blending will soften the lights and lighten the darks as the colours interact, so it is important to continuously reintroduce the colours to achieve the best mixes. Additionally, I pay attention to the neutrals I can create, as these will play a vital role in establishing quieter areas within my work. I also experiment with my transparent colour, observing how it interacts with both the lights and darks, and how it changes their appearance.

This blending exercise helps me evaluate whether the overall colour combinations align with my ideas and how effectively I can control the colours during the blending process. My next step is to return to colour mixing on my palette to explore how vibrant I can make my colours, and what variations in tints are available. While a lot of blending occurs on the surface of the painting when working with a squeegee, it is crucial to ensure that I can recreate those colours on my palette for the detailed refinement part of the painting process.

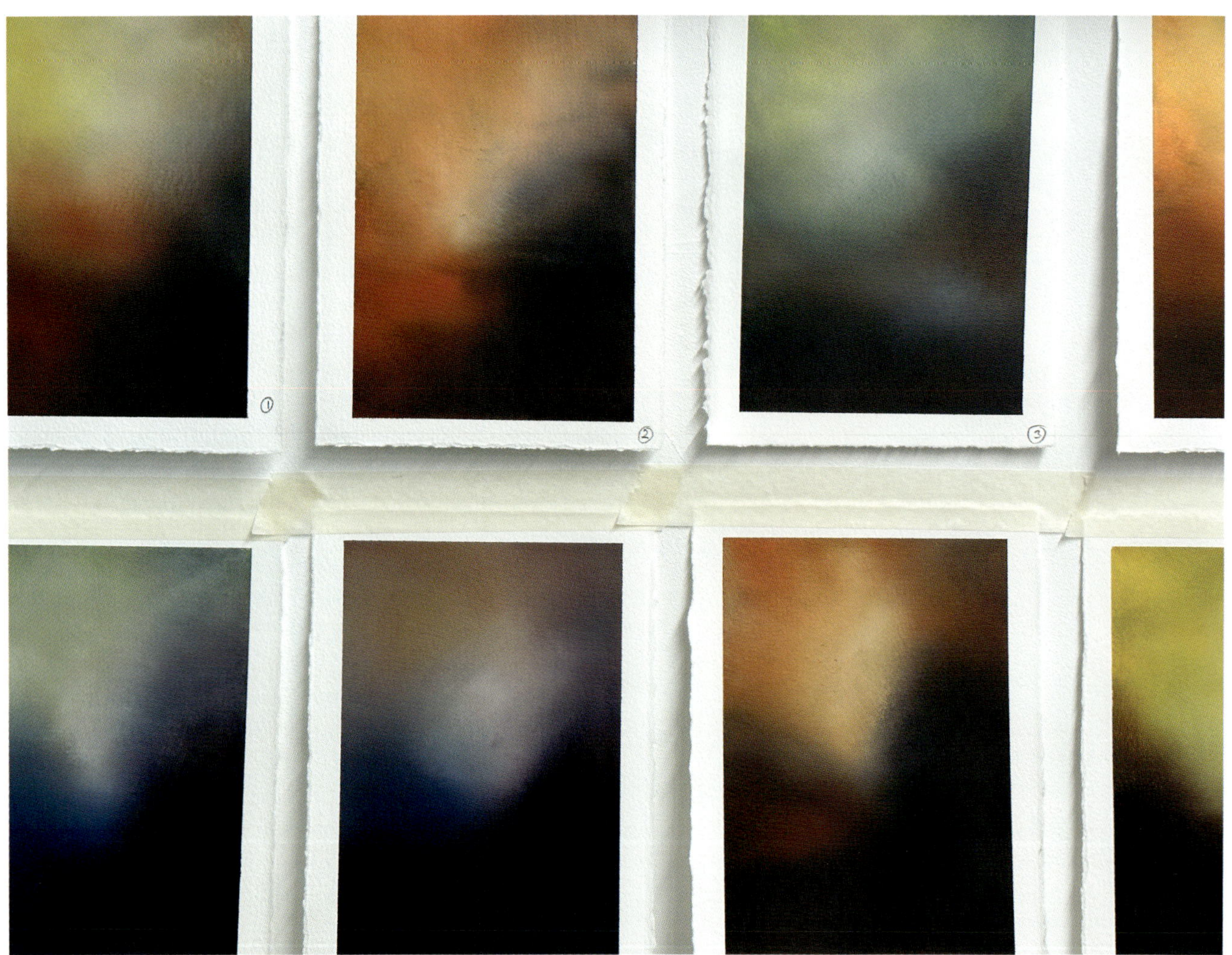

A selection of colour blends featuring vibrant primary hues alongside muted earth tones. Wet-on-wet blending on paper is a fluid and dynamic way to explore your palette and discover the range of colours you can achieve. Experiment with substituting a saturated colour for a muted one to observe how it transforms your colour combinations and overall palette harmony.

COLOUR HARMONY IN PRACTICE

Caroline Mackintosh is an oil and cold wax landscape artist living in the flatlands of East Anglia, where her inspiration largely stems from the Norfolk and Suffolk marshes and coastal estuaries that surround her. She starts her paintings with loose blocks of colour and strong free marks, working quickly from sketches and photographs, focusing on tonal value and contrast. Starting with a vibrant, warm pink base colour, she then incorporates deep purple and black to establish tonal variations. This pink base infuses warmth and glow into subsequent layers, allowing hints of pink, purple, and black to emerge when she scratches back through the paint. From this base, she explores colour further, adding more defined shapes and lines to give the painting structure, while striving to retain some of the initial loose marks.

The colours Caroline uses are exaggerated versions of what she sees. She adopts a limited palette that includes Payne's grey, cerulean blue, cadmium red, cadmium yellow, and yellow ochre, often adding small amounts of violet, pink, yellow, or green gold. This limited palette aids colour cohesion and harmony. As she paints and moves between colours, she adds the tiniest amount of the previous colour to the next. At the end of a painting session, she mixes the remaining scraps of paint together, using this mixture, much like a sourdough starter, to create new colours the following day. This method ensures that all the colours carry a bit of each other, fostering cohesion despite their differences.

Pink plays a significant role in her work. The pink she favours is a mix of cadmium red, cadmium yellow, yellow ochre, and white. To this mixture, she adds the tiniest dot of green gold or Payne's grey, both of which have strong tinting strengths, to knock back the pink, and create a colour that harmonises more readily with the greens and blues of the landscape. For her sky blue mixes, she often introduces hints of violet, pink, yellow, or green gold to further integrate the sky with the surrounding landscape colours.

If Caroline finds that a completed painting lacks colour cohesion, she will glaze the entire piece with a highly diluted tint to achieve harmony. She often opts for Payne's grey to create a moody effect, while Indian yellow and green gold provide a warm glow. For an added touch of warmth, she may also use alizarin crimson.

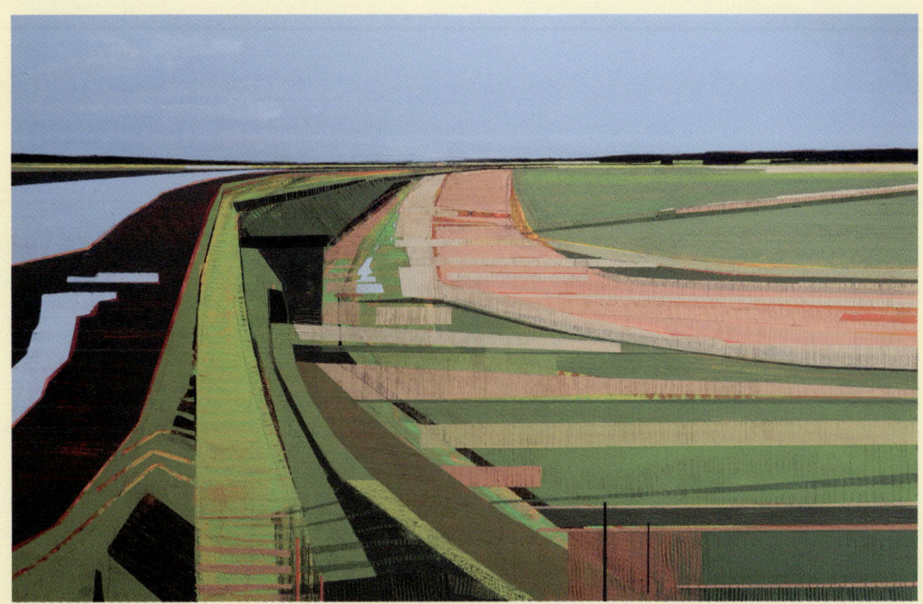

Marshlands, 70 × 113cm (27½ × 44½in), oil and oil and cold wax on canvas by Caroline Mackintosh.

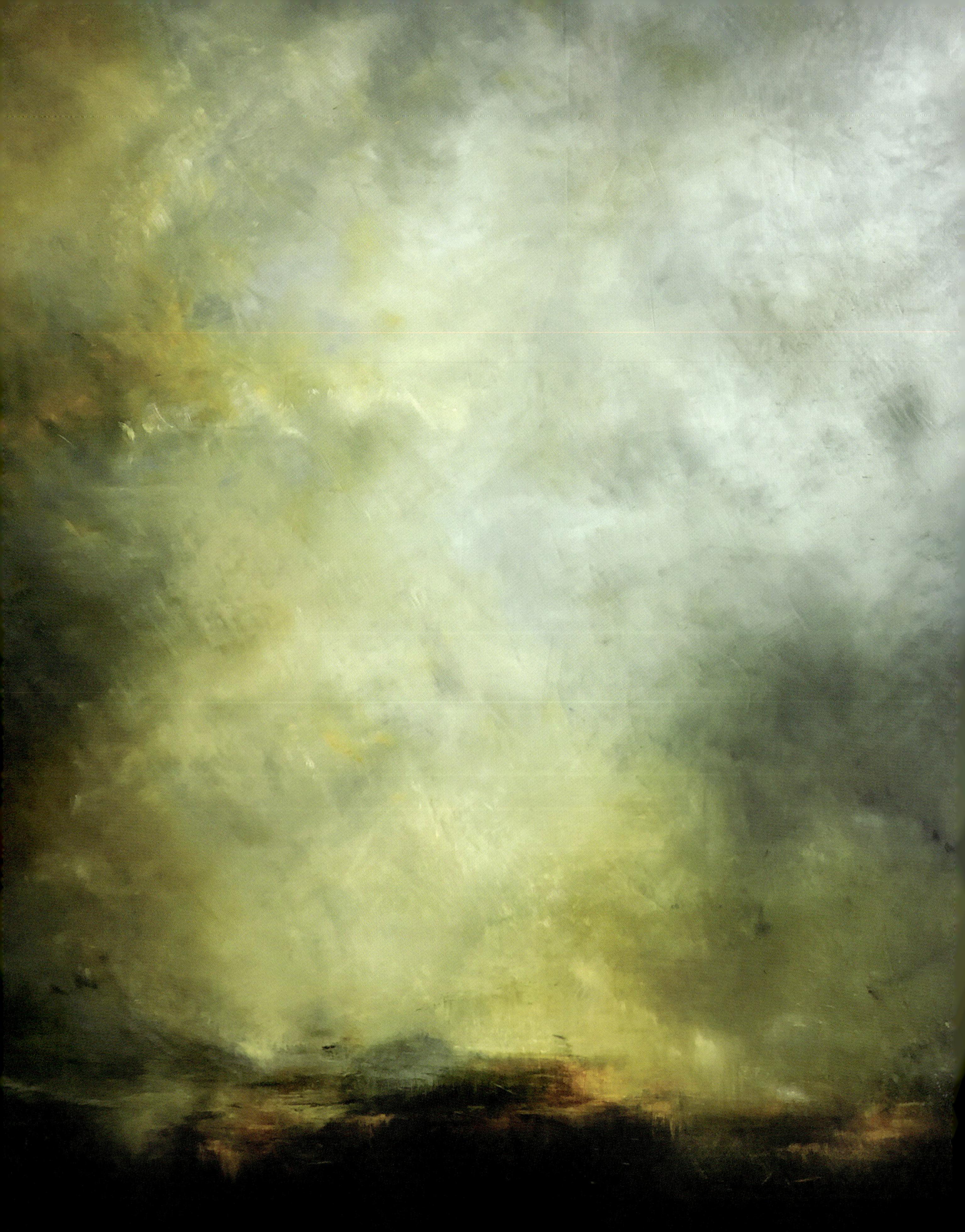

CHAPTER 5

CREATING RICH SURFACES

In this chapter, we explore how to create a rich surface of colour, pattern, and texture, and how these elements contribute to adding depth and visual interest to a painting. Adding and removing paint is a fundamental part of this process. Whether it involves layering opaque and transparent colours, delicately scratching back with sgraffito techniques, scraping large areas with a palette knife, or dissolving layers with solvent, we are actively engaging in the process of removing paint to reveal unique marks, patterns, and shapes. At the same time, we add paint to unify the surface and build depth. The process requires an element of faith, as you make decisions about what to keep, what to tone down, and what to cover up. This experimental approach encourages boldness and playfulness, creating a surface rich with marks, textures, and colours unique to your painting.

Being able to use a rich and complex surface to create a painting with depth and atmosphere does require an element of skill and practice. Knowing when to stop making marks, which colours to use to enhance those marks, and how to push through even when the painting feels chaotic are key challenges in the process. The work may become loud and messy at times, and you may struggle to find direction, but then, a single new mark will spark an idea, or a layer of a transparent glaze will completely change the mood of the painting. It is important to remember that at this stage, the goal is not a finished, polished painting, but rather to focus on creating a rich, engaging base layer from which the painting can evolve.

Start by adding some initials marks and colour to your surface, but once you have done that, there is no order to the techniques covered in this chapter. You can use all of them or a selection, and you may find that you want to repeat some depending on what you are trying to achieve and, ultimately, the direction in which you want to take your painting. These techniques can also be applied as your painting progresses, and are not limited to creating base layers.

What makes this approach so powerful is its flexibility. The process of adding and removing paint, whether through layering or removal, allows the painting to unfold organically. Each technique you apply builds a surface full of texture, complexity, and energy. As the painting develops, it will be increasingly difficult to replicate. The unpredictability of the process, combined with a willingness to experiment, ensures that each mark you make contributes to a final work that feels both resolved and alive.

Ultimately, this chapter is about embracing the fluid, experimental nature of the creative process. By layering, scratching back, and dissolving, you create a surface that invites depth and visual intrigue. This approach may feel messy or uncertain at times, but it is through this iterative process of trial, error, and discovery that you will find the richness and atmosphere that make a painting truly compelling.

OPPOSITE: *Tempest* (detail), 100 × 100cm (39½ × 39½in), oil, cold wax and gold leaf on wooden panel.

MAKE SOME MARKS

When faced with a blank canvas, it is easy to overthink which marks to make, what tools to use, and whether they are the 'right' ones — often leading to a reluctance to commit. I try not to spend too much time on this stage, as the temptation is to keep second-guessing the marks you are putting down. Instead, see this part of the process as a warm-up — a way to get yourself moving, to start working on the blank surface, and create something to react to. These initial marks may end up being covered up and might not appear in the final piece, but they will subtly influence the direction of your painting, whether by altering the colour of your base layers, by being scratched back to be revealed, or by allowing them to gently shine through.

For my initial marks, I like to use oil and pigment sticks. They offer the richness of oils, while allowing me to make expressive marks, working across and over the edges of the surface. You can smudge your marks with paper roll, your fingers, or even a little solvent. Some oil and pigment sticks, particularly those with high tinting strength, can bleed through subsequent layers, and a white or pale colour will produce a luminous glow even when covered with a dark transparent or opaque layer.

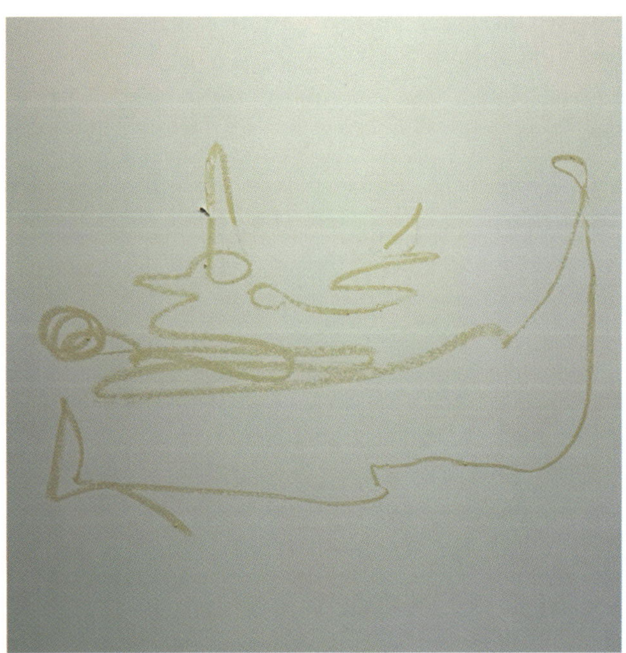

When starting a painting, I often begin by making marks on the surface using charcoal, soft pastels, pigment sticks, or oil bars. These initial marks help kick-start the painting process through action and provide a foundation to build upon. The marks are expressive and spontaneous, made with little thought beyond the intention of starting the process.

COLOUR

Once you have some marks on your surface, your next step is to cover it with a base layer of colour. For this layer you want to choose a bright, clean, saturated colour — avoid white, as we are aiming to cover the white surface, and steer clear of light colours such as pale blue, which will appear white when scratched back. Also, stay away from dark opaques such as browns, blacks, and purples, as these will be difficult to see unless you intend the top layers of your painting to be lighter and brighter (*see* Caroline Mackintosh's work in Chapter 4). Saturated, dark transparent colours, such as alizarin crimson, shift in luminosity and transparency when moving from masstone (a thick mix of paint) to a thin layer, making them excellent for base layers. Ultramarine blue, when applied thinly, produces a glowing lilac colour on a white surface. Bright oranges, yellows, pinks, and reds are perfect for this. If you prefer a cooler base layer, a bright blue such as cerulean blue stands out beautifully against dark colours. Your base layer can be either transparent or opaque, as long as it is a strong, bold colour.

Next, use your squeegee to apply the colour, making sure you have a good amount of your oil and cold wax mix as you pull it across the surface. When you apply the first layer, you may notice it smudges or blends with the oil bar and pigment stick marks underneath. This is perfectly fine — just ensure the entire surface is covered with a thin layer of colour. If you are unsure about the thickness of your paint, pull your squeegee across the surface at a 90-degree angle to remove any excess. We want to create rich colours that can be blended and scratched back into, so we need to add further layers of colour on top of the base layer. You can do this by working wet-on-wet or let the layers dry, but ultimately, we want to create colour blends which will require the paint to be wet. This can be achieved through wet-on-wet techniques or by using dissolving and pouring methods, which we cover later in this chapter.

Adding a second layer of colour will deepen and enrich the first layer, creating a more complex composition. The choice of transparent or opaque colours can change the look and feel of the painting. For example, try layering alizarin crimson over lemon yellow or Indian yellow to create a beautiful glow. Alternatively, layering alizarin crimson over ultramarine blue will produce a rich, dark purple. Once you have chosen your second colour, add your oil and cold wax mix to the squeegee and gently pull it across the first layer, keeping the layer as thin as possible.

At this stage, you might want to introduce a small amount of white. This will add a lighter, more opaque area to your painting, not only introducing a lighter tonal value, but also creating the opportunity to start adding depth. Let the squeegee mix the white with your base colours in some areas of your painting, and experiment to see what colour blends you can achieve. The combination of transparent and opaque colours will help you add more depth to your work. Take a transparent colour from your palette and sweep it across the whole surface with the squeegee. This will push everything back, creating a sense of depth and distance and will unify the surface, reducing the tonal contrast.

Do not be afraid to experiment with layering different colours as you may discover some striking combinations. For example, lemon yellow will still shine through a thin sweep of transparent magenta, creating a rich, warm glow. Start with a consistent base layer and explore the effects of transparent and opaque hues applied on top. As you build layers, observe how the underlying colour shifts, especially when scratched back. This technique reveals the interplay of transparency and opacity, offering endless possibilities for depth, texture, and visual complexity in your work.

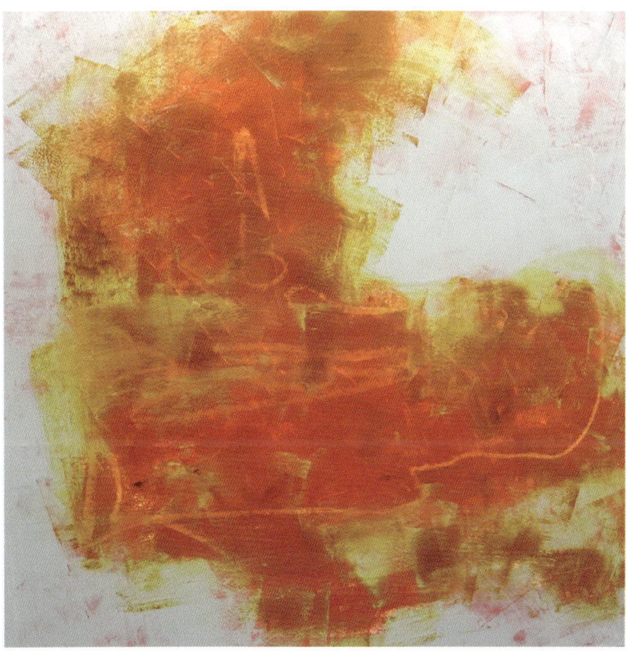

A bright pink base layer was applied, followed by a second layer of transparent orange. A pale, opaque colour was then introduced, blending subtly with the underlying layers. The R&F Pigment Stick® remains visible, glowing through the pink and orange, yet is largely obscured where the pale opaque paint has been applied.

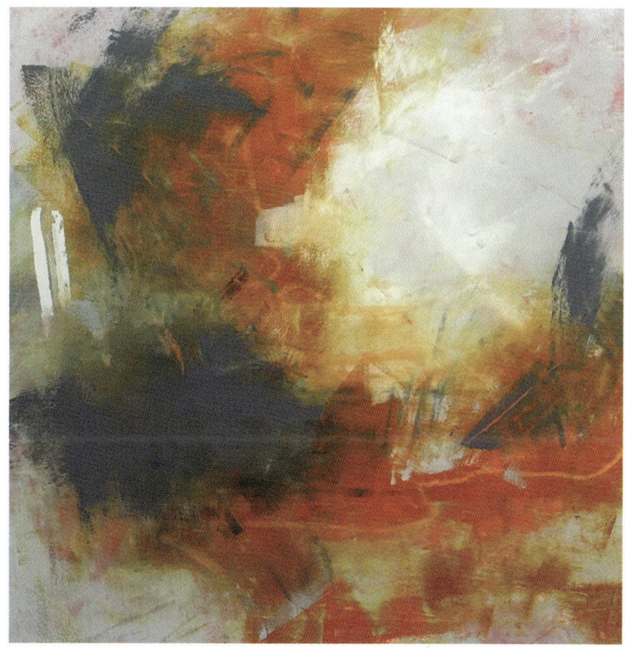

A violet-grey was introduced to add depth and darkness, its opacity concealing the underlying base layers and marks. Notice how this grey deepens when transparent orange is layered over certain areas, creating a subtle greenish shift. Meanwhile, marks made with the R&F Pigment Stick® remain visible in sections left untouched by the opaque layers, adding texture and dimension.

SGRAFFITO

Sgraffito, from the Italian word *graffiare* meaning 'to scratch', is a technique where you score into the paint with a rigid tool to reveal the underlying layers of colour. By experimenting with different tools, you can create controlled, purposeful marks, carefully selecting the type of line and where to place it. Almost anything that allows you to scratch a line into the paint can be used — whether it is the pointed end of a brush, a palette knife, a fork, a credit card, or even your squeegee.

The quality of the marks depends on both the thickness and dryness of the paint. Cold wax increases the viscosity of oil paints, making the marks sharper and more defined. If you use oil paints directly from the tube, they are more fluid, and your marks may blur as the oil seeps back into them. Experiment with various tools to discover different types of marks — from gestural and controlled to more free-form. For straight lines, you could try using a ruler or even a barbecue stick. Aim to create a range of marks, as variety will make your surface more dynamic and interesting.

Sgraffito can be applied at any stage of your painting, from building texture in the early stages of creating base layers, to adding intricate details as you resolve your work. It is perfect for scratching back to reveal vibrant base layers and create patches of light in a sky, reflections on water, distant lights, or pathways through the landscape.

TOOLS

While colour is my main love with cold wax, the variety of tools and the mark-making possibilities come a very close second. When I first started using cold wax, I often

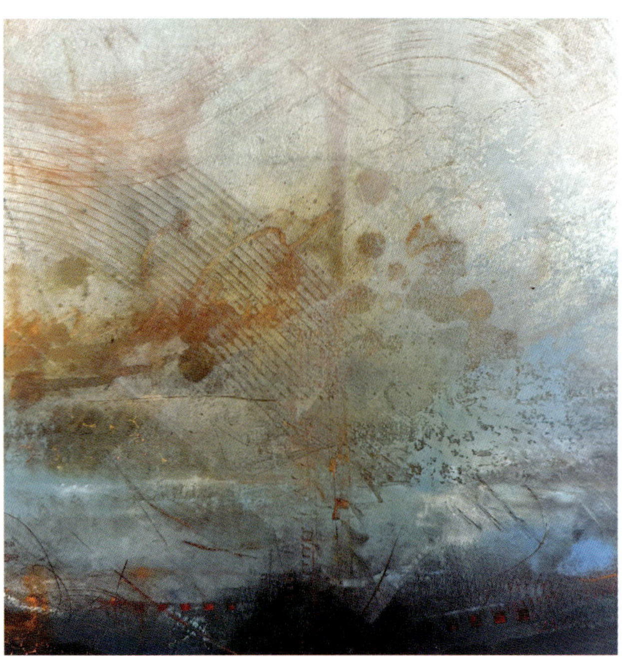

Lines and marks can be scratched into the paint, cutting through layers of colour to reveal the base layers, and then covered again with transparent glazes. In this example, the marks were created using a brush comb, Princeton Catalyst contour tools, barbecue sticks, and organic patterns formed with solvent drops.

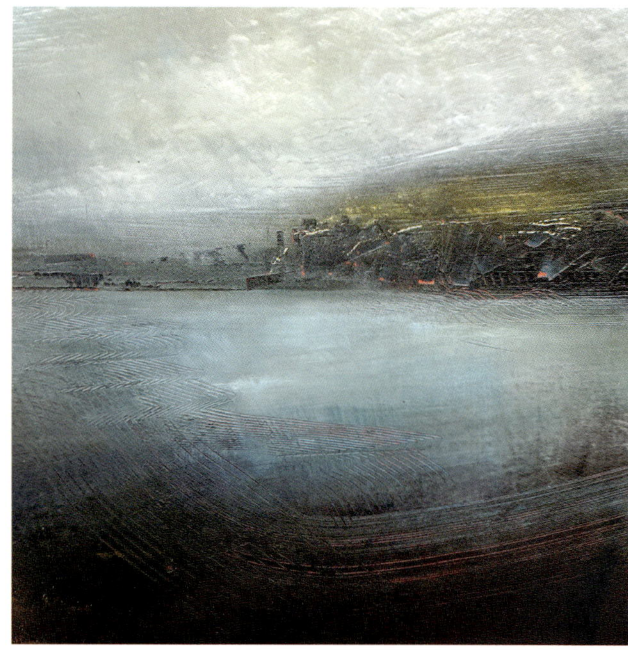

Detail of *Where the curlew calls*, 60 × 60cm (23½ × 23½in), oil, cold wax, and gold leaf on board. A brush comb has been used to uncover underlying layers of colour, creating dynamic, energetic marks that evoke movement and rhythm. These gestural marks draw the viewer's eye around the painting, leading them through the composition and adding a sense of fluidity.

found myself rummaging through kitchenware and DIY stores, searching for tools to experiment with and seeing what effects they might create. Some art tools I bought, initially promising to revolutionise my painting, generally did not live up to expectations. However, on returning to them years later, I discovered they had become essential to my process. One of my most treasured tools for mark-making is a brush comb. Though it was designed to clean hairbrushes, I have found it perfect for creating beautiful, dynamic marks in my paintings. You will see the marks made by this tool in many of my works, where I use it to scratch back to base layers to inject energy and movement into my compositions.

Other tools that may be useful include the Princeton Catalyst contour tools, which come in a range of shapes and edges. These tools are firm enough to scratch back into your work as well as scraping off paint. They can also be used for adding gold leaf when resolving your painting (*see* Chapter 7).

London-based artist and printmaker Bina Shah incorporates natural earth pigments, handcrafted inks, and plant-based materials into her work whenever possible. She has created a range of tools from black bamboo that she grows in her garden, including brush pens, dip pens with both pointed and flat nibs, and various mark-making tools. These bamboo tools are excellent for scratching into oil and cold wax paintings at various stages of painting. They are also perfect for use with carbon papers (*see* Chapter 7) to create fine, detailed marks with a loose, energetic feel.

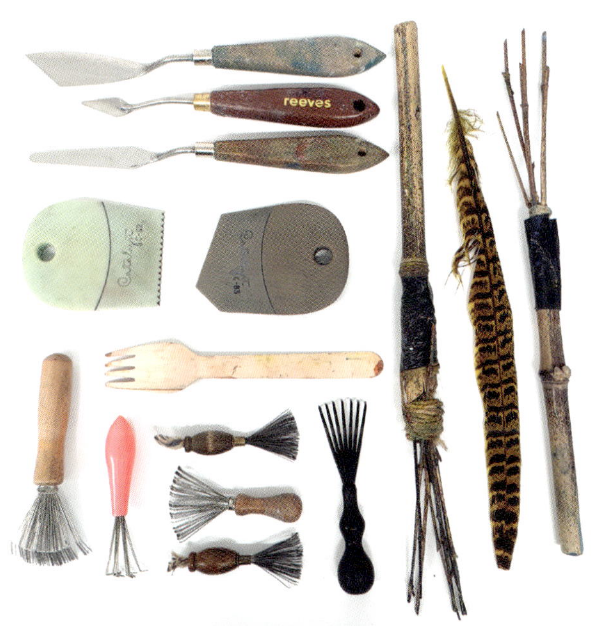

Collect an array of tools to create a wide range of interesting marks on your surface, from delicate, fine lines to bold, expressive strokes. Use palette knives, squeegees, and blades in various shapes and sizes, along with unconventional items like sticks or brush combs, to add complexity and visual interest to your artwork.

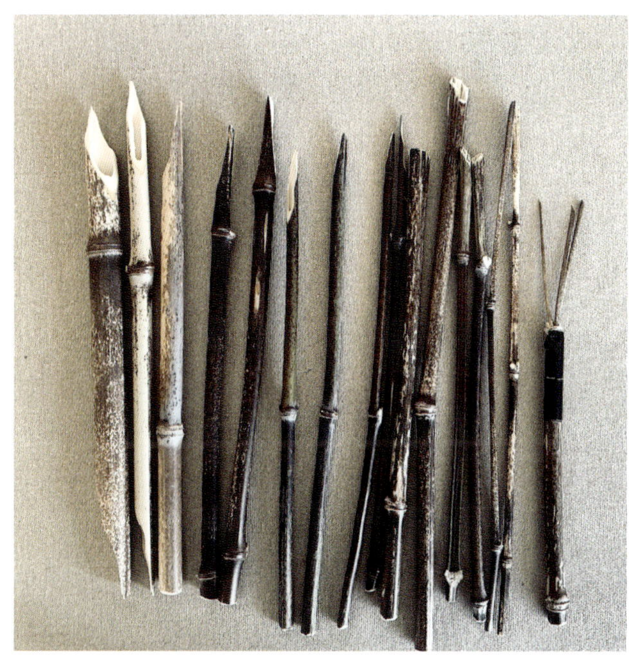

Bina Shah's bamboo tools are ideal for mark-making throughout the painting process. Hand-carved from black bamboo, each tool is carefully shaped to create a wide variety of expressive marks allowing for dynamic, fluid strokes as well as intricate, detailed lines.

IMPRINTING

Sometimes, the marks created with brushes or palette knives may not fully meet your needs, or you might simply want to explore other methods. As cold wax thickens your oils, it offers more opportunity to add texture to your painting by pressing various materials or objects into the surface to leave imprints. Almost anything can be used for this — from natural materials such as leaves to everyday items such as papers and bubble wrap. Imprinting can either become a main feature of your work or serve as an underlying texture, contributing to the richness and complexity of the surface.

Tissue Paper

Tissue paper, or any lightweight paper (including paper roll), is particularly well suited for imprinting and can also be useful for removing paint from your surface. Tissue paper works effectively because it is lightweight and generally has one side that is waxy, which prevents it from absorbing too much oil, resulting in crisper, cleaner marks. It is advisable to use lightweight papers, as heavier papers (such as glassine) can stick to the surface, potentially removing more paint than you intend.

When you press tissue or lightweight paper onto your painting, it will leave behind a crackle effect, revealing flashes of colour from the underlying layers. The outcome can be quite beautiful, but it will vary depending on factors such as the wetness or dryness of your surface, the thickness of the paint, and the pressure you apply. The best results are often achieved by scrunching up the tissue and gently dabbing the surface. Alternatively, scrunch up the tissue, then unfurl it and press it onto the surface. Use your hand or a brayer to apply pressure before lifting the paper to reveal the marks. Light pressure typically

The effects of using scrunched-up tissue paper to create imprints in your work can be extraordinarily beautiful, adding both texture and depth to the surface. Once you have created imprints with the tissue paper, you can reuse it to create a mono-print, either by printing it onto a separate piece of paper or back onto the surface of your painting.

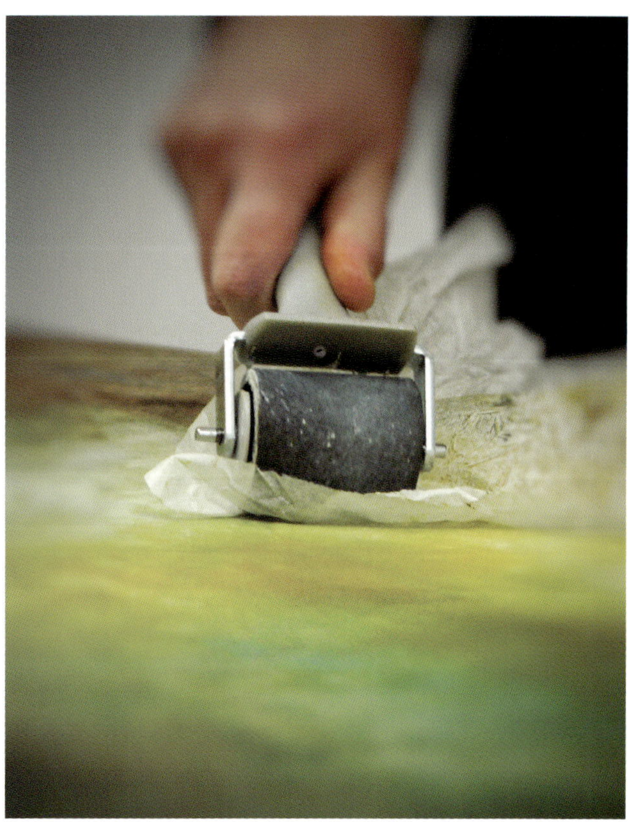

By using scrunched-up tissue paper and a brayer you can create unique textures in your painting. By varying the pressure applied, you can achieve different effects and introduce intriguing layers of texture and colour. This technique can spark fresh ideas and inspire new directions in your painting, encouraging experimentation and spontaneity.

New Lands, 26 × 26cm (10¼ × 10¼in), oils and cold wax on Arches Huile paper. Scrunched tissue paper has been used to create subtle, organic marks that reveal the base layers of colour. These impressions can range from soft, feathered textures (as in *New Lands*) to more defined, bold marks, depending on how wet the paint is, and the amount of pressure applied.

produces delicate marks, while firmer pressure pulls off more paint, creating bolder, more defined imprints.

If your paint is touch-dry, you may need to apply more pressure to create a clearer imprint. Do not be discouraged if the result is not what you expected — factors such as paint thickness, pressure, and surface conditions will all affect the texture and quality of the imprint. Experiment with different effects before committing to any part of your painting.

DISSOLVING AND POURING

Using solvents to dissolve your paint is an experimental technique that can produce unpredictable results. The application of solvent thins the paint, causing some colour mixing and blurring, but it allows you to expose underlying layers of colour and texture. The effects depend on how dry or wet the surface is, the solvent's strength, and the specific marks (such as sgraffito or imprints) the solvent interacts with.

For best results, ensure the paint is still soft on your surface. If it is touch-dry, apply a thin layer of paint over it using your squeegee or brayer — a complementary or neutral colour can work well for contrast. Then sprinkle, splash, or drip solvent onto your painting with a brush or dropper, and gently wipe it away with the squeegee. Once you have wiped away the solvent, try adding a transparent layer to the surface to see how it unifies and pushes back the previous layers. Drip, brush, or splash

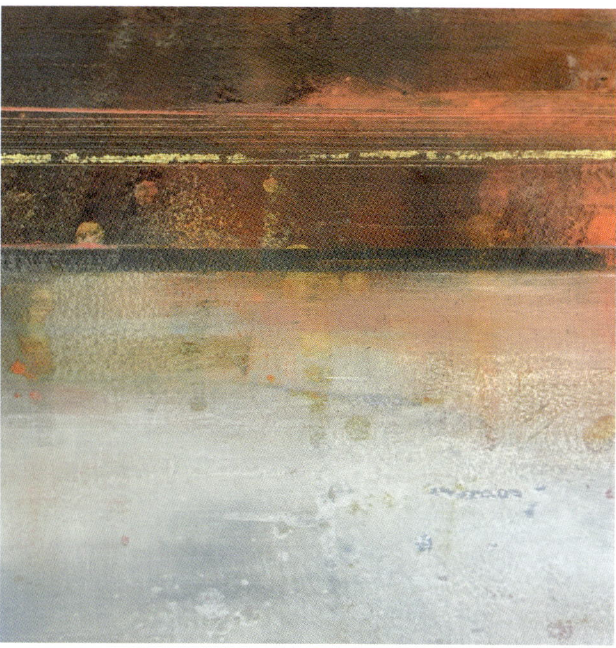

Solvent splashes are an excellent way to reveal underlying colours and create organic, textured marks. This technique can be used effectively at various stages of the painting process, and you do not always need to return to the base layer to achieve interesting effects. Sometimes, simply exposing the previous layer can add just the right amount of depth and visual intrigue.

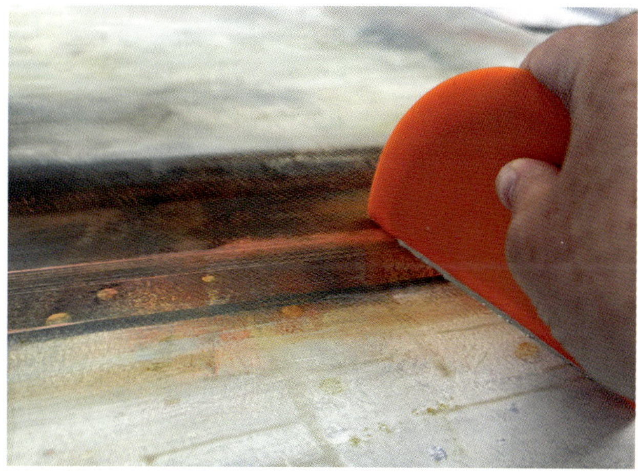

The squeegee is ideal for wiping away solvent splashes and dribbles, leaving more defined marks compared to sponging off the solvent with paper towels. It allows for controlled removal of excess dissolved paint, producing clean, sharp edges on the surface. As you work, move the excess dissolved paint towards the edges of your painting and wipe away to prevent spills.

more solvent to further reveal hidden layers, deepening the painting's overall complexity.

As the solvent dissolves the surface layer of paint, it also starts to soften the rest of the painting, causing colours to blend. If you are working on top of sgraffito marks, the

CREATIVE USE OF SOLVENTS

Sophie Velzian is a landscape artist based near the Helford River in Cornwall, UK. Living and working in this uniquely Cornish environment, she draws inspiration from its crystal-clear waters, soft light, and distinctive trees. Working with oil and cold wax, Sophie uses solvents to uncover the rich, muted colours of her base layers, which are often concealed beneath thin layers of a titanium buff or dark transparent hues. Using a paintbrush, she splashes solvent, varying the height at which she holds the brush, the amount of solvent, and the intensity of the flicking to create a range of splash marks. She lets the solvent sit for a few seconds before using a squeegee to wipe it away, revealing delicate, drop-shaped marks in the top layer of paint. To expose additional layers of colour, she lets the solvent sit longer, allowing it to cut through to the underlying base layer. In *Serpentine Waters*, Sophie used solvent to create the pebble-like marks along the tideline of this Helford-inspired landscape.

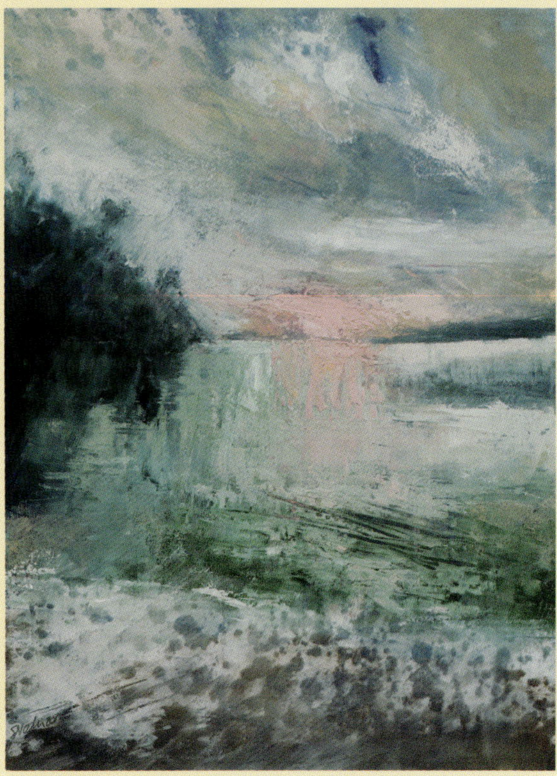

Serpentine waters, oil and cold wax on Arches Huile paper, 76 × 56cm (30 × 22in) by Sophie Velzian.

thinned paint will sink into these lines, creating delicate effects. This process can make the painting wet and soft very quickly, making it easy to overwork. If this happens, allow it to rest for a few hours and let the solvent evaporate before returning to it. Be mindful that working with solvents can be messy, so protect yourself from splashes and fumes. Ensure your workspace is well ventilated and take breaks when needed.

If you are working vertically, consider switching to a flat surface to prevent the solvent from running down your painting. On the other hand, if you want dribble effects, tilting the painting can help achieve the desired effect.

Solvent Pours

Once you have explored solvent splashes, you can create bold dribble effects by applying solvent directly onto your painting and allowing it to flow across the surface. Place your painting on a flat surface and then use a brush or a dropper to apply a generous amount of solvent. Tilt the painting to guide the movement of the solvent. As the solvent runs, it dissolves and lifts the paint, revealing the base layers beneath. Tilting in different directions can create additional dynamic effects. Use a squeegee to cleanly remove any excess solvent and to reveal the dribble marks. Applying a transparent glaze over the marks will subtly push them into the background and unify the surface.

Pigment Pours

Solvent can also be used to carry dry pigments across your painting, leaving them embedded in the surface as the solvent evaporates. To prepare the mixture, add powdered pigment and odourless solvent to a small bottle with a lid (a squeezy bottle works well). Shake it well to mix the pigment and solvent thoroughly. Be sure to keep

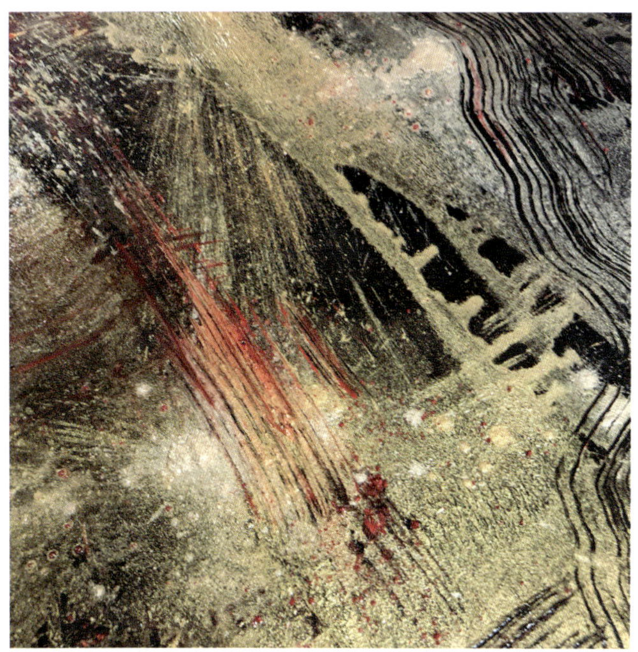

Pigment pours differ from solvent pours in that the solvent is used to carry and embed the pigment into the painting and is typically applied in the later stages of painting. This technique works especially well with metallic pigments on a dark colour, as the contrast amplifies the shimmering effect, allowing the pigments to stand out beautifully.

shaking the bottle as the pigment will settle at the bottom when left. Pour the mixture across your painting and tilt the surface to allow it to flow in different directions. As the solvent dissolves the paint, the pigment will stay behind, becoming embedded in the surface. When using this technique, avoid wiping the solvent away with your squeegee, as it will also remove the pigment. This is important if you plan to apply more solvent later, as wiping could inadvertently remove some of the pigment you have just laid down.

Paint Pours

Certain techniques, such as paint pours, benefit greatly from a more fluid paint mix, enabling organic marks and a dynamic flow across the surface. By diluting your paint with solvent or other mediums, you can make it thinner and easier to pour, allowing it to run across your painting and leave behind dribbles that add movement and energy to your composition.

Solvent is a popular choice for thinning paint due to its ability to significantly increase flow. However, it can produce a less flexible paint film that may crack over time – an effect you may intentionally seek for certain artistic results. To maintain flexibility in your paints while achieving a fluid consistency, you can incorporate mediums such as cold-pressed linseed oil, Liquin, Galkyd, Galkyd Lite, or Solvent-Free Fluid. Each of these mediums provides varying levels of fluidity and drying times.

While these mediums enhance flow, they may not achieve the extreme thinness that solvent alone provides. If a fluid, dramatic pour is the desired effect, you can combine a small amount of solvent with your chosen medium. This approach allows you to tailor your paint mix to your specific needs, ensuring a stronger, more flexible paint film while still achieving the desired consistency.

The versatility of these mediums opens up a wide range of possibilities for creating dynamic, fluid effects. As you pour the paint across the surface, its movement will depend not only on the medium you have chosen, but also on factors such as the texture of the surface and the angle at which you tilt it. Whether aiming for controlled, smooth dribbles or more spontaneous, unpredictable streaks, experimenting with different combinations of solvents and mediums will help you achieve the desired effect.

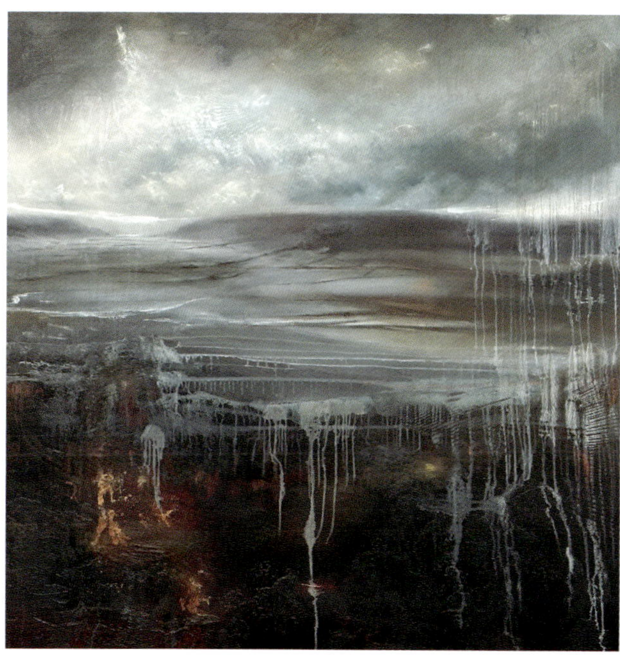

The wetlands shall rise again, 125 × 125cm (49¼ × 49¼in), oils and cold wax on board. This work-in-progress photo illustrates how paint and solvent pours generate unpredictable marks and depth. As the painting evolves, the textures left by the pouring process create intricate layers that enhance the composition.

EMBEDDING

The thickness of cold wax and its adhesive qualities make it an excellent medium for embedding lightweight materials into your work. This approach adds texture, colour, and narrative elements, particularly when using collage techniques to introduce patterns, shapes, or text.

Textural materials

Oil paint, by its very nature, provides texture to a painting. However, additional techniques can enhance or alter the texture of your work. These include imprinting, but in this section, we focus on incorporating materials such as marble dust, sand, ash, or slate dust into your paint. Such additions not only change the character of the paint, but also provide varied tactile qualities. Marble dust and sand give your surface a coarse, granular feel, while finer materials such as ash and slate dust create a smoother, raised surface. Both work well to create a contrast with the smoother areas of your painting.

To create a marble dust mix, fold it into your oil and cold wax, then apply it with a palette knife. If you are working on a larger surface, a trowel or a large palette knife makes the application easier and quicker. Mix thoroughly, as marble dust is highly absorbent and can create a crumbly texture if insufficient oil and cold wax are used. This will ensure the mixture bonds securely to your surface. If you do not mix thoroughly, loose grains may scratch the surface, which can be extremely frustrating if you are aiming to create sections in your painting with a smooth finish.

Before adding your marble dust mixture to the surface, make sure you have a base colour applied to avoid leaving patches of unpainted surface, which can be extremely difficult to cover. To ensure consistency, use the same colour in the marble dust mix as the base layer. Spread the mixed marble dust with your palette knife or trowel and scratch any marks or textures into the mixture while it is still wet. If you apply a thick layer of marble dust, add a coating of oil colour and cold wax with a squeegee to ensure it stays in place, then

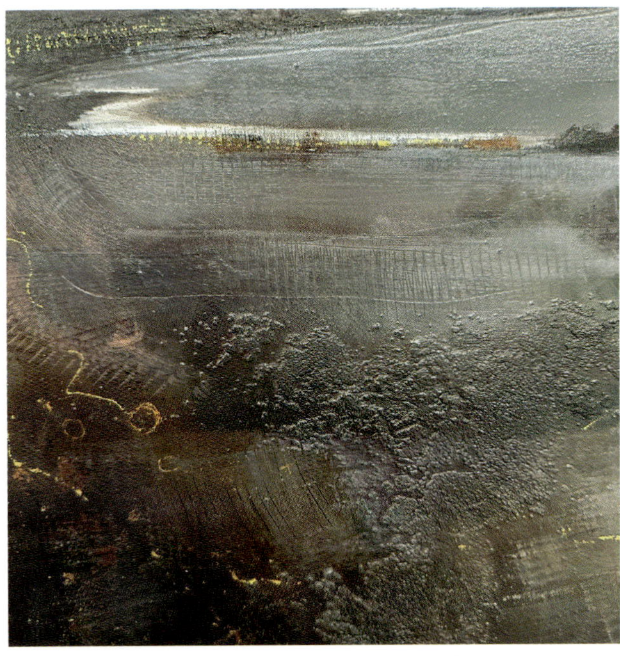

The wetlands shall rise again, 125 × 125cm (49¼ × 49¼in), oils and cold wax on board. Marble dust mixed with oil and cold wax has been applied to the painting, creating a rich, textured surface that contrasts with the smoother areas. This textured effect has been used to emphasise the foreground, adding depth and visual interest to the composition.

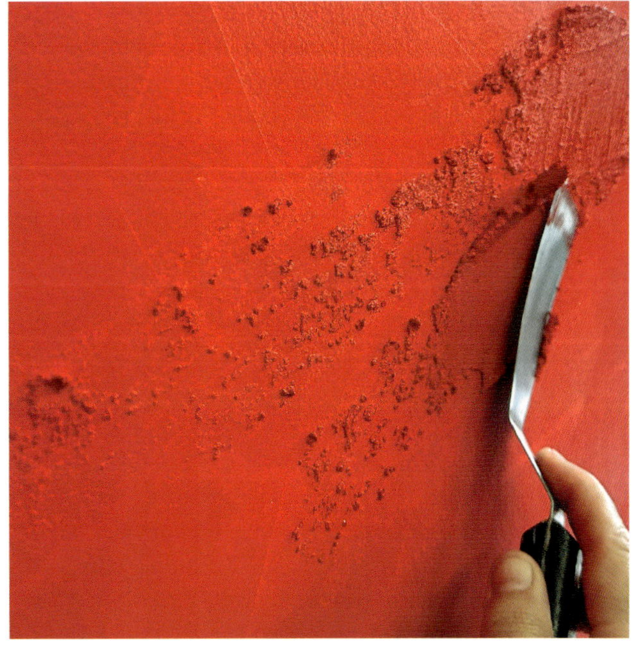

Adding texture with marble dust mixed with ample oil and cold wax ensures proper bonding. In this approach, a base layer of colour is applied first, followed by a mixture of the same colour and marble dust. This prevents unpainted areas from appearing, which can occur if it is applied directly to the surface before a layer of colour.

leave it to dry and harden overnight before continuing with your painting. This process also applies to sand; however, ensure the sand is fully dry, before you start mixing with it, especially if sourced from a beach. Other ingredients, such as ash or slate dust, can also be used to create a raised surface, but they will not provide the same granular texture as marble dust.

Dry pigments

Pigments are the colours that make up your paints, whether oil, acrylic, watercolour, gouache, and so on. To create paint, pigments require a binder to hold them together. For oil paints this binder is typically a drying oil, the most common being linseed oil, along with an additive such as aluminium stearate, which provides the paint's buttery texture (Coles, 2018).

Pigments are generally derived from natural or synthetic sources and vary in density, chemical composition, size, and shape, all of which affect their behaviour, including their transparency or opacity. Smaller pigment particles sizes often result in better coverage, making the pigment more opaque. Pigments fall broadly into organic and inorganic categories. Inorganic pigments include naturals salts and minerals extracted from the earth, whereas organic pigments are derived from living organisms such as plants, animals, or insects. Traditional organic pigments (such as indigo from plants or cochineal from insects) were once common but are known for being more fugitive, that is, prone to fading when exposed to light or air. Modern synthetic pigments, such as quinacridones, are more stable and have largely replaced their natural counterparts (Casey, 2022).

Dry pigments are readily available as many artists like to make their own paints. As well as being used for making paint, they are also excellent for adding a splash of colour to a painting. If you want to incorporate pigments into your work, it is essential to ensure they are properly embedded into the painting. To achieve this, brush the pigments onto the surface, pushing them into your oil and cold wax and then, using a squeegee

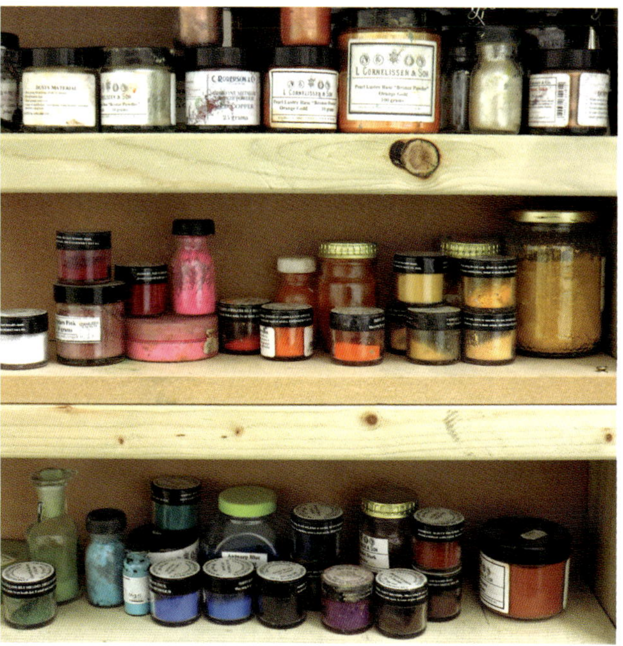

Pigments are available in a wide spectrum of colours, each with its own unique properties, depth, and intensity. Incorporating dry pigments into your artwork is a powerful way to introduce bold splashes of colour and texture. Whether sprinkled or brushed directly onto the surface, dry pigments can create striking visual effects that infuse your work with energy and movement.

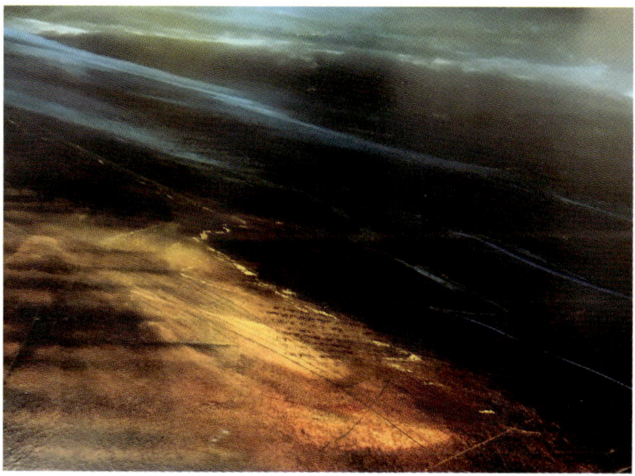

Turning Tides, 120 × 90cm (47¼ × 35½in), oils, cold wax, and gold leaf on board. In this detail of the foreground, bright gold pearl lustre pigments were carefully brushed into the painting, then layered with a transparent colour. This process is repeated until the desired glow, depth, and luminous quality is achieved.

or palette knife, adjust the shapes or cover with a transparent colour. This technique works particularly well with pearl lustre pigments and bronze powders, which can add light and a shimmering metallic effect to your painting.

Another method for adding dry pigments is to create a splash effect. Add a small amount of pigment to the end of your brush and let it drop randomly on to some print paper. Spread a thin layer of cold wax onto a piece of tissue paper and press it face-down onto the splashed pigment, applying gentle pressure. When you lift the tissue, it should have picked up the pigment. You can then use the tissue to transfer the pigment onto specific areas of your work by pressing it face-down onto your painting.

Collage

Collage is a versatile technique for introducing visual interest and narrative to your work. Lightweight papers, such as tissue, patterned papers, including handmade collage papers, can be seamlessly embedded into layers of oil and cold wax.

To begin, place the paper onto the wet surface of your painting, or apply a layer of cold wax to the desired area before positioning the paper. Press the paper firmly to ensure good adhesion, then apply a thin layer of cold wax on top to secure it in place. This not only binds the paper but also protects it. To further integrate the collage elements into your painting, apply a thin layer of transparent colour over the top. This technique will help to unify the different components of your artwork and create a cohesive look. The transparency of the colour allows the patterns and textures of the handmade papers to remain visible, adding complexity to the overall composition.

As with all materials you incorporate into your work, it is crucial that the collage elements contribute meaningfully to the painting. Consider whether your artwork would benefit from the inclusion of these papers and if the answer is yes, then consider carefully where it is best placed in your work before committing.

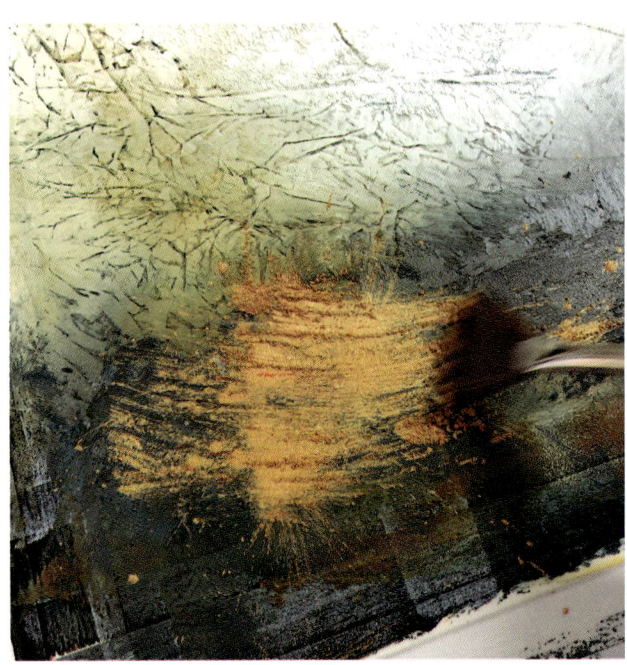

Bronze powders differ from pearl lustre pigments in that they consist of metallic particles made from copper and zinc alloys, designed to replicate the appearance of bronze. However, they can achieve the same shimmering, metallic effect, whether brushed onto your painting surface or used to create a splash effect.

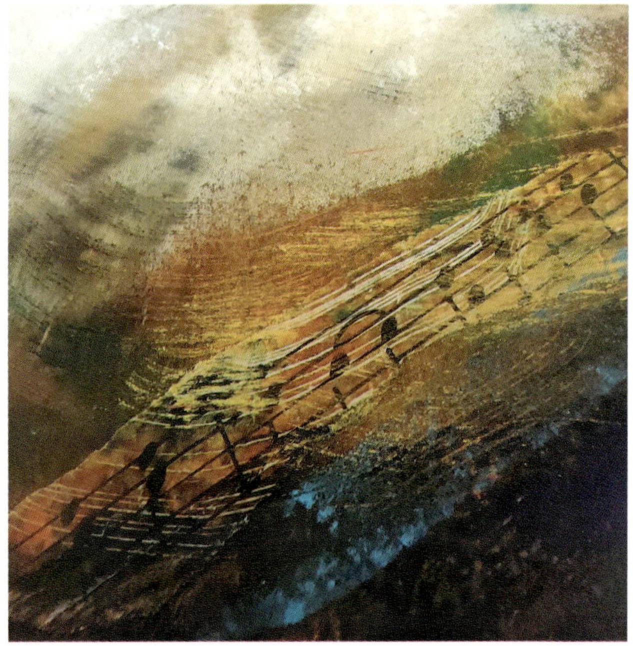

Adding collage to your painting can strengthen the narrative and enrich the composition, but it is crucial to fully integrate the elements so they become an integral part of the piece. Use lightweight papers and materials, such as decoupage papers, to ensure that the cold wax can effectively hold them in place.

ADDING EXPRESSIVE MARKS

Adding expressive marks to your painting can significantly contribute to texture, energy, and visual complexity. Working with a dry surface provides you with more control, allowing you to create marks that might not be achievable on a wet surface. By experimenting with different tools – brushes, transfers, and brayers – you can introduce a range of dynamic, textured effects, each offering unique possibilities for enhancing your composition.

These techniques not only introduce new textures, but also allow you to engage with the painting surface in a dynamic way, adding energy, contrast, and cohesion to your work. Using brushes of various sizes can create everything from delicate, flowing lines to bold, structured marks. Transfers offer the chance to bring print-like textures into the mix, while brayers help unify the surface with thin layers of colour, or they can block out specific areas for contrast. As you layer these marks, you create a rich, complex surface that not only reflects the iterative process of painting, but also invites the viewer to engage with the work on multiple levels.

Brushes

Once your surface is dry, using a variety of brushes allows you to introduce a wide range of expressive marks, creating energy in your painting – especially when you work across the borders and edges of your surfaces.

- A long-haired liner brush is ideal for creating flowing, delicate lines that can add movement and fluidity to your painting. They are perfect for adding fine details or for creating lines that contrast with larger, more gestural marks.
- A medium flat brush creates squared or angular edges, offering a more structured, precise type of mark. This kind of mark is great for creating contrast with the softer, more fluid lines produced by the liner brush.
- A large mottler, mop or decorator's brush can be used to make bold, sweeping marks that cover larger areas of the surface. The softness or stiffness of the bristles allows for different textural effects, from soft, feathery strokes to more abrupt, impactful marks.

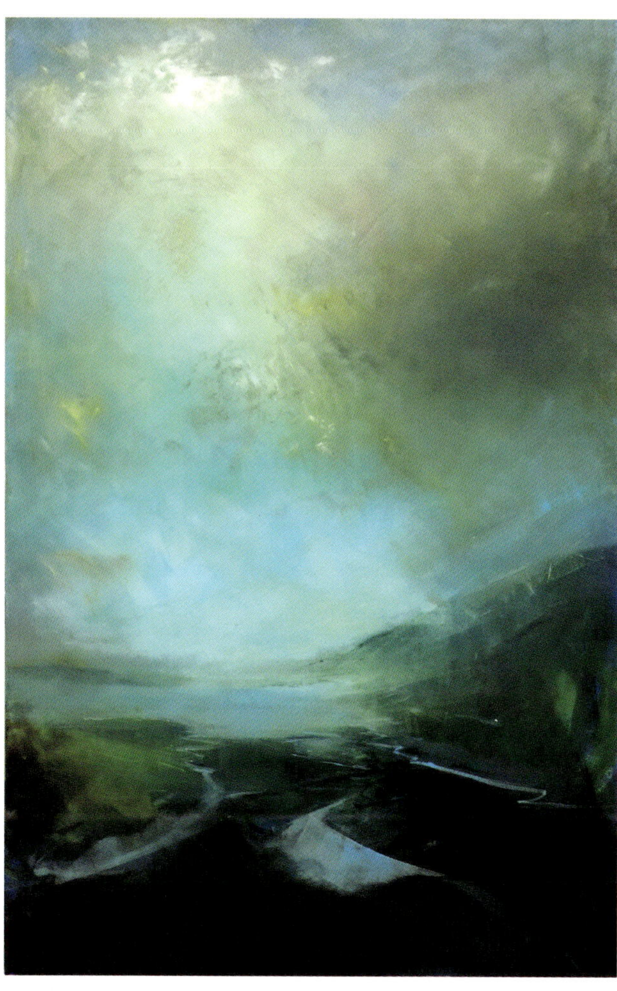

Waterlines, 60 × 91cm (23½ × 36in), oils and cold wax on board. The dynamic marks in the foreground were created early in the process using a brayer. A thin layer of colour was applied with the brayer to create sweeping lines that evoke the movement of water, establishing the tone for the rest of the painting.

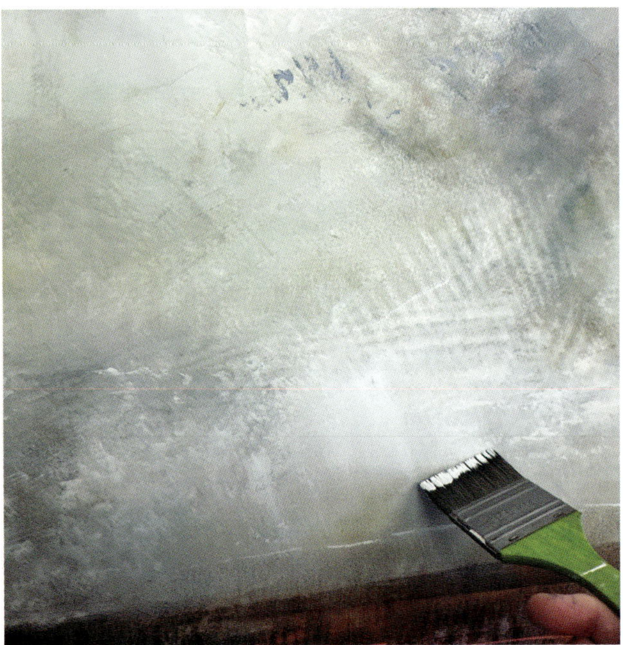

A range of marks can be achieved using different types and sizes of brushes. You can create expressive, dynamic marks, adding bold strokes to your painting or refining details to tighten up the composition. The variety of marks made with different brushes helps establish a contrast between areas of boldness and subtlety, introducing both tension and harmony to the composition.

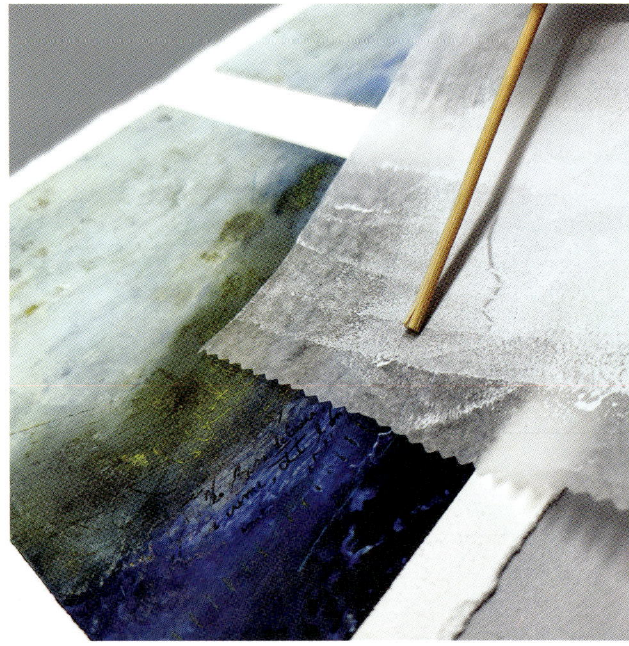

Creating a transfer with paint is a great way to generate unique marks that bring a spontaneous, expressive quality to your work. This technique involves applying paint to a surface such as greaseproof paper, and then transferring it to your painting by rubbing or mark-making on the reverse side. The resulting marks often evoke the textures and effects of printmaking.

Transfers

Transfers are a creative way to introduce additional textures and patterns into your painting. By using materials such as tissue paper or print paper, you can transfer your painted marks onto the dry surface of your painting in a way that gives them a print-like quality. Apply a thick layer of paint to a piece of tissue or print paper and then place it onto your painting. By pressing the paper onto the surface, the paint will transfer, leaving behind a textured, print-like effect. This method can create both unexpected print-like textures and layered visual effects that can add depth to your work. Similarly, you can use an oil bar or a pigment stick to draw directly onto tissue, greaseproof paper or freezer paper. Place the paper onto your dry surface and gently rub, or scratch with the end of your brush, to transfer the pigment. This process adds a drawn or sketched quality to the surface, which can contrast beautifully with more fluid, painterly marks.

Brayers

A brayer (a type of roller) is a great tool for creating expressive marks; however, it is advisable to let your surface become touch-dry before using it. This means the paint should be dry enough so that it does not lift or blend as you roll the brayer across the surface. It is best to apply a thin layer of paint over your surface with the brayer so that the marks and textures underneath remain visible. This technique helps unify the surface, creating a soft, delicate film across the surface, while allowing the underlying marks to show through. Alternatively, you can use the brayer to block out specific areas of the painting, pushing back textures or colours and adding space within the composition.

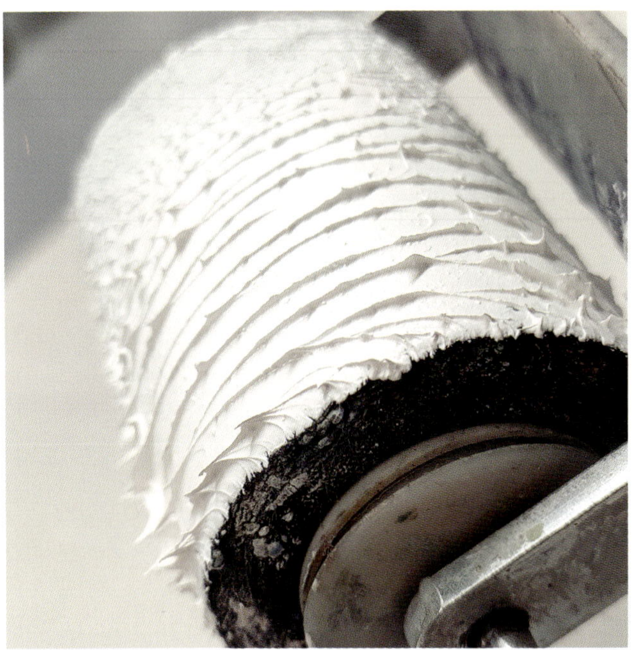

If you end up with peaks of paint on the roller, as shown, it means there is too much paint to achieve a thin, delicate film of colour. Instead, you will end up with a thick, opaque layer that may unintentionally obscure areas you want to push back.

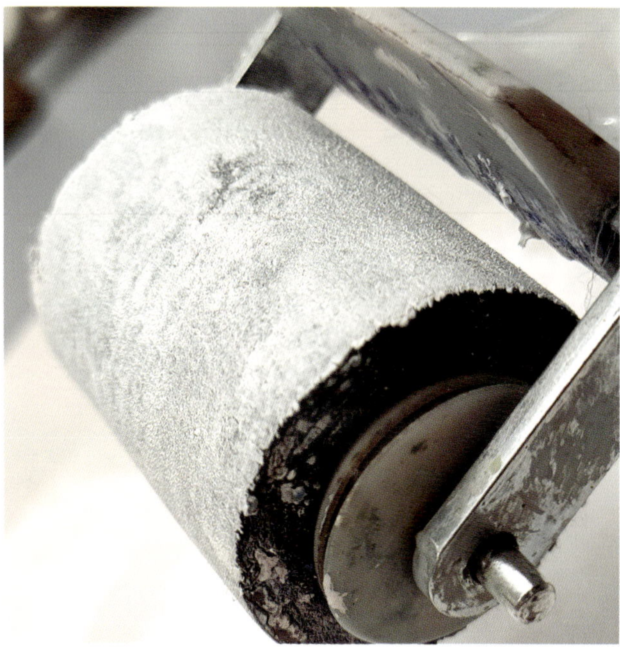

To fix this, roll your brayer over a piece of print paper to remove excess paint until only a thin, even layer remains. This will help you create a fine, controlled application that allows the underlying surface to show through, while maintaining subtle transparency.

MASKING

Masking enables you to define specific shapes and conceal parts of your painting, adding structure and visual interest. By incorporating painted shapes, you can create contrast and enhance the composition. Hard-edged shapes provide sharp contrast to softer, blurred areas, while colour blocks can help define form, create areas of calm, or push back sections to suggest depth. These shapes can also enrich your base layers, especially when painted with a light colour and then covered with a transparent layer. This technique pushes the shapes into the background while still allowing them to subtly emerge through the top layer. The interplay between the light base and transparent overlay can evoke a sense of depth, with shapes appearing to recede or come forward depending on how much of them is revealed.

If you want to mask off certain areas of your painting, start by covering them with newsprint paper. For crisp, straight edges, you can use the edge of your newsprint paper or carefully apply masking tape.

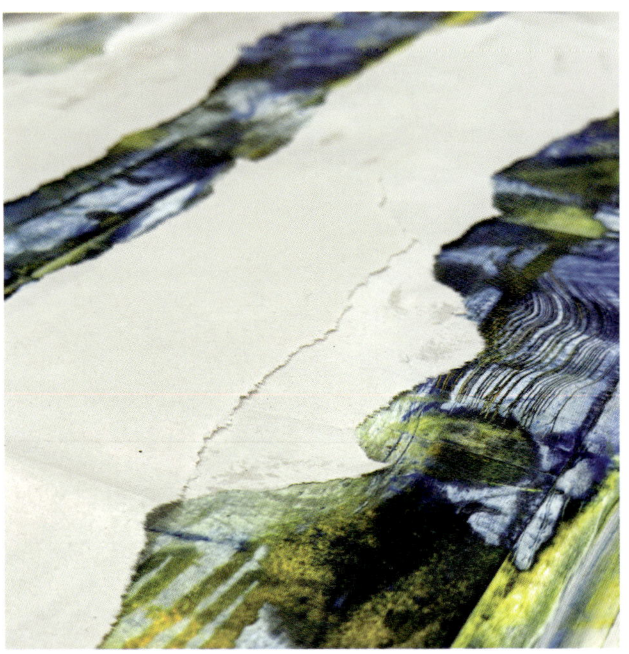

Mask off sections of your painting, then paint over the areas that remain exposed to create shapes, push back areas, and add depth, all of which help develop your composition. You can either create your own shapes using torn newsprint (or cut newsprint for sharper edges) or use pre-made stencils, especially useful if you want to incorporate letters or numbers.

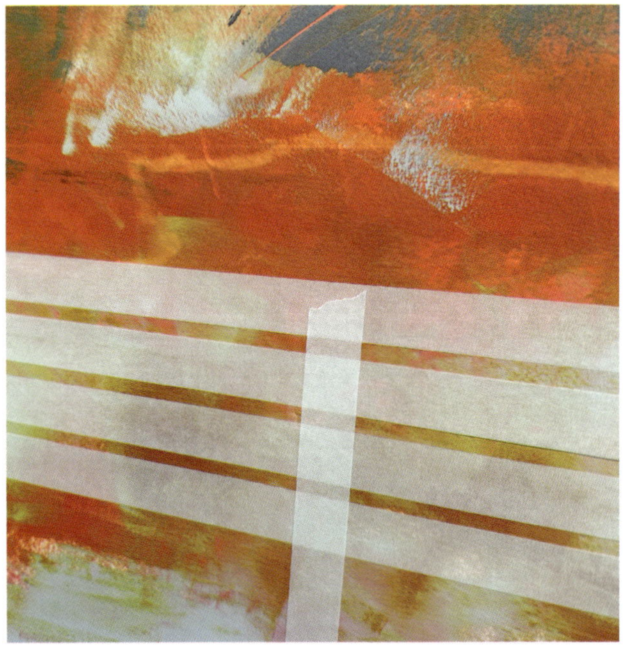

With the surface of the painting touch-dry, low-tack masking tape has been applied to create shapes and section off areas before adding a layer of paint. In this example, the tape is used to introduce straight lines, creating contrast against the more organic marks made through blending with a squeegee, thereby adding visual interest to the composition.

Ensure the masking tape is not too sticky to avoid lifting any paint when removed. Once the areas you want to protect are covered, use either a squeegee or a brayer to apply paint over the exposed sections. The squeegee will create a thinner, smoother layer of paint, while the brayer will give a slightly textured finish – both are effective. To add visual interest, you can scratch into the surface before removing the masking tape or print paper. At first, the newly painted areas may appear disconnected from the rest of your painting, but you can integrate them with mark-making across areas, or adding a transparent layer over the entire painting to create a more unified surface.

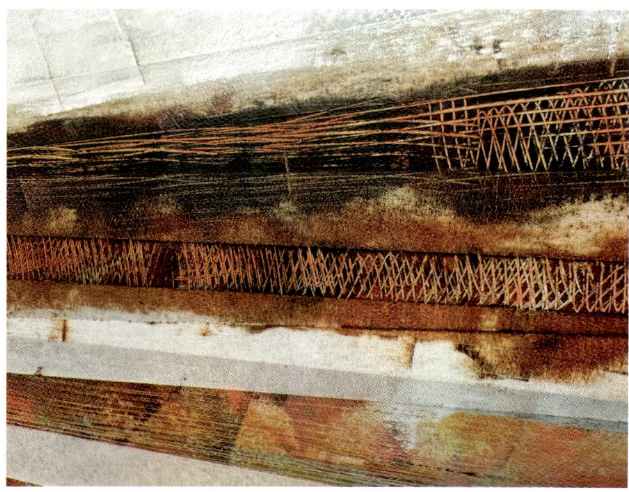

Blocking out sections of your painting enables you to begin organising and composing the overall piece, helping to create a sense of balance and structure. In this example, masking tape has been used to create sections, which have then been scratched into, creating textured marks that add visual interest and enhance the depth of the surface.

PAINTING WITH MASKING TAPE

Caroline Mackintosh is drawn to the strong shapes, lines and patterns formed by the complex interplay of water and land in the marshes and coastal estuaries that surround her. Her work attempts to portray the vast horizons of this landscape, using diagonal lines and carefully positioned verticals to guide the viewer's eye through the landscape and into the distance. She will start her paintings with a framework of dark lines and shapes, emphasising the tonal contrast, which provides her with a guide over which she can work loosely and boldly with colour. As the painting takes form, she defines the shapes and lines she sees in the landscape with masked off areas. 'I think of it as painting with masking tape, using the tape as a tool to sculpt the contours of the landscape, creating curves as well as straight lines and bands, organic alongside geometric shapes.' Sometimes, tears in the masking tape are used to leave a ragged edge and softer blurred lines. The contrast between the defined edges provided by the tape, against the more organic loose marks and areas of colour, provides interest and definition, allowing Caroline to emphasise the geometry she sees in the landscape.

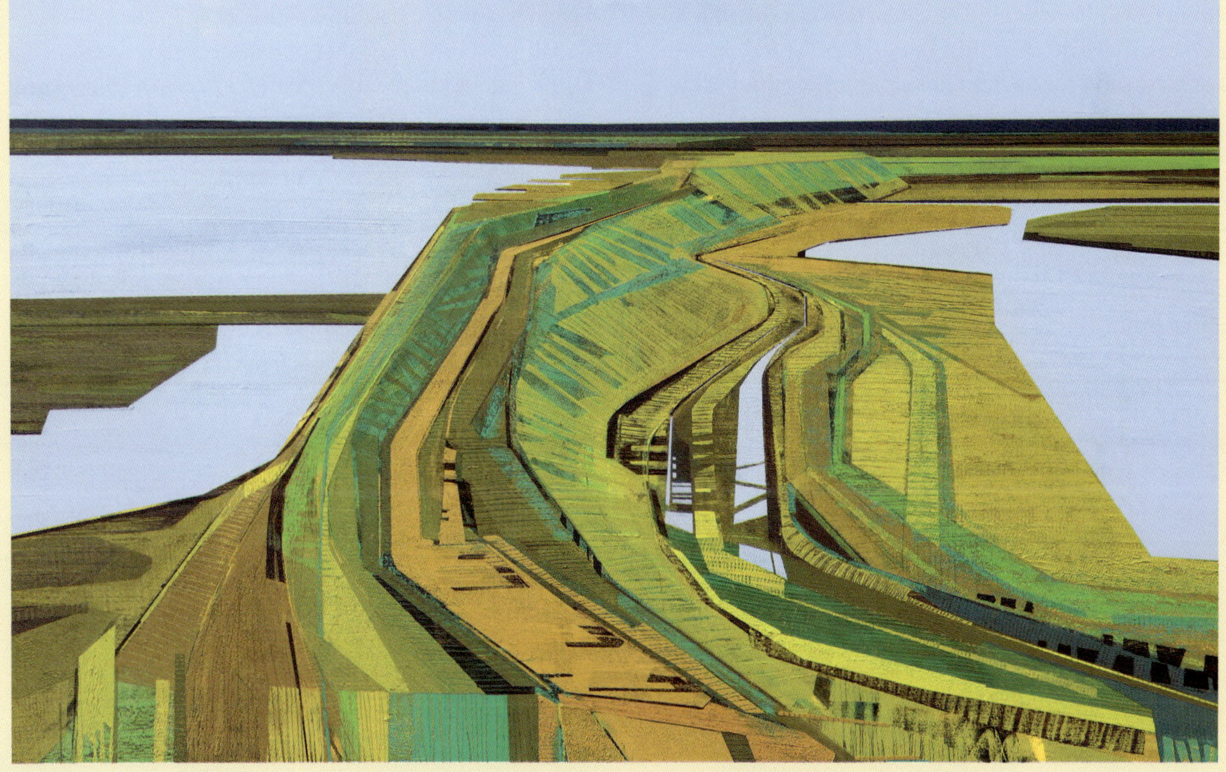

The Footpath, 100 × 160cm (39½ × 63in), oil and oil and cold wax on canvas by Caroline Mackintosh.

UNIFYING

This chapter offers techniques for building texture and depth in painting through an experimental, iterative process of adding and removing elements. Central to this process is the concept of unifying the work – transforming what may initially appear chaotic or unresolved into a cohesive and engaging whole. The process begins with experimentation and flexibility, pushing and pulling, adding and subtracting elements, allowing the painting to evolve organically. This dynamic process often leads to stages that feel 'messy' or even 'ugly', but such phases are a normal, necessary part of discovery. The key is to push through these challenging moments, understanding that they serve as a stepping stone for what will eventually emerge.

Glazing plays a critical role in unifying. When a painting feels disconnected or rough around the edges, a glaze can quickly transform the surface. Transparent glazes are useful for harmonising the composition by integrating the various elements, softening contrasts, and creating a sense of atmospheric depth. The right glaze can bring balance and can help to refine shapes, adjust tones, and make disparate parts of the painting feel more connected. The contrast of light and dark values is crucial for effective glazing, as this contrast serves as a strong foundation for the layers of transparent glazes and will add depth and complexity to your painting. The interplay between transparent and opaque layers contributes to a painting's tactile quality, enriching the visual experience and giving the surface life. By adjusting the intensity of glaze layers, artists can create different moods, enhance luminosity, or create the illusion of distance and space.

When a painting lacks direction, glazing can act as a transformative tool. A glaze can create new connections and introduce unexpected colour shifts. It provides an opportunity to recalibrate the painting, shifting its energy, and reinvigorating the process when it feels stuck. Glazing is a powerful way to tie all the elements in your painting together – whether it is reconciling contrasting areas, enhancing depth, or enriching texture. Through the careful balance of addition and subtraction, opaque and transparent layers, you can create a harmonious composition that feels both resolved and alive. This flexible, experimental approach to surface development should help to achieve a richly layered, and visually cohesive painting.

Ultimately, the goal is not to achieve perfection immediately, but to embrace the process of trial, error, and discovery. Each mark, each layer, and each decision contributes to the painting's evolution. By using the techniques covered in this chapter, and by balancing the addition and subtraction of elements while allowing the painting to evolve organically, you will create a composition that feels both resolved and alive. This flexible, experimental approach ensures that the final work is not only visually cohesive, but also rich in energy, depth, and texture.

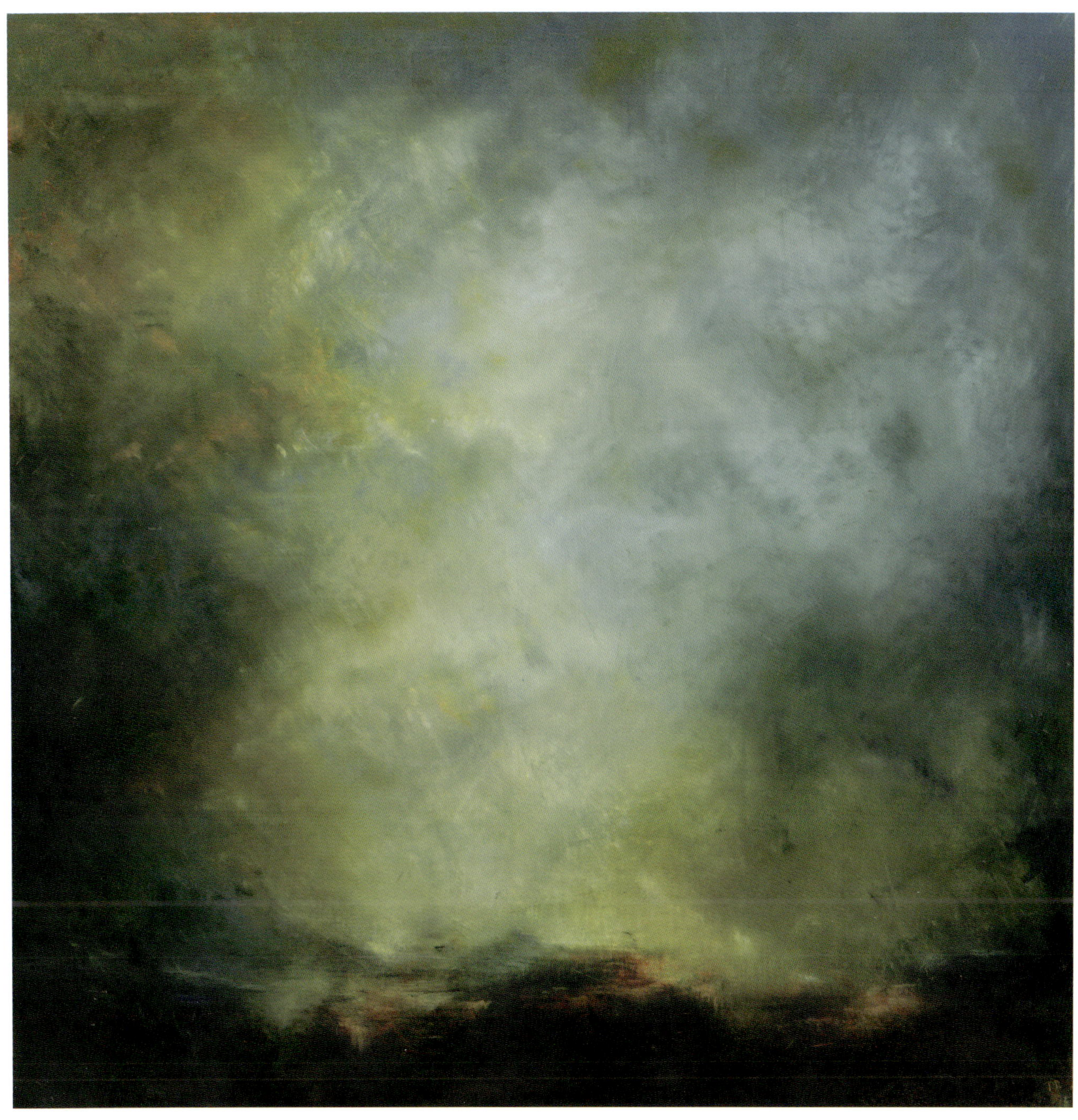

In *Tempest*, a warm transparent orange glaze was applied during the painting process, unifying the surface and subtly shifting the overall mood of the piece. This glaze helped push elements back, creating a greater sense of depth and atmosphere. It also refreshed the surface, providing a new layer for blending and allowing for scratching back to reveal underlying textures.

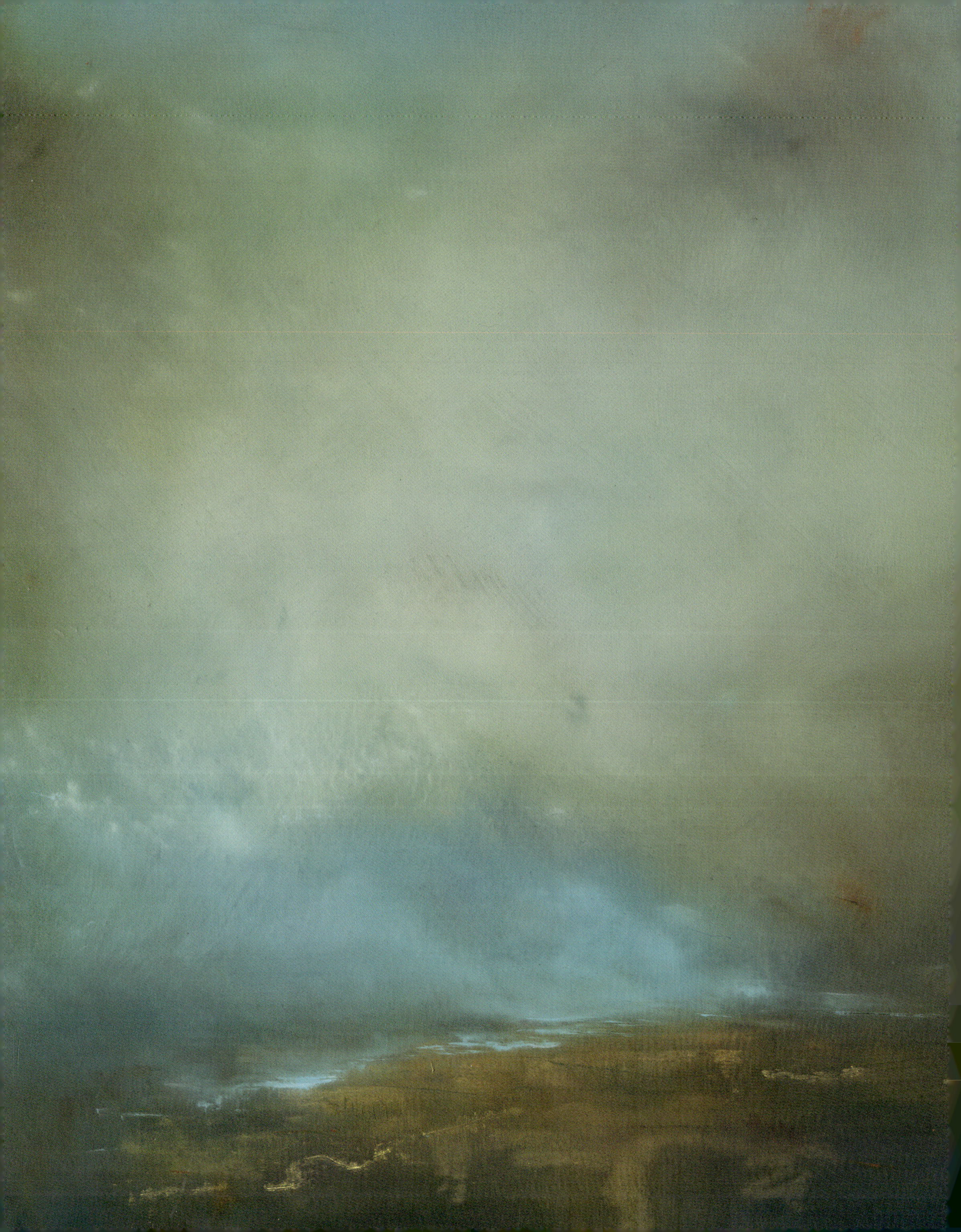

CHAPTER 6

CREATING ATMOSPHERE

Atmosphere in a painting refers to the mood, tone, or emotional resonance evoked by the work. This intangible quality conveys a sense of place, emotion, or environment and is often described as the essence of the painting. It immerses viewers, drawing them into the scene and establishing a connection with the artist's vision.

Creating atmosphere involves the deliberate interplay of light, colour, texture, and composition. While representational art uses recognisable subjects to evoke mood, abstract or non-representational works rely on visual elements to achieve similar effects. This process emphasises subtlety and balance; by thoughtfully considering these components, artists can infuse their work with impactful feelings that resonate deeply with the audience.

In my work, I employ various techniques to achieve atmosphere. I use glazing with thin, transparent layers of paint to add depth and luminosity, enhancing the overall mood. Intuitive painting allows the creative process to unfold organically, fostering authenticity and dynamic interactions among colours, forms, and textures. Manipulating light and tone is essential for defining depth, mood, and narrative. A careful balance of tonal values, from highlights to deep shadows, greatly contributes to the overall atmosphere. Additionally, contrasting smooth and textured areas enhances visual interest and evokes specific emotions, enabling me to create compelling atmospheres that resonate with viewers.

This chapter explores how key decisions in the painting process contribute to creating atmosphere. We examine the interplay of intuitive methods, tonal values, and various techniques to inspire dynamic and emotionally resonant work. Ultimately, the power of atmosphere lies in its ability to transcend the canvas, inviting viewers into a world shaped by the artist's vision and emotional intent.

SUBJECT MATTER

The choice of subject in a painting plays a pivotal role in establishing its atmosphere, as it serves as the foundation for the viewer's emotional and sensory response: as an example, a stormy landscape or seascape inherently conveys drama, intensity, and perhaps even a sense of foreboding. The inclusion of elements to suggest a rolling mist or darkening clouds further enhances this emotional resonance, drawing the viewer into the scene.

OPPOSITE: *Storm Chasing* (50 × 50cm/19¾ × 19¾in, oils and cold wax on Arches Huile paper) is an abstracted landscape with muted tones, evoking mist gently enveloping the shoreline. Delicate lines of gold leaf and turquoise lead the eye towards the horizon and the subtle colour transitions in the clouds.

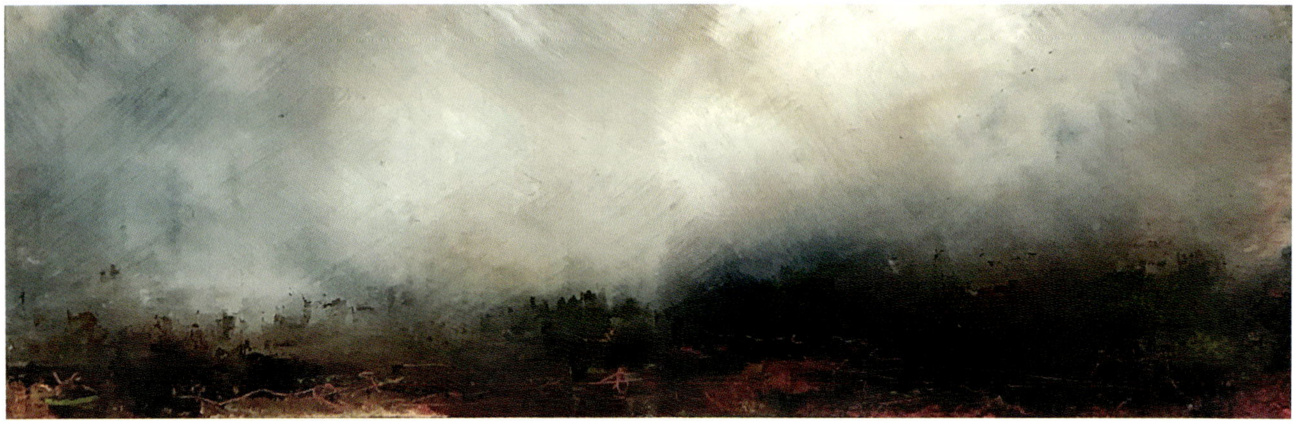

Misty Moorland (37 × 12cm/14½ × 4¾in, oils and cold wax on Arches Huile paper) captures a soft, atmospheric landscape with seamless transitions between sky and land. Marks created with a fan brush pull colour down into the foreground, enhancing the sensation of mist drifting over the terrain. Subtle scratches reveal glimpses of the pink base layer, adding depth and texture to the composition.

Weather elements such as fog, rain, sunlight, and snow profoundly influence the mood of a landscape, each bringing its own emotional and visual qualities. Fog softens edges and reduces visibility, creating an ethereal, mysterious, or introspective atmosphere.

In the painting *Misty Moorland*, muted colours evoke a strong sense of atmosphere. Soft tones in the sky suggest a mist cloaking the moorland, enhancing depth and space. The earthy browns of the landscape are beautifully complemented by subtle pops of muted pinks, reinforcing the impression of mist enveloping both the viewer and the landscape. This composition fosters a quiet, still ambiance, inviting you to imagine walking across the moorland, embraced by its tranquillity. The harmonious palette deepens the sense of peace conveyed by the scene.

Sunlight can dramatically transform a scene based on its intensity, direction, and warmth, creating various moods, including a sense of gloaming. Harsh midday light may feel stark and unforgiving, while the softer glow of sunrise or sunset induces warmth, comfort and tranquillity. Additionally, crepuscular rays can introduce drama, drawing attention to specific areas of the work and enhancing the overall composition. In *Cloud Shadows*, sunlight reflects off large clouds, creating a lively sense of movement as they bustle across the sky. Shadows envelop the land below, while areas illuminated by sunlight are brought to life with accents of gold leaf, emphasising their brightness.

Bright blues capture the essence of a summer's day, and carefully placed highlights accentuate the details of the clouds, guiding the viewer's gaze throughout the composition. The wispy texture of the clouds, achieved through brushstrokes, conveys a sense of lightness and airiness, as though propelled by a gentle breeze. Their diagonal placement enhances the dynamic energy, reinforcing the impression of movement and imbuing the scene with vitality and a sense of exploration.

In contrast, using movement and texture to introduce the suggestion of rain can evoke feelings of melancholy, renewal, or vitality. In *New Lights I*, the impression of rain emerges through the downward pull of sunlit clouds, which blur the boundaries between land and sky. This effect is further emphasised by the visible brush marks left within the composition. The disrupted horizon line hints at a gentle drizzle moving across the shoreline, while diagonal light illuminates the clouds, infusing the scene with energy.

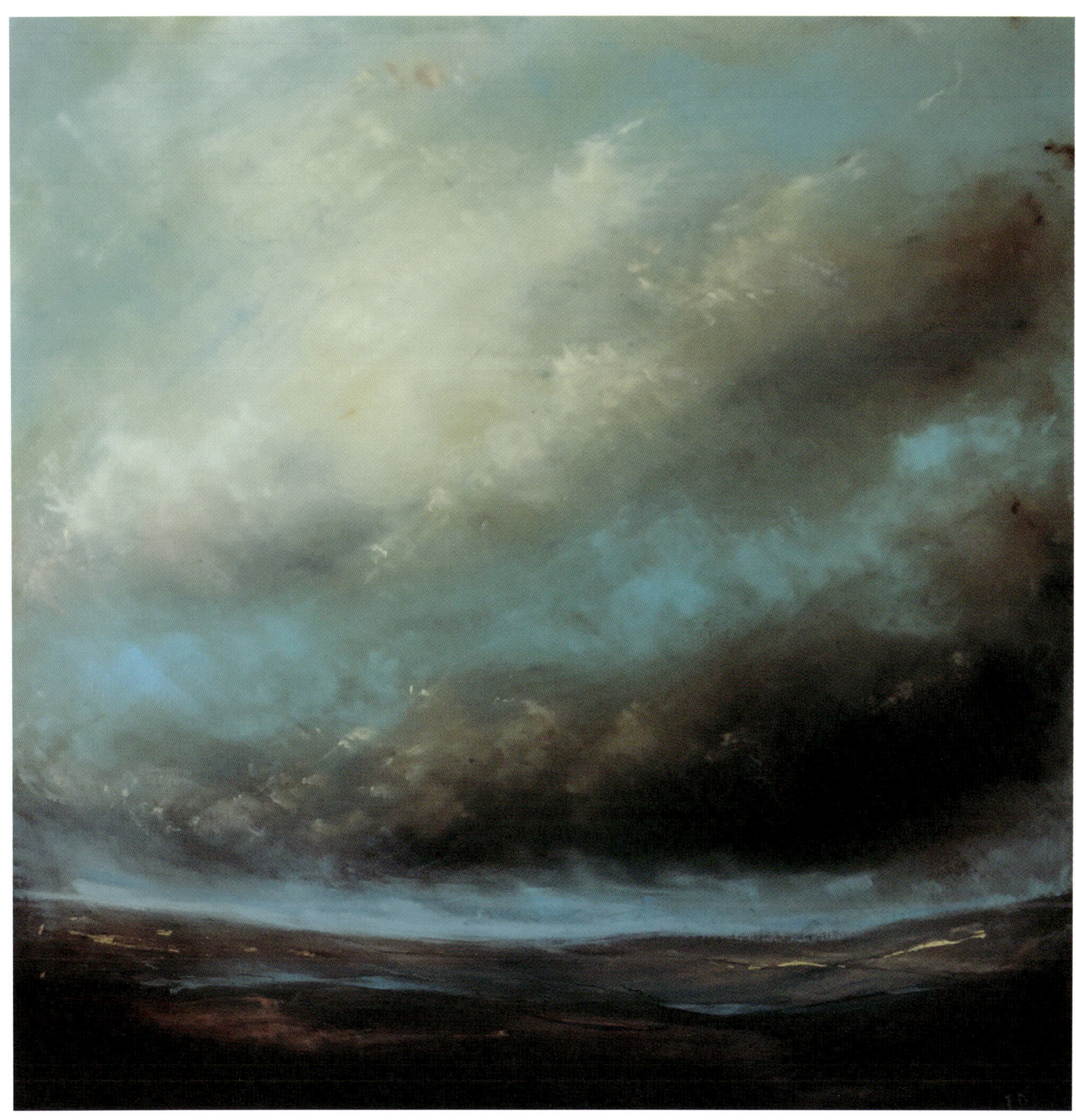

Cloud Shadows (50 × 50cm/19¾ × 19¾in, oils, cold wax and gold leaf on wooden panel) offers a sweeping perspective, inviting the viewer to look down and across the landscape. Delicate traces of gold leaf meander across the terrain, catching the light and guiding the eye through the composition. Subtle scratches carved into the surface further enhance movement, drawing the viewer deeper into the scene.

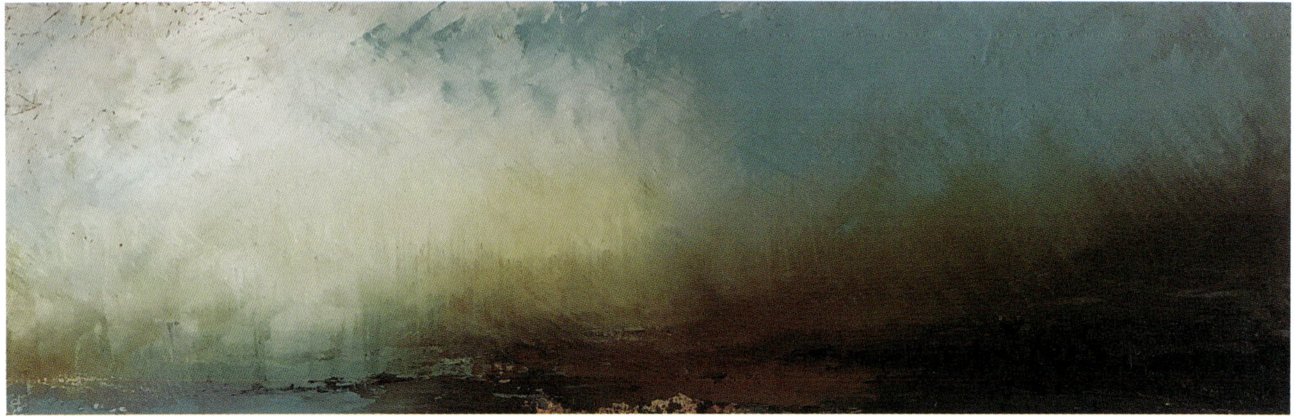

New Lights I (37 × 12cm/14½ × 4¾in, oils and cold wax on Arches Huile paper) explores movement and atmosphere through expressive palette knife work. Chopping into the paint blends the colours seamlessly, creating smooth transitions while accentuating the downward pull of rain sweeping across the landscape. This dynamic technique enhances the sense of weather and shifting light within the scene.

The transitions between colours are seamless, ensuring that each hue retains its individuality, while softly blending into the next. Bright tints add a dazzling, shimmering quality, allowing the muted turquoises and oranges to resonate harmoniously. Meanwhile, the dark foreground incorporates metallic pigments that complement the warm oranges in the sky, creating a sense of balance throughout the composition.

In *Haar*, the suggestion of rain is conveyed through the downward pull of colour from the clouds, which blurs the boundaries between land and sky. This disruption of the horizon line implies sheets of rain cascading onto the shoreline as clouds roll ominously towards the shore. Diagonal light illuminates the clouds, infusing the painting with energy, while leading lines created by brushstrokes draw the viewer in, offering perspective amidst the diffused edges between land and sky. Transitions between colours ensure that each hue occupies its own space, while softly blending into the next. The lighter tints in the upper section create a tranquil atmosphere, while the warm greys provide a muted effect, allowing the muted blues, yellows and oranges to sing. The dark foreground incorporates metallic pigments to harmonise with the yellows and oranges in the sky and create balance in the composition.

Seasonal changes can be reflected by transitions in colour and light, with each season offering a unique palette and emotional resonance. Spring's vibrant greens and bright sky blues evoke growth and renewal, bringing a sense of optimism. In contrast, autumn showcases warm tones, from deep oranges and fiery reds to muted browns and golden yellows, amplifying feelings of transformation and introspection. By capturing the essence of these seasonal shifts in artwork, you can convey deeper narratives that resonate with viewers, inviting them to connect with the emotions and experiences associated with each phase of the year.

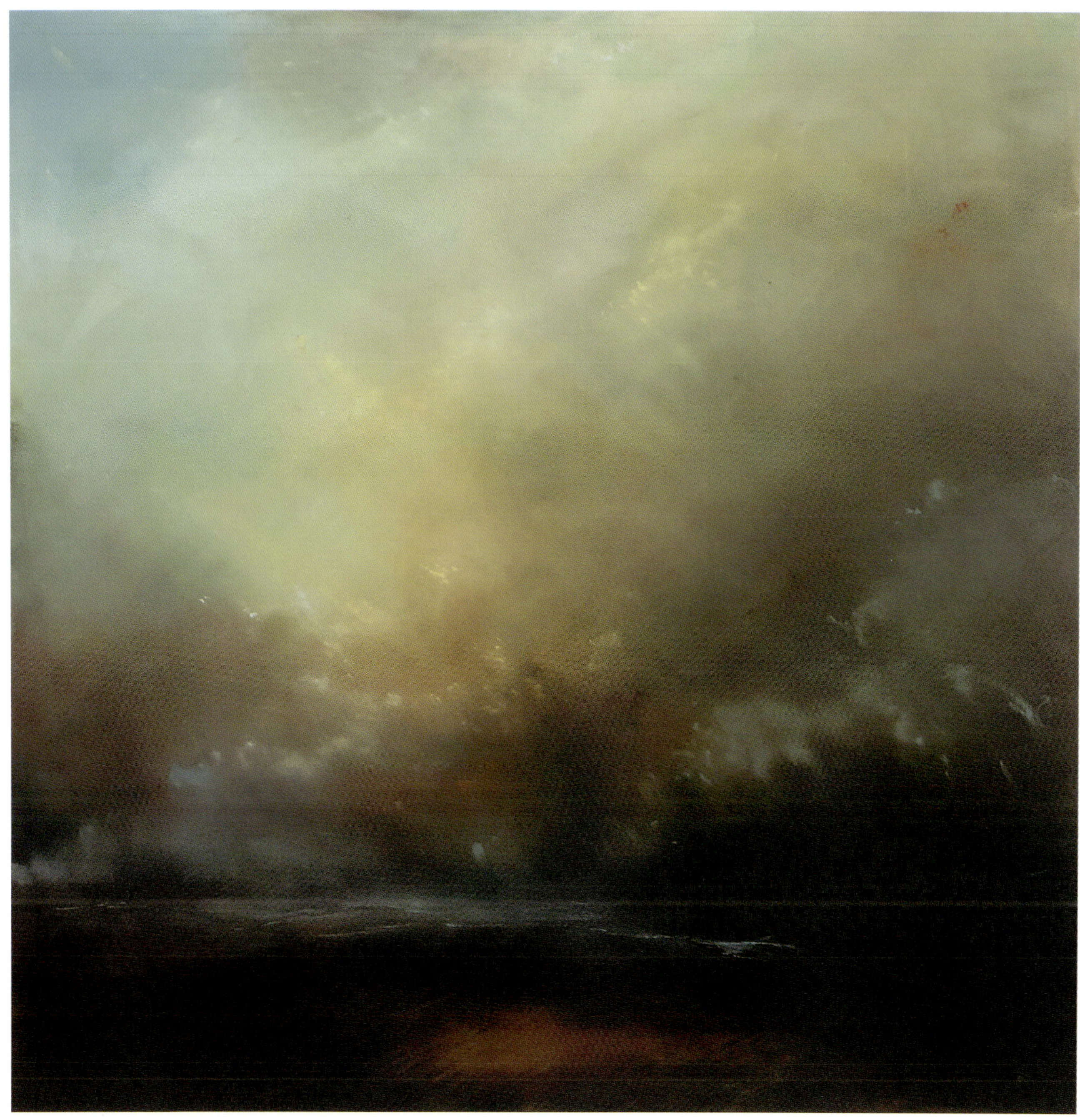

Haar (80 × 80cm/31½ × 31½in, oils, cold wax and gold leaf on Arches Huile paper bonded to a wooden panel) evokes a serene atmosphere through a restrained, muted palette, even as a storm looms on the horizon. Subtle details emphasise the shifting forms of the clouds, enhancing their movement across the sky. Highlights are deliberately confined to a small area, hinting at the promise of a brighter day ahead.

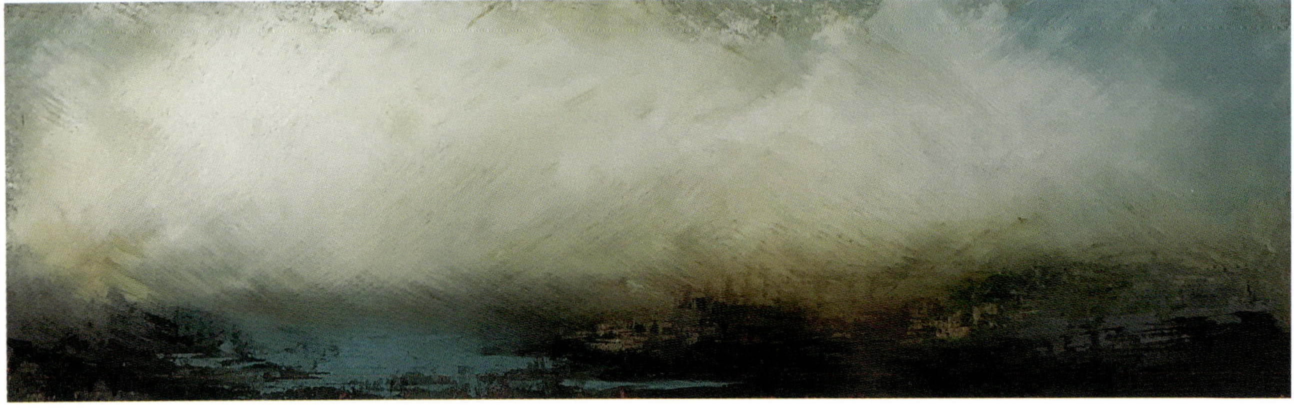

New lights II (37 × 12cm/14½ × 4¾in, oils and cold wax on Arches Huile paper) presents a striking contrast to *New Lights I*, with deeper, darker tones adding weight and structure to the clouds, suggesting the presence of heavier rain. Expressive brushwork and palette knife marks enhance the movement of the storm-laden sky, emphasising the shifting weather and dynamic energy of the landscape.

COLOUR CHOICES AND THEIR IMPACT ON ATMOSPHERE

Colour choices play a vital role in shaping the mood and atmosphere of a painting, though individual reactions to colours often vary, based on personal experiences and associations. For instance, blues and greens typically evoke feelings of coolness and calm, while reds, pinks, and oranges create warmth and energy. Warm colours such as reds, oranges, and yellows convey intensity and vibrancy, whereas cool colours often inspire a sense of melancholy or mystery. Interestingly, paintings dominated by blue and green hues are frequently more popular among collectors, most likely due to their soothing qualities and versatility.

Incorporating muted or desaturated colours can enhance the sense of distance and depth within a composition. These softer tones create an atmospheric effect, particularly in landscapes, by simulating the natural fading of colour that occurs in the distance. This technique not only adds complexity to the painting but also encourages viewers to engage more deeply with the scene, evoking emotions and memories allied to their own experiences with colour and light. By thoughtfully considering your colour choices, you can effectively manipulate the atmosphere of your artwork and forge an emotional connection with your audience.

In *January,* cool greys, greens, and blues capture the essence of a winter landscape. Mist rising from the land suggests a chilly, overcast day, with clouds descending to envelop the moorland and valley. The rich, dark foreground, painted with indigo and burnt umber, is punctuated by luminous accents of metallic bronze powders and gold leaf. These shimmering details trace a path toward the horizon, drawing the viewer further into the scene.

This cold, atmospheric composition conveys the stillness of a dark winter's day. The richly dark foreground contrasts beautifully with the muted grey-greens in the top left corner, amplifying the sense of encroaching weather. Delicate porcelain-like blues,

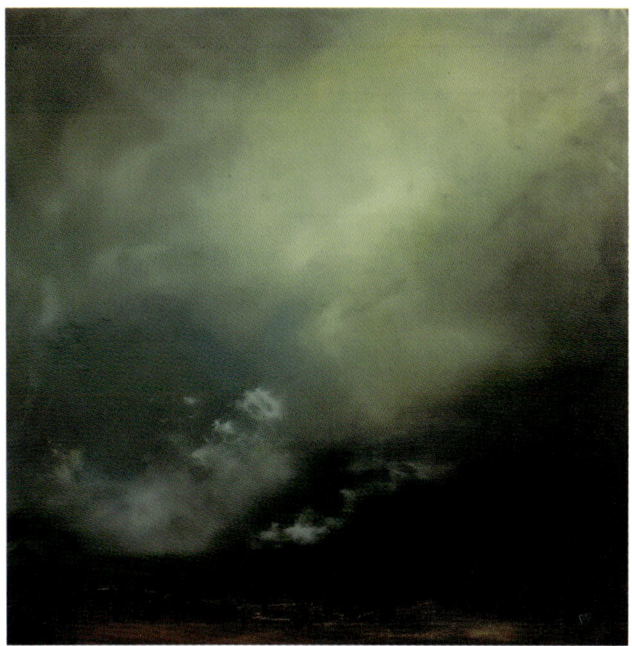

January (50 × 50cm/19¾ × 19¾in, oils, cold wax, and gold leaf on Arches Huile paper bonded to a wooden panel) creates a sense of depth by softening the transition between land and sky with the presence of low-lying clouds. This atmospheric effect gently guides the viewer's eye into the distance, enhancing the painting's sense of vastness and tranquillity.

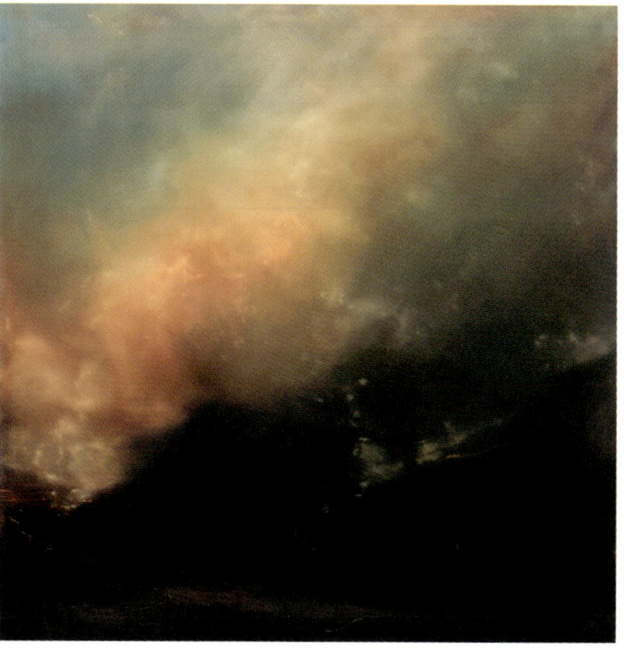

Tempestuous (70 × 70cm/23½ × 23½in, oils, cold wax and gold leaf on Arches Huile paper bonded to a wooden panel) lives up to its name, capturing a powerful sense of drama and movement. The dynamic energy of the composition conveys intensity, while delicate, almost luminous pinks introduce a contrasting sense of serenity and balance, softening the turbulence and adding depth to the scene.

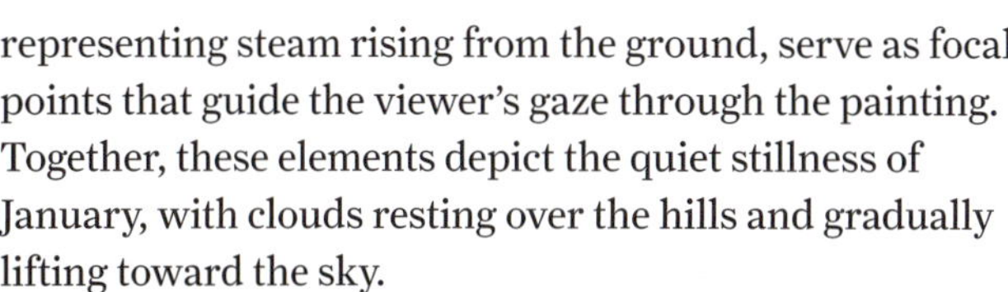

representing steam rising from the ground, serve as focal points that guide the viewer's gaze through the painting. Together, these elements depict the quiet stillness of January, with clouds resting over the hills and gradually lifting toward the sky.

In contrast, *Tempestuous* explores a similar subject matter, but evokes a completely different atmosphere. Similar to *January*, rolling clouds cascade from the hillside with darkness dominating much of the composition. However, light breaks through to illuminate the clouds ahead, suggesting movement and a dramatic shift in the scene. The warm palette intensifies the drama, infusing the painting with energy and vibrancy.

The darker areas of the composition extend upwards, creating a sense of enclosure, as if the storm is unfolding directly before the viewer. Bronze powders in the foreground reflect the warm hues of the clouds and are accented by leading lines of gold leaf. These shimmering details guide the eye toward the light source on the horizon, where highlights draw the viewer deeper into the scene.

The title, *Tempestuous*, perfectly captures the mood of the painting. The dynamic interplay of drama and movement generates a feeling of energy and intensity, which is balanced by the delicate, almost luminous pinks that introduce a sense of serenity creating an overarching harmony in the scene.

MANIPULATING LIGHT AND TONAL VALUE

Light and dark values are essential for creating depth and atmosphere in paintings. Successful paintings often incorporate a balanced range of tonal values (dark, medium, and light) to enhance the visual and emotional impact. Introducing lighter areas into a painting fosters a sense of openness, evoking brightness and spaciousness, while darker areas add mystery, hinting at unseen elements within shadows. These tonal contrasts work together to create atmosphere, drawing viewers into the painting and immersing them in its mood and narrative. A broad range of tonal values is critical for achieving depth and visual interest. Tonal contrast establishes depth and mood, and a well-balanced tonal range enhances the overall structure and impact of a painting, inviting viewers to engage more deeply with its emotional resonance.

Tonal values are crucial for creating the illusion of three-dimensionality on a two-dimensional surface. Dark tones tend to recede, while lighter tones come forward, effectively defining spatial relationships. Atmospheric perspective relies heavily on tonal gradation; distant objects appear lighter and less defined, whereas closer ones are darker and more detailed. A variety of tones guides the viewer's eye through the composition, with strong contrasts emphasising focal points. Intermediate tones – those that fall between the lightest and darkest values – create gradual, seamless transitions between contrasting areas. These mid-tones act as a bridge, softening contrasts and making shifts between light and dark appear more natural and cohesive. Without a wide tonal range, a painting risks feeling flat, monotone, or unengaging.

Moreover, tonal values not only enhance spatial relationships but also convey subtle emotional shifts. High-contrast paintings with strong darks and

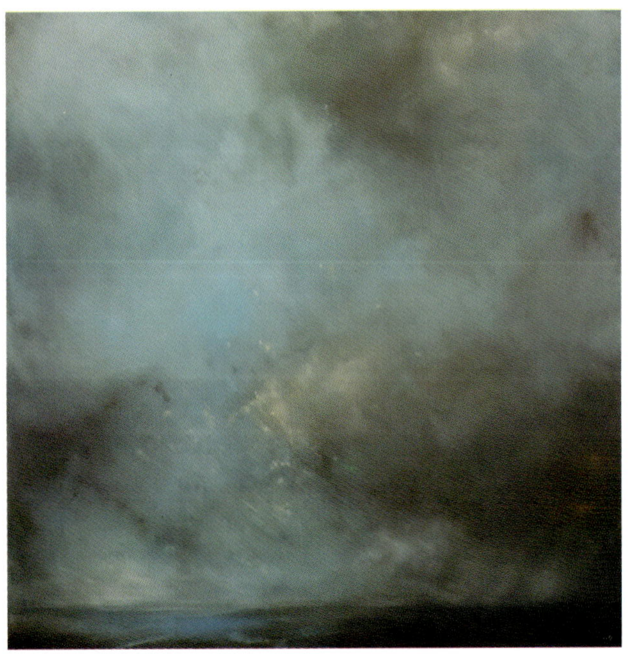

Drisk I (61 × 61cm/24 × 24in, oils and cold wax on wooden panel) embodies the essence of its title – 'drisk' refers to drizzling mist – a weather phenomenon where sunlight filters through thin clouds or a delicate mist. This interplay of light and moisture creates a luminous, shimmering effect that evokes a sense of tranquillity.

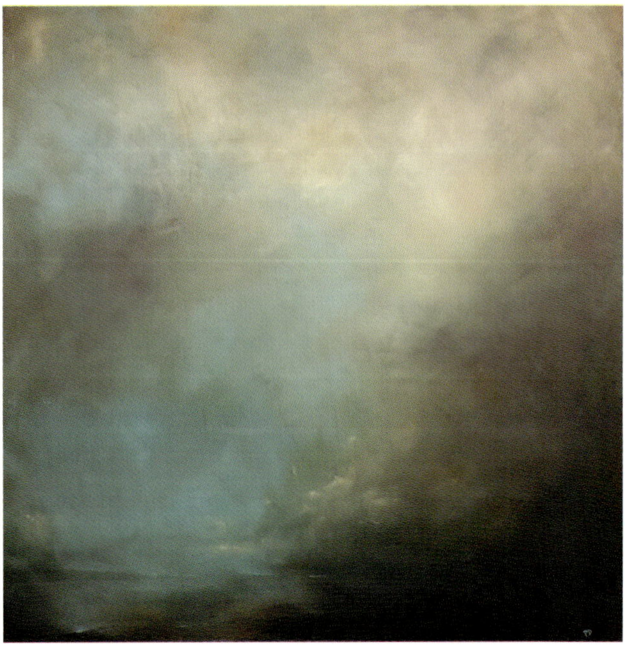

Drisk II (61 × 61cm/24 × 24in, oils and cold wax on wooden panel) much like its counterpart *Drisk I*, showcases the use of a squeegee and fan brush to create delicate, nuanced colour mixes and seamless transitions. This technique enhances the ethereal quality of the piece, evoking the gentle interplay of light and mist, inviting viewers to immerse themselves in the serene atmosphere.

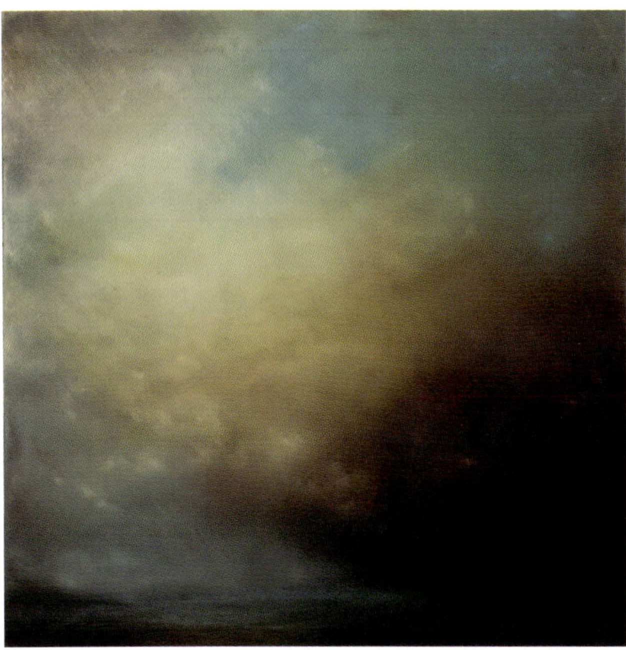

Cloud burst (45 × 45cm/17¾ × 17in¾in, oils and cold wax on Arches Huile paper bonded to a wooden panel) contrasts with *Drisk I* and *II* by drawing more on colours with a yellow bias. This approach creates soft peach and pink tints that, when combined with darker elements, enhance the shape and weight of the clouds, adding depth and visual interest to the composition.

PRACTICAL STEPS FOR CREATING A BALANCED RANGE OF TONAL VALUES

Enhance depth: Utilise a strong range of light and dark values to create a sense of depth in your painting. Strategically placed highlights can guide the viewer's eye, while shadows add a three-dimensional quality, making the composition feel more dynamic and engaging.

Build tonal depth: Experiment with transparent layers of oils and cold wax to gradually build your tonal values. By layering, you can achieve a smooth transition between light and dark, enhancing the overall atmosphere.

Avoid flatness: To prevent a composition from feeling flat or monotone, ensure there are distinct areas of darks and lights. A well-defined contrast between these tonal ranges will draw attention to focal points and create visual interest. Be mindful of incorporating a variety of tones to keep your composition lively and engaging, steering clear of a dominance of mid-tones, which can dilute the emotional impact of your painting.

lights can invite feelings of drama or tension, while softer tonal transitions create a tranquil or dreamy atmosphere. Juxtaposing dark and light areas amplifies intensity, and gradual tonal shifts introduce subtlety and complexity, enriching the overall atmosphere of the painting.

My paintings often feature dramatic tonal contrasts, with a predominant use of dark values. However, in *Drisk I* and *Drisk II*, I wanted to capture the lightness and breeziness of a Cornish seascape, along with the ethereal mist that emerges as cooler, denser air from the moors cascades down the cliffs towards the sea. In contrast, *Cloud Burst*, painted during the same period, carries a heavier, stormier feel. Darker tones dominate the composition, particularly in the bottom-right corner, balanced by darker elements suggesting land in the bottom left. Lighter tonal values in the clouds suggest sunlight reflecting off them, adding a soft glow and visual interest. Muted blues along the horizon give depth and perspective, while the towering cloud envelops the viewer in the scene. Smooth transitions between colours and tones enhance the painting's softness, with the interplay of light and shadow creating a delicate range of tints.

SCALE AND ATMOSPHERIC PERSPECTIVE

Scale and atmospheric perspective are powerful tools for shaping the perception of space and mood in a painting. By immersing the viewer in the scene, you not only reinforce the atmosphere, but also foster a deeper emotional connection. Enlarging key elements, such as a mountain range that dominates the frame, can heighten drama and intensity. Similarly, shifting the perspective by placing the viewer on top of moorland looking down into a valley can evoke a sense of exploration.

Atmospheric perspective emphasises how light, colour, and details change with distance to create depth and mood. Softened details and lighter, cooler colours in the distance can evoke vastness, mystery, or tranquillity. This draws the viewer further into the scene, enhancing the illusion of space and reinforcing the painting's overall atmosphere. In *Squall*, this technique is illustrated through soft, muted tones of cool blues and greens, complemented by pink tints in the clouds. The composition suggests clouds rolling across an estuary or shoreline, with dark elements in the foreground grounding the painting. Gold leaf and turquoise brushstrokes draw the eye toward the

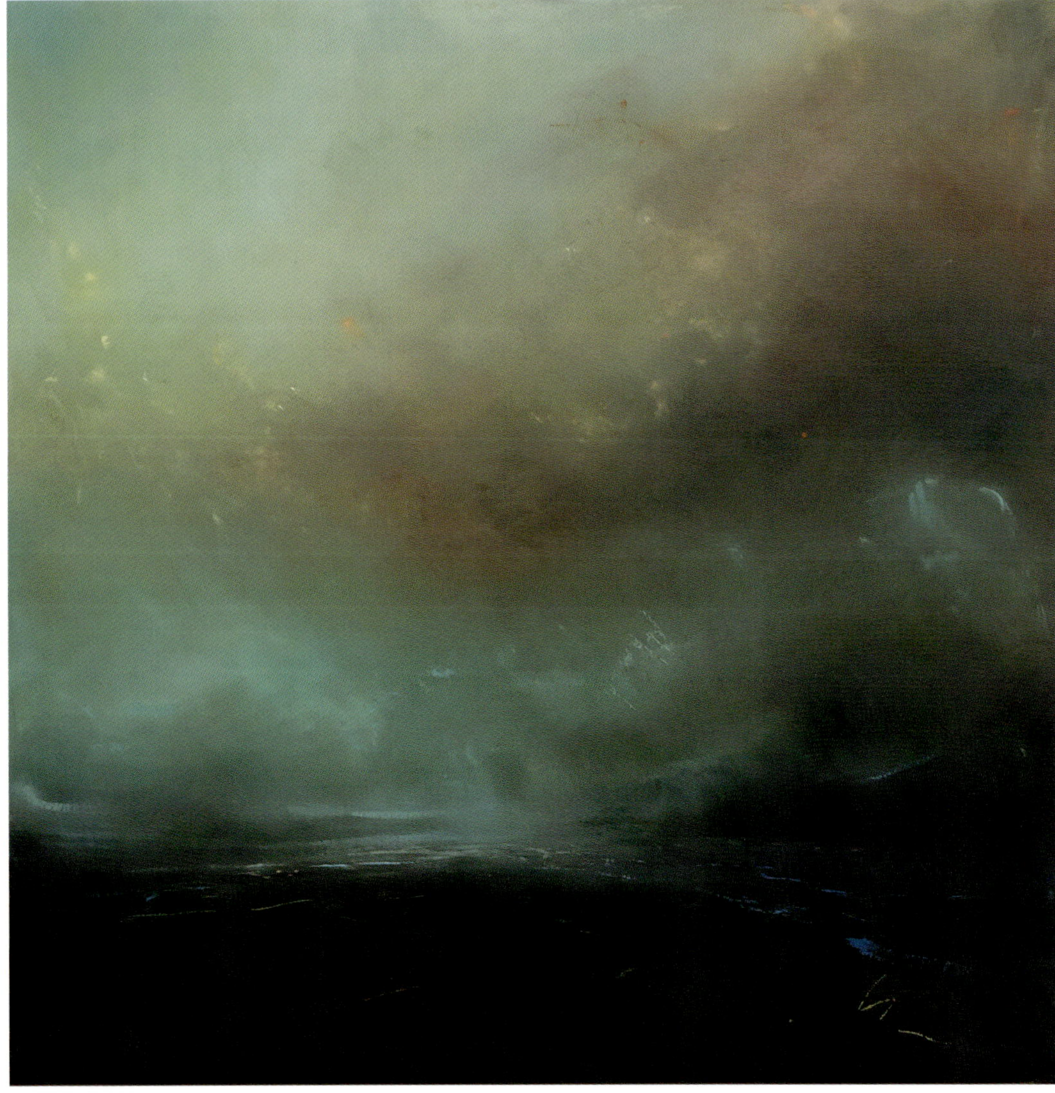

Squall (50 × 50cm/19¾ × 19¾in, oils, cold wax and gold leaf on Arches Huile paper bonded to a wooden panel) pulls the viewer in with its cool turquoise hues along the horizon, evoking a sense of distance. The warm dusky pinks in the clouds leap forwards, creating a striking contrast that further emphasises depth and enhances the painting's atmospheric quality.

horizon, where cool turquoises imply light filtering through the clouds. Soft hints of yellow, peach, and pink suggest sunlight attempting to break through, adding to the sense of movement as leading lines guide the viewer towards the horizon and the low-hanging clouds drifting along the shoreline. The dominant sky creates a sense of scale, evoking the impression of billowing clouds moving above and around the viewer. Despite the energy and movement within the piece, the cool turquoise tones impart a sense of calm and quietness.

Manipulating space within a painting, whether to convey expansiveness or intimacy, also plays a critical role in shaping its emotional impact. Quiet spaces can enhance feelings of openness or isolation, depending on the intended mood, while densely packed compositions might feel dynamic or overwhelming. Balancing composition with atmospheric elements is key to creating a cohesive and engaging work. The arrangement of elements, space, and tonal contrasts influences how the viewer perceives the scene and its mood. Leading lines and focal points guide the viewer's eye through the painting, shaping their emotional response and ensuring a dynamic interaction with the artwork.

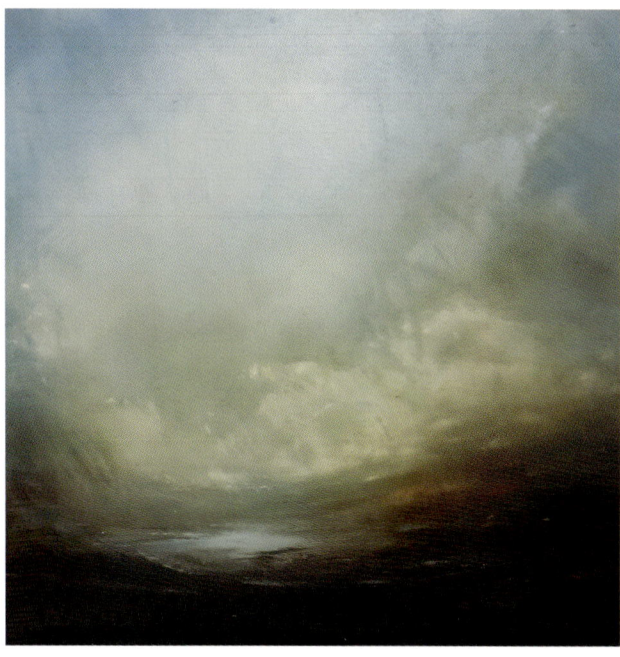

Lakeland Lights (30 × 30cm/12 × 12in, oil, cold wax and gold leaf on Arches Huile paper bonded to a wooden panel), demonstrates the thoughtful use of scale and atmospheric perspective to draw the viewer into the scene, gazing down upon the valley below. The composition's quiet spaces and a balanced palette of cool blues, greys, greens, and soft yellows evoke the crisp, uplifting brightness of a winter's day.

Lakeland Lights places the viewer at a height, overlooking a scene that suggests a tarn or lakeside, surrounded by hills and mountains shrouded in clouds. The painting exudes a light, ethereal quality, with diffused light filtering through thin, pale blue-grey clouds, creating a hazy, contemplative sky. The foreground anchors the composition and is counterbalanced by darker blue tones in the top left corner. This tonal interplay evokes a cool day, despite the brightness of the sky.

Copper hues in the land hint at the autumnal die-back of vegetation, while cool blue, green and yellow tints complete the impression of a crisp autumn morning. The mood is uplifting, inviting the viewer to imagine standing at the viewpoint, ready to descend and explore the landscape below. Strategically placed highlights suggest reflections in the water or perhaps the presence of distant buildings, adding subtle visual interest. Energy emanates from the sparkling light on the water and a cool winter sun reflecting off the clouds.

Sweeping brushstrokes emphasise the contours of the land, guiding the viewer's eye from the foreground towards the lake, beyond to the horizon, and finally upwards to the sky. Softer details and lighter tones in the distance enhance the illusion of space, reinforcing the painting's atmospheric depth and immersing the viewer in the beauty of the scene.

EMOTIONAL CONNECTIONS THROUGH INTUITIVE PAINTING

Drawing from your own memories and feelings associated with specific places or moments and being able to convey these will infuse your work with emotion and depth. When your experiences are reflected in your work, it creates a shared understanding that enhances the emotional impact, forging a deeper bond between the artwork and its audience.

The power of intuitive painting

Working intuitively, allowing the painting process to unfold organically, fosters a dynamic atmosphere. By trusting your instincts and emotions to guide you, you invite spontaneity and authenticity into your practice. This approach encourages unexpected interactions between colours, forms, and textures, giving each brushstroke and colour choice a narrative quality that reflects your emotional state. As the painting evolves, it takes on a life of its own, enhancing its emotional resonance.

Embrace risk

Take risks and embrace the unpredictability of the creative process. Rather than starting with a rigid plan or fixed outcome, cultivate an openness to the evolving composition. Let the painting guide your decisions, responding to its cues with flexibility and curiosity. This organic approach invites discovery, uncovers deeper emotional connections, and infuses the work with authenticity. By paying close attention to the visual and emotional cues within your painting, you create a dialogue between yourself and the work. This fluid, responsive process transforms the act of painting into a meaningful act of exploration, where the process of painting is as significant as the finished piece.

Atmosphere and emotional impact

The atmosphere of a painting plays a crucial role in shaping the emotional response it evokes. By combining personal insights with thoughtful techniques and artistic choices, you can create an atmosphere that resonates deeply with viewers. This harmony between atmosphere and emotion enhances the narrative and essence of the artwork, drawing the viewer into a shared emotional experience. When artists integrate intuitive methods, emotional depth, and responsive techniques, their work transcends mere visual appeal. It invites viewers on a shared experience that elevates the artwork beyond its physical form.

Autumn Mist exemplifies the power of simplicity and emotional connection achieved through intuitive painting. Created with a limited palette and guided by instinctive blending and mark-making, the composition strikes a delicate balance between light and dark. The tonal contrast between the shadowed land and the luminous sky naturally draws the viewer's eye upwards, giving the impression that the land seamlessly blends into the clouds.

The light catches on the billowing clouds, emphasising their momentum as they tumble across the sky. Shades of blue in the top left corner add visual interest, balancing the darker tones of the land pulling

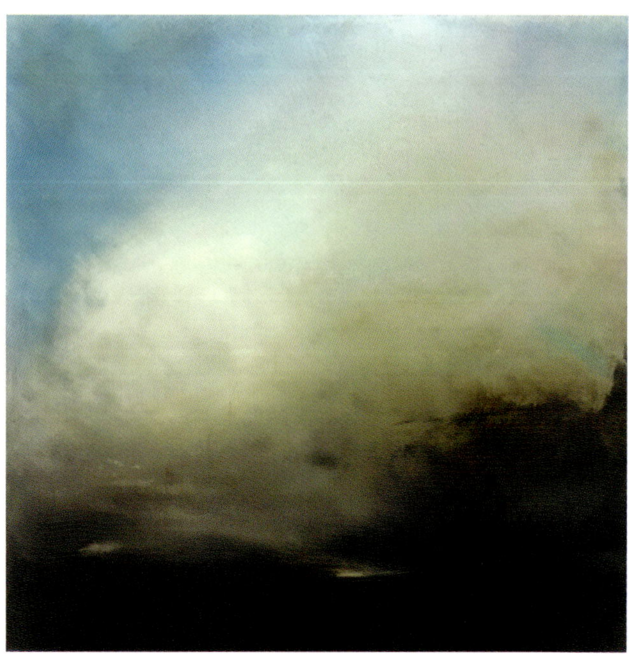

Autumn Mist (20 × 20cm/8 × 8in, oils and cold wax on a deep cradled panel) employs a limited palette of cerulean blue, titanium white, transparent orange, burnt umber, and indigo. The transparent orange infuses a warmth into the clouds, creating a harmonious balance that effectively captures the tranquil essence of an autumnal landscape.

upwards into the clouds on the opposite side. A sweeping brushstroke along the horizon ties the tonal elements together, creating perspective, depth, and a touch of light within the composition's darkest areas.

Despite its restrained mark-making and simplicity, *Autumn Mist* captures a compelling interplay of light, shadow, and movement. The carefully blended colours and atmospheric effects immerse the viewer in the scene, demonstrating how even a modest composition can provoke a profound emotional connection.

TECHNIQUES FOR CREATING ATMOSPHERE

Creating atmosphere in an oil painting involves a combination of techniques that influence mood, depth, and emotion. Here are some key methods to achieve a sense of atmosphere in your work.

Sfumato

Sfumato is a painting technique that emphasises creating soft, seamless transitions between colours and tones that create a hazy atmospheric effect, which adds depth to a painting. By subtly blending edges and lines to eliminate sharp boundaries, the technique results in a smooth, harmonious effect with a hazy or smoky quality.

The essence of sfumato lies in finding the right balance, allowing colours to mingle without losing their identity, while forming a harmonious union. These soft edges and blurred lines give sfumato its characteristic ethereal quality.

Sfumato is a slow, meditative process which works well with the wet-on-wet techniques using cold wax described in this book. It is a technique I frequently use in my work to achieve the soft transitions between colours and tones. I will use a variety of tools, including a squeegee, a fan brush, an assortment of soft synthetic flat brushes, and even my fingers. The process involves adjusting contrasts, refining details, and continuously blending until the desired effect is achieved. A light touch and patience are key to mastering this approach.

Call of the Moor demonstrates how blending and softening colour transitions allow each hue to maintain its place within the painting, while contributing to an overall ethereal quality. In this piece, I utilised a squeegee to facilitate intuitive colour blending, responding to cues from the painting as I refined the composition. I focused on enhancing contrasts and improving transitions between tones and colours. When the squeegee became too unwieldy, I shifted to blending with a fan brush, adding details with further brushwork and a sweep of vibrant colour to suggest light on the horizon, adding energy to the overall piece.

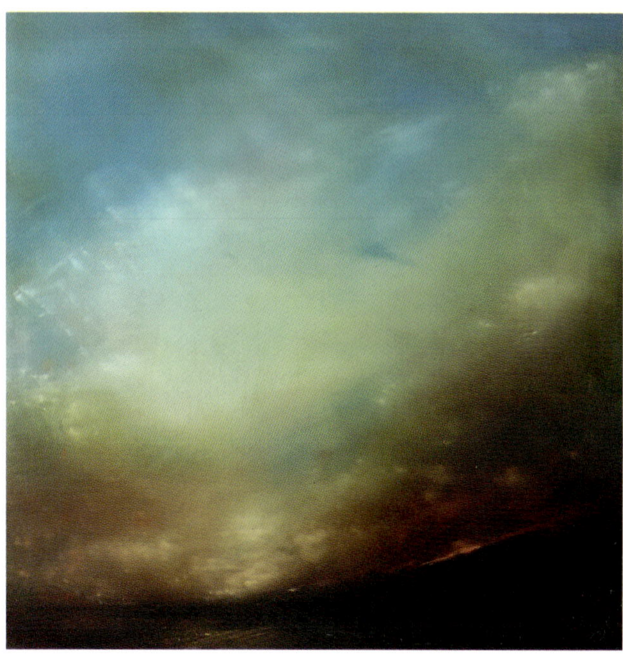

Call of the Moor (30 × 30cm/12 × 12in, oils and cold wax on a wooden panel) highlights wet-on-wet blending techniques to create soft colour and tonal transitions. The initial layers were refined with brushwork, incorporating repeated adjustments to tonal values. This process enhanced the composition's subtle gradations, atmospheric depth, and interplay of light and shadow, creating a serene and harmonious effect.

Texture

Employing different textures in a painting significantly contributes to its overall atmosphere. By using thicker applications of paint in certain areas of your work or by incorporating dry materials such as marble dust or sand, you can create contrasts that enhance visual interest and add dimension, giving the work a sense of depth and space.

Textures can evoke specific emotions; for example, a rough surface may convey tension or chaos, while a smooth surface suggests calm and tranquillity. Additionally, texture influences how light interacts with the painting's surface. A heavy impasto texture can create highlights, adding drama and movement, whereas a smooth surface reflects light uniformly, contributing to a harmonious atmosphere. Furthermore, textures can carry symbolic significance that enriches the painting's narrative. For instance, a cracked surface might symbolise decay or fragility, while a rich, layered texture may suggest complexity and depth.

In my work, I contrast smooth sections with a textured focal point by incorporating materials such as marble dust, sand, or ash mixed with oils and cold wax to create a thick paste. Marble dust, in particular, produces an effective texture that scatters light due to the irregularities in its particles, enhancing its vibrant quality. By incorporating contrasting textures, I can create visual interest and tension, enriching the overall atmosphere of a painting.

Glazing

Glazing is a powerful technique for building depth, luminosity, and atmosphere in your work. By layering thin, transparent paints, you can transform underlying colours, creating a glowing, multi-dimensional effect. This method is particularly effective as it mimics the way light interacts with colour and texture, evoking a sense of vibrancy and atmosphere.

Transparent layers serve multiple purposes: they allow colours to transition softly, push back textures, soften edges, and unify the surface, bringing harmony to the composition. These layers enhance depth and help establish distance and focus within the painting. To create a luminous atmosphere, use transparent colours that either replicate, complement or contrast with the base layers. Thin, even applications of oil and cold wax – whether working wet-on-wet or on a dry surface – are essential for achieving this effect. By building up transparent layers, you allow light to pass through and reflect from the underlying surface, inviting the viewer to explore the painting more deeply. Glazing also adds complexity by balancing areas of light and shadow, refining transitions, and emphasising focal points.

For even greater richness, combine glazing with techniques such as soft blending or detailed mark-making. These approaches smooth transitions and introduce a dynamic interplay between transparency and texture, resulting in paintings that feel both visually intricate and emotionally resonant.

Winter's Light exemplifies the transformative effect of glazing. Midway through the painting process, a transparent orange glaze was applied over cool blues and greys, completely altering the mood of the piece. While the painting retains its cooler, autumnal atmosphere, the glaze unified elements, adding depth, cohesion, and harmony to the composition. Highlights in the sky were created through brushwork, which was then softened and blended using a squeegee and fingertips to achieve a seamless, ethereal effect. Additional brushstrokes introduced simple yet dynamic lines that guide the viewer's eye towards the horizon, enhancing the sense of movement and focus.

The harmonious interplay of glazing, blending, and mark-making in this piece demonstrates how these techniques can come together to create a painting that is both immersive and emotionally resonant.

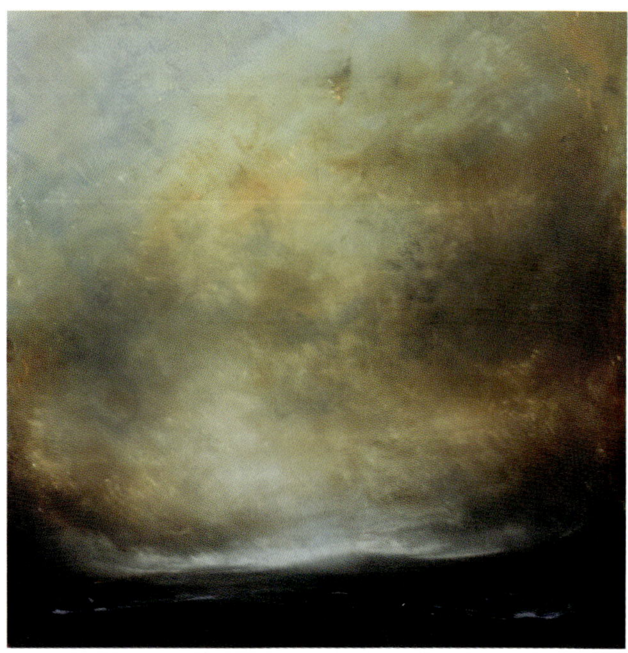

Winter's Light (80 × 80cm/31½ × 31½in, oils, cold wax and gold leaf on Arches Huile paper bonded to a wooden panel) captures a dynamic energy through the careful placement of highlights that suggest sunlight catching the clouds. The darker tones interspersed within the clouds suggest movement and the presence of heavy, brooding skies, add to the painting's overall atmospheric depth.

Brushwork and mark-making

Experimenting with a variety of brushwork and mark-making techniques can bring movement, energy, and emotion to your artwork. Loose, expressive strokes convey a sense of dynamism and vitality, while smoother, more deliberate marks evoke calm and tranquillity. By blending colours with intentional brush marks, pulling one hue into another or transitioning seamlessly between light and dark tones, you can create striking contrasts that enhance the atmosphere of your piece.

Allowing paint to flow naturally across the surface can also introduce organic shapes and forms, further enhancing the mood and depth of your piece. Techniques such as solvent reduction (*see* Chapter 5), can produce drips or flowing trails of paint that form intricate, organic marks, adding an unplanned, raw energy to the work.

Carried on the Wind shares similarities with *Winter's Light* in its use of glazing to transform the composition. In this instance, the glaze introduced a much warmer tone, working harmoniously with the blue-greys already present. Brushwork was used to add highlights to the clouds, creating an energy in the work and guiding the viewer's eye across the composition. A signature technique of thin, straight, stepped lines, created with a flat-edged tool, draws the viewer's gaze downwards into the land and establishes a connection between the sky and the earth. This motif appears repeatedly throughout my work, with its prominence shifting based on the use of colour.

Gold leaf was also incorporated and allowed to form organic shapes, which were then pushed back and softened with the glaze. This interplay of materials created a spontaneous, natural quality, enriching the overall texture and atmosphere of the piece. Together, these elements illustrate how combining brushwork, mark-making, and glazing can create layers of depth and texture, enriching the overall atmosphere of your artwork.

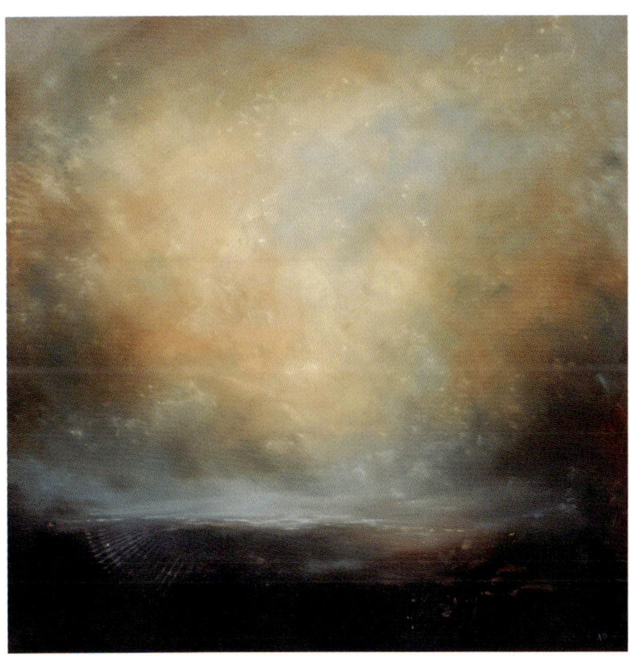

Carried on the Wind (80 × 80cm/31½ × 31½in, oils, cold wax and gold leaf on Arches Huile paper bonded to a wooden panel) features gold leaf that has been applied and then veiled with a transparent colour, resulting in a soft glow beautifully highlighted by the surrounding darker hues. This interplay adds depth and intrigue to the painting.

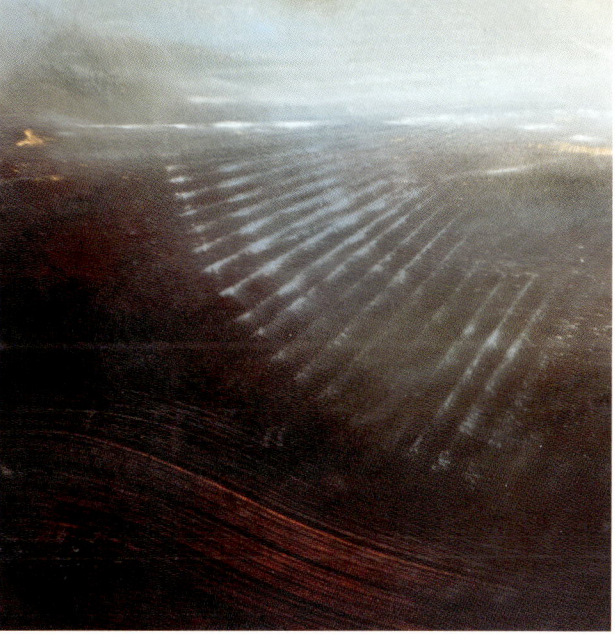

A detailed section of *Carried on the Wind* illustrates mark-making techniques, which guide the viewer's eye downwards into the landscape. Using a squeegee, hard lines are created with a mid-tone colour that flows from the sky into the land, establishing a connection, while emphasising the downward pull of the clouds and blurring the horizon line.

Final touches for creating atmosphere

The final touches of a painting can significantly enhance its atmosphere, giving it a polished and cohesive feel. Softening and blending edges in key areas can create an ethereal quality, adding a sense of depth and harmony to the composition. This technique is particularly effective in areas where light transitions, or where you want to imply movement.

Use highlights sparingly and intentionally to draw the viewer's eye to specific focal points. A few well-placed accents can illuminate the composition and create moments of intrigue without overpowering the overall atmosphere. Experiment with the intensity and placement of these highlights to strike a balance between subtlety and emphasis.

In addition to blending and highlights, consider refining textures and colour transitions to enhance the mood. For example, applying a transparent colour which has been heavily diluted with cold wax to the surface of your painting can create subtle shifts in hue, enhancing the sense of depth and mystery. Similarly, incorporating fine, delicate details or marks in selective areas can introduce a tactile quality that complements the broader atmospheric elements. By thoughtfully combining these techniques, you can create a painting that feels rich, immersive, and resonates with the audience.

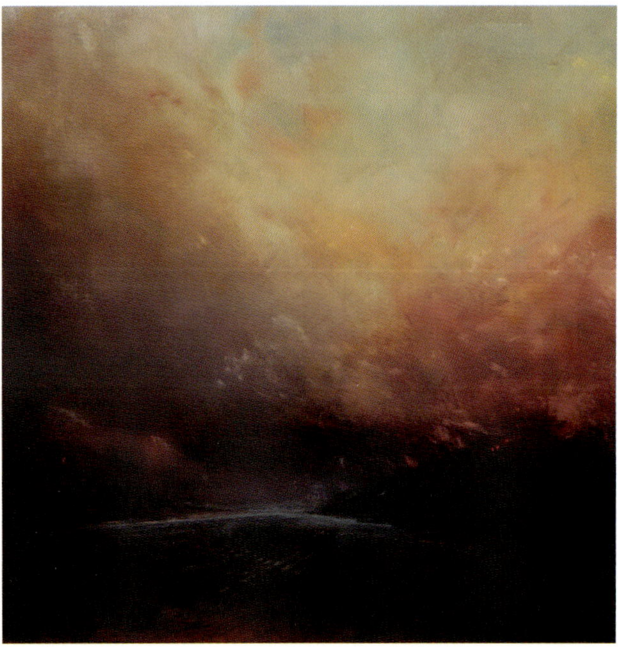

Audra (80 × 80cm/31½ × 31½in, oils, cold wax and gold leaf on Arches Huile paper bonded to a wooden panel) employs darker pinks to evoke a sense of enclosure. The deep tones in the foreground heighten the feeling of being surrounded, with clouds rushing towards the viewer. The sumptuous rich pinks and oranges further draw the viewer in.

Freyr exemplifies the dramatic interplay of light and shadow within a dynamic landscape. This composition captures the energy and movement of a passing storm, with the land occupying a prominent space in the painting. Its darkness suggests the land lies in the shadow of storm clouds, heightening the contrast against the illuminated horizon. Shafts of light break through the clouds, hinting at movement and the promise of clearing skies, while subtle highlights reveal the presence of a loch or river. A single, purposeful brushstroke of bright blue emphasises this water feature, linking it to glimpses of blue emerging in the sky.

The pinks, oranges, and browns in the clouds amplify the sense of drama, while the darker areas of the painting stretch upwards, visually connecting the land and the sky. Brushstrokes create leading lines toward the horizon, where shafts of light pull the viewer's gaze towards the clouds. These highlights and details guide the eye through the composition, ultimately lifting it to the brighter areas of the sky.

The land remains understated, with minimal detail, ensuring the focus stays on the stormy sky and its dynamic energy. This simplicity prevents the painting from feeling overcrowded, maintaining a sense of balance, while preserving its emotional intensity. The overall effect immerses the viewer in the heart of the storm, while the emerging blue skies hint at resolution and calm.

The title, *Freyr,* references the Norse god associated with good weather, sunshine, summer, and rain, perfectly encapsulating the dual nature of the scene, storm and serenity, shadow and light. Through the use of blending, brushwork, and carefully balanced elements, *Freyr* demonstrates how final touches can transform a painting into a deeply atmospheric and emotionally powerful work.

THE POWER OF ATMOSPHERE

The power of atmosphere lies in its ability to transcend the canvas, forging a deep emotional connection between the artwork and the viewer. Through thoughtful integration of subject matter, colour, light, texture, and tonal values, artists can create an immersive experience that captures the viewer's eye and fires their imagination.

Creating atmosphere requires both artistic skill and emotional insight. Techniques such as glazing, sfumato, and intuitive painting allow for the subtle interplay of elements, enriching the mood and depth of the work. This dynamic balance invites emotional engagement, transforming a painting into more than merely a pleasant image or scene; instead, it becomes a lasting feeling, almost a lingering memory that stays with the viewer long after they have left the gallery.

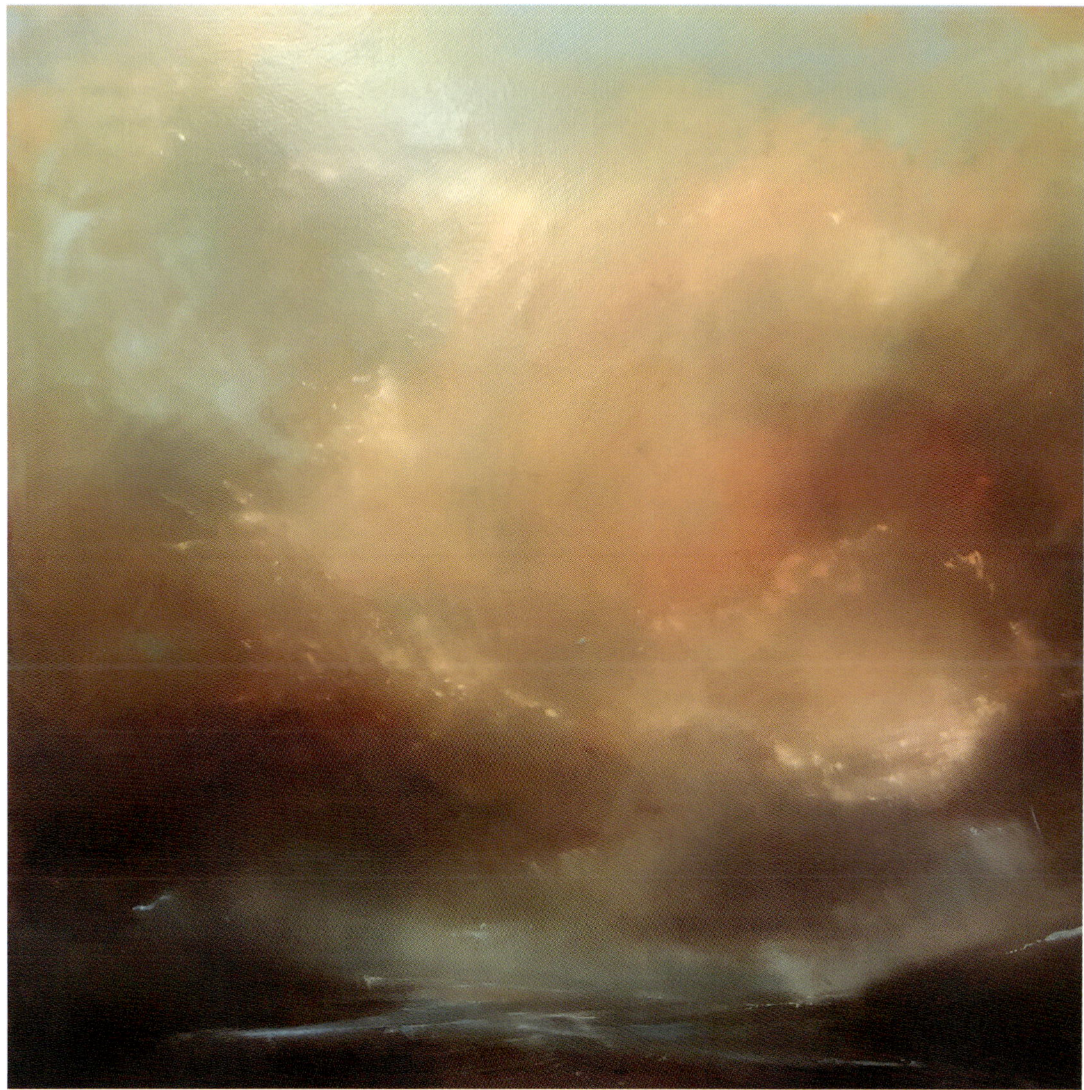

Freyr (80 × 80cm/31½ × 31½in, oils, cold wax and gold leaf on Arches Huile paper bonded to a wooden panel) uses cool blues to draw the eye towards the horizon line, evoking the sense of distance. In contrast, warm pinks in the clouds leap forwards, drawing the viewer into the scene and enriching the painting's overall atmosphere.

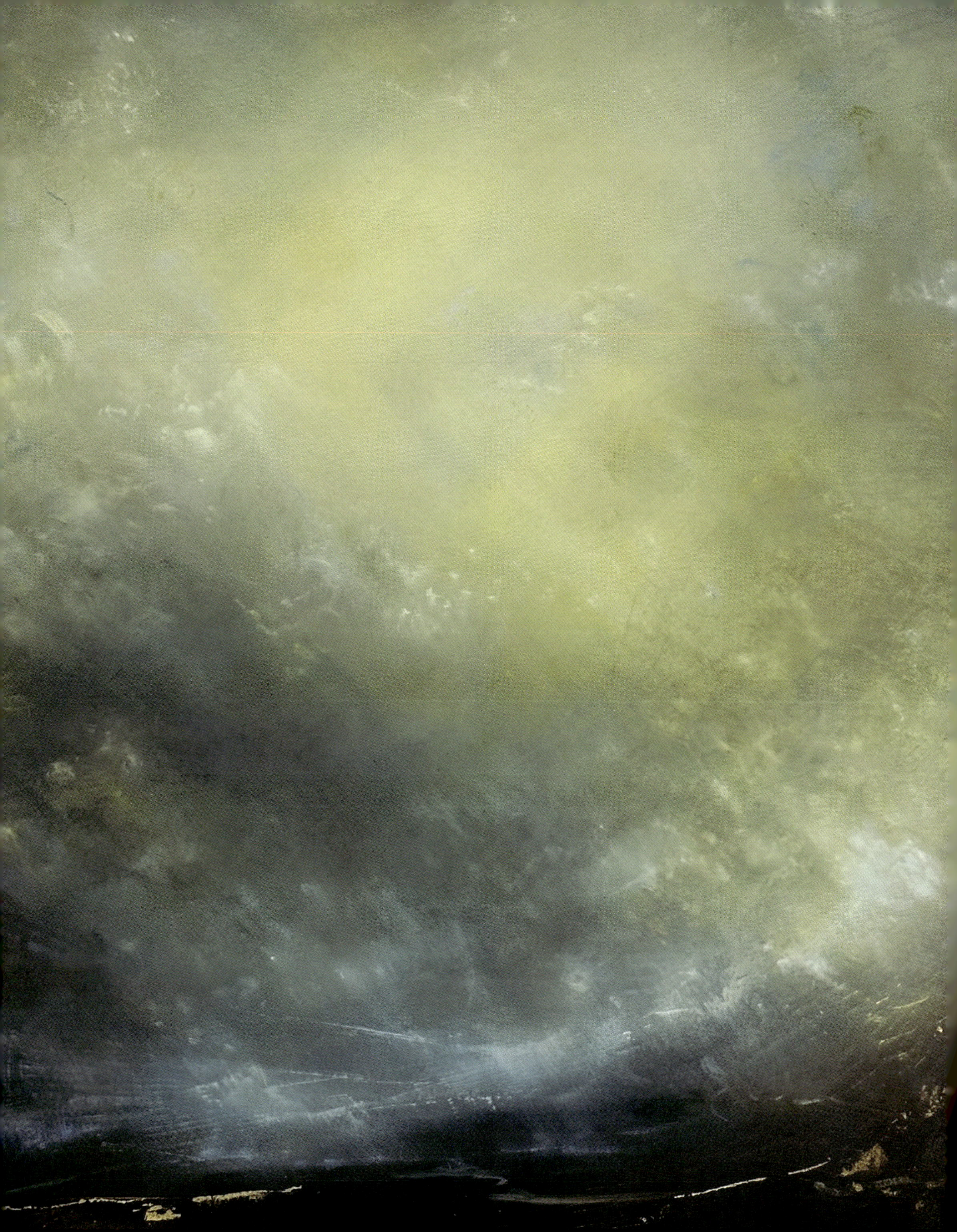

CHAPTER 7

RESOLVING AND REFINING

The previous two chapters highlighted the importance of experimenting with layering colours, adding texture, and painting intuitively to create depth and atmosphere. This experimental phase is essential for developing the rich foundations of your painting, allowing for exploration and creative freedom. However, it is easy to lose sight of the overall composition and structure during this intuitive process.

In this chapter, we focus on restoring balance and order to your work, ensuring the composition serves as a solid framework. We explore techniques for critically evaluating your painting, helping you identify areas that need improvement or refinement to enhance its overall impact. Additionally, we delve into specific strategies for incorporating detail into your painting. Fine elements can elevate your work, creating focal points that draw the viewer's eye. Techniques such as glazing, applying thin, transparent layers of paint, can add depth and luminosity, while precise line work defines shapes and edges, bringing clarity to your composition.

We also examine the importance of balance and harmony in your work. Understanding how colour, texture, and form interact is vital for creating a cohesive whole. For example, a harmonious colour palette can evoke specific emotions, while a balanced distribution of visual weight can make a composition feel stable. By considering elements such as scale, proportion, and spatial relationships, you can ensure that each part of your painting contributes meaningfully to the overall composition.

By the end of this chapter, you will have a clearer understanding of how to enhance your paintings through critical evaluation and more intentional mark-making, ultimately resulting in work that is richer and more impactful.

COMPOSITION

There are numerous rules associated with composition, and plenty of reference material readily available if you wish to delve deeper into the subject. To keep it simple, I offer suggestions on what to avoid, what to look for, and what to emphasise to help resolve your work and create a stronger painting.

Horizon line

Experimenting with the position of your horizon line can significantly impact the composition of your painting. Placing the horizon below the centre emphasises the sky, creating an expansive, open feeling and adding a sense of scale and drama. Conversely, placing it above the centre draws attention to the land or water. Ideally you want to avoid a central horizon line, as this can divide the painting in half, diminishing its visual impact. If you find yourself with a central horizon that you feel cannot be easily adjusted, consider disrupting it by blurring the distinctions between land and sky. You can achieve this by using similar colours to blend these sections, adding an element of atmosphere and haziness.

OPPOSITE: *Autumn's light* (cropped), 60 × 60cm (23½ × 23½in), oils, cold wax and gold leaf on Arches Huile paper bonded to a wooden panel. Gold leaf is a prominent feature in this autumnal-themed piece, helping to capture light and movement throughout the composition. Its reflective quality enhances the warmth and depth of the scene, adding a luminous, dynamic presence.

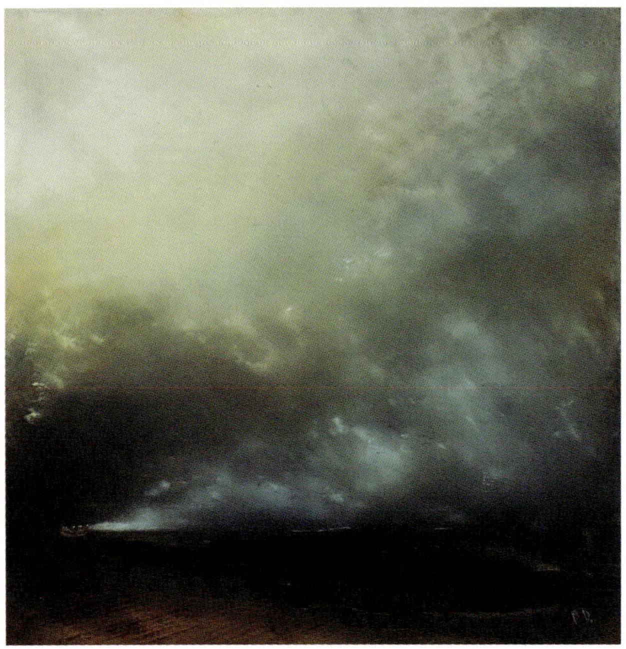

After the rain (30 × 30cm/12 × 12in, oil, cold wax and gold leaf). In this piece, the horizon line is softened by low-lying clouds and mist, blurring the boundary between land and sky. The subtle suggestion of a horizon is drawn down into the lower third of the composition, allowing the expansive sky to take centre stage as the dominant element.

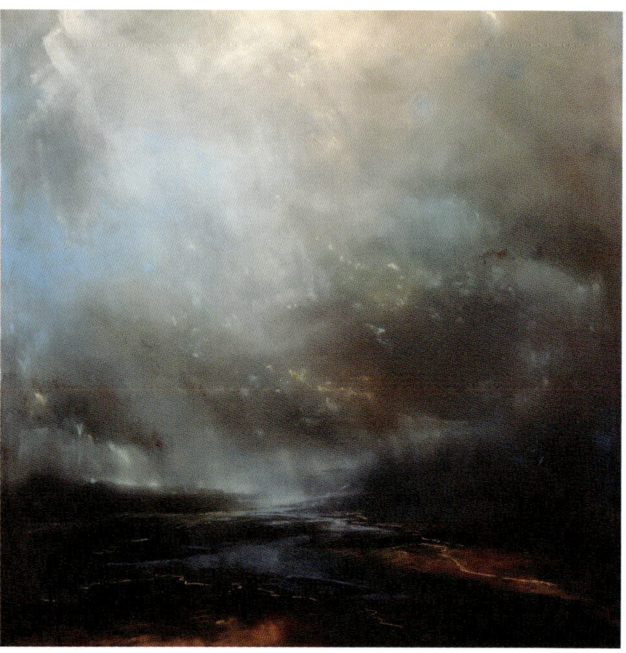

Where the Loch Meets the Sea (cropped), 90 × 120cm (35½ × 47¼in), oil, cold wax, and gold leaf on board. Gold leaf is used to guide the viewer's eye across the painting. Representing a pathway or road through the landscape, it draws the viewer inwards, while subtle tints in the sky lift their gaze upwards.

Focal point

Creating flow and points of interest in your painting is essential for guiding the viewer's eye. Use lines to represent rivers, pathways, or roads to draw the viewer in, while strategically placed accent colours can lead their gaze. Although establishing focal points is important, you must ensure they vary from one another. Avoid unwanted symmetry caused by similar shapes; instead, incorporate contrasting shapes, colours, and textures to enhance depth and visual interest. Position focal points, horizon lines, and other key elements off-centre for a more dynamic composition.

Creating balance

Balance refers to the visual weight of objects within your painting and how they relate to one another. A large object or a cluster of objects in one section may create an impression of heaviness, leading to a feeling of imbalance, especially if there is a large empty space nearby. The visual weight of an object is not solely determined by its size: details, contrasts, and colours also play significant roles. You can adjust the visual weight of an object or area by adding more contrast, which can either draw attention or diminish it.

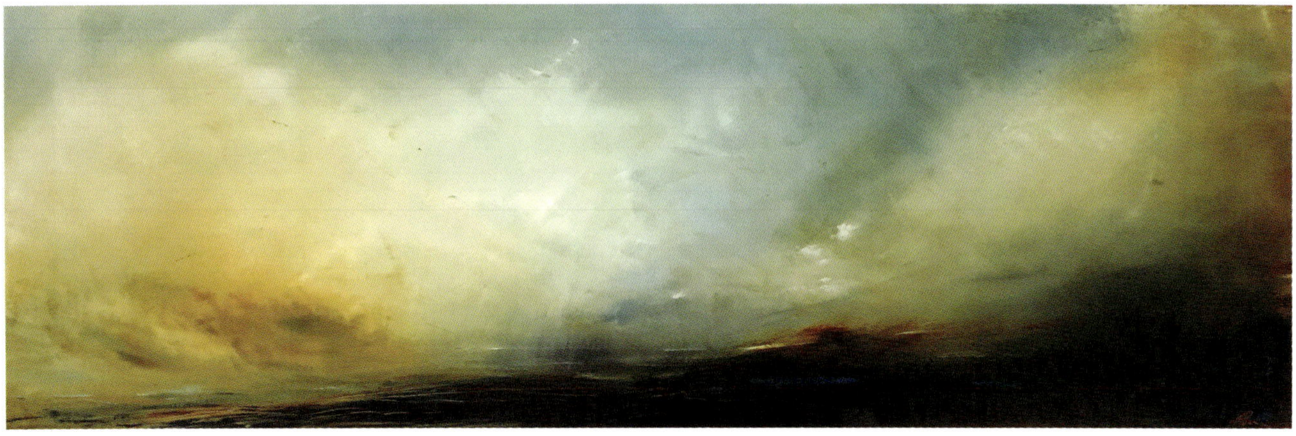

Darkened Hills are Dreaming, 71 × 23cm (28 × 9in), oils, cold wax on paper presents a simple yet striking landscape dominated by billowing clouds. The darker tones at the base of the clouds on the left create balance, countering the larger, darker shapes of the land on the right. This interplay prevents the composition from feeling weighted to one side.

Contrasts

A painting becomes more engaging when it features a variety of contrasts and differences. When elements within your painting begin to resemble each other, the composition can become monotonous and a bit 'samey'. Evaluate your focal points for similarities in size, shape, and repetition. Make small adjustments by varying their dimensions and spacing to enhance the overall feel of your painting. Additionally, check the tonal values and colours of your largest shapes to ensure they are not too dark or saturated. A large, dark element can dominate the composition, while a saturated colour may look beautiful and jewel-like when it is small or used sparingly, but can be overpowering when used as a dominating colour.

Quiet spaces

Conversely, too many contrasts can lead to a busy painting unless offset by quiet spaces, which provide a place for your eyes to rest. Quiet areas are essential for structuring the composition, establishing focal points, and maintaining balance. If your painting feels cluttered, consider adding a larger shape with minimal texture and a mid to low tonal value. This neutral element allows the viewer's eye to rest within the painting, enhancing overall harmony.

Cohesion

Lack of links between elements in your painting, such as colours and marks, can result in a disjointed appearance. Unity plays a crucial role in creating a cohesive painting and refers to the way elements in a composition work together, in harmony. Achieving cohesion can involve repeating colours or shapes, but be careful not to overdo it, as this can make areas look overly uniform.

Fill the frame

Encouraging your mark-making to extend beyond the boundaries of your surface can result in a more dynamic and expressive painting. Allowing your composition to spill beyond these edges prevents it from being confined by the edges of your painting. This approach not only enhances the drama, but also adds a sense of scale, effectively placing the viewer within the landscape.

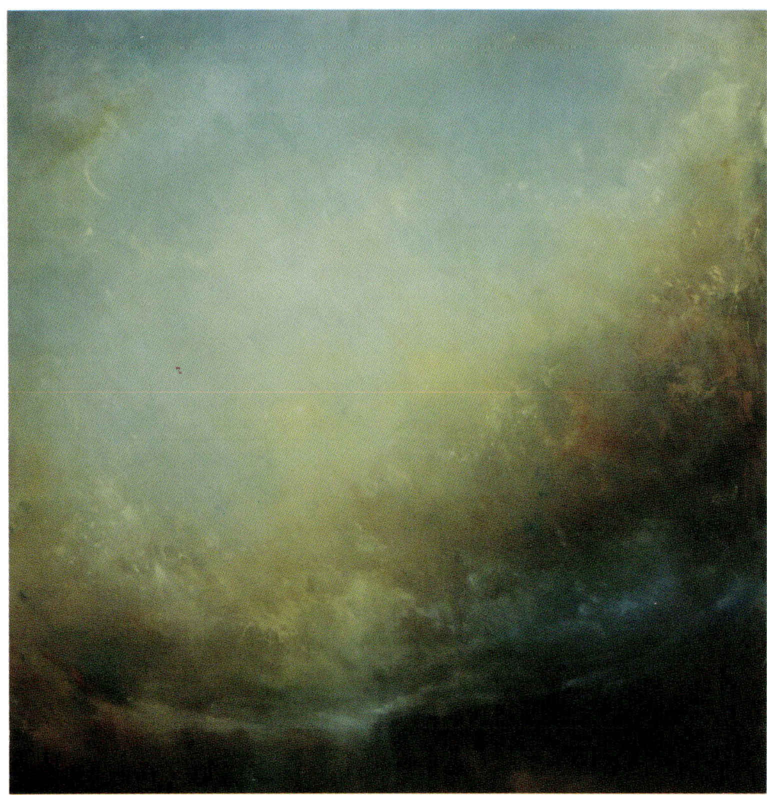

Smoke on the Water (90 × 90cm/27½ × 27½in, oils, cold wax on board) balances the detailed brushwork and rich colours of the lower-lying clouds with the quieter, more subdued areas of the sky offering the viewer a visual resting point. As the clouds merge with the land, they subtly disrupt the horizon line, creating depth and intrigue.

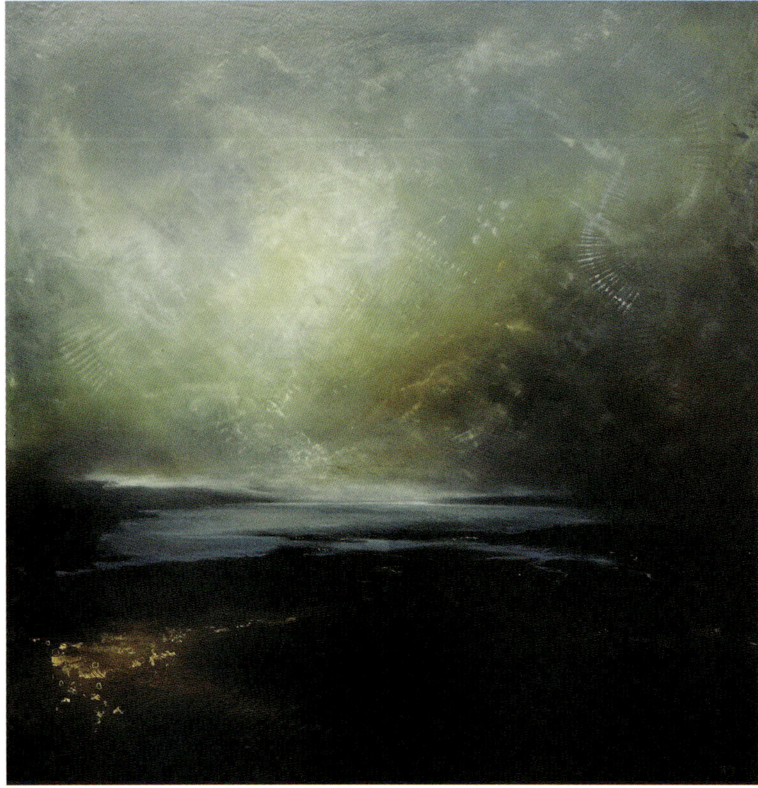

Changing the vantage point in your painting can immerse the viewer more deeply in the landscape. In *Between the River and the Sea* (70 × 70cm/23½ × 23½in, oils, cold wax, and gold leaf), the perspective looks down from an elevated viewpoint towards the water. This angle evokes a sense of standing on top of moorland, with the scene unfolding below.

PROBLEM-SOLVING

Take a step back from your painting, or even leave it overnight, and return with fresh eyes. This break allows you to view the entire composition and assess whether all the elements work together cohesively before finalising your work. Ask yourself: Does the composition flow? Are there strong tonal values (light and dark), colour contrasts (warm, cool, complementary, light, and dark colours), and varied marks and shapes? Consider what could be added or adjusted to enhance the overall piece.

Try not to be too attached to your work. Be bold and willing to correct mistakes. It can be disheartening to make significant changes to a painting when you feel you are close to finishing, but do not shy away from those adjustments. Moving a shape, covering an area, or editing elements that seem off can make a substantial difference. Simple changes, such as altering the colour or value of an element, or incorporating lines to depict paths or streams to guide the viewer's eye, can have a significant impact on your work.

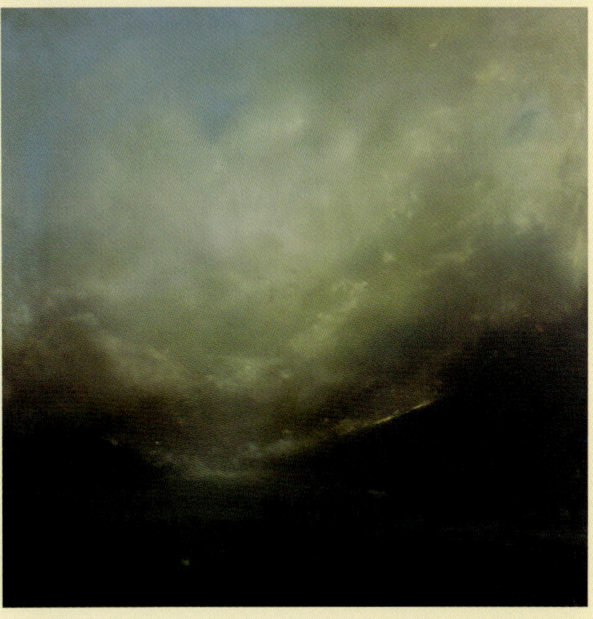

Darkness and Light (60 × 60cm/23½ × 23½in, oils and cold wax) underwent a process of refinement. After allowing the painting to rest, it was revisited a few days later.

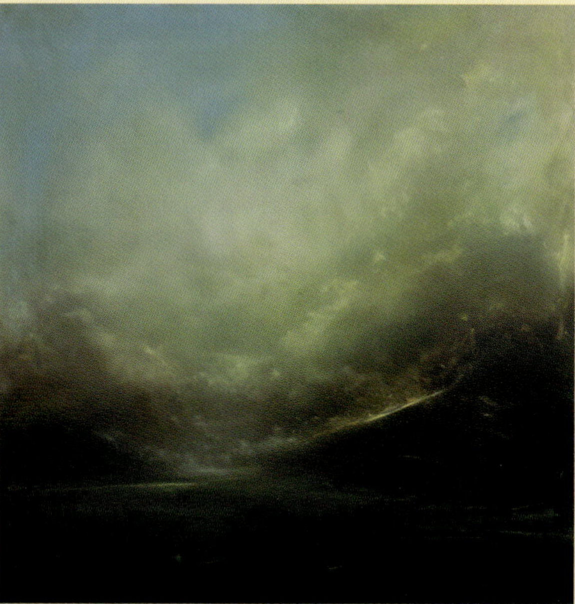

Additional definition was added to the land, enhancing perspective, while highlights were introduced to create greater contrast, bringing balance and depth to the composition.

REFINING

As you approach the final stages of your painting and focus on refining details, it is worth considering whether additional elements, such as collage, pigments, or metal leaf, could enhance your composition. These materials can add texture, depth, or even a touch of brilliance that elevates your work. Carbon papers, for instance, might be just what you need to introduce a vibrant pop of colour, while techniques such as scratching into the surface could extend lines or reveal intriguing base layers, adding dimension and visual interest.

Does your painting require the precision of fine brushwork to introduce and highlight details, or would a bold flourish of colour with a large dry brush inject the energy and dynamism it needs? Whatever you choose to add, consider each element thoughtfully. Does it contribute meaningfully to the overall composition? Does it enhance the painting, or is it distracting? The final touches should work in harmony with the rest of your piece, reinforcing its impact rather than overwhelming it. By approaching these decisions with intention, you can ensure that every addition strengthens your painting.

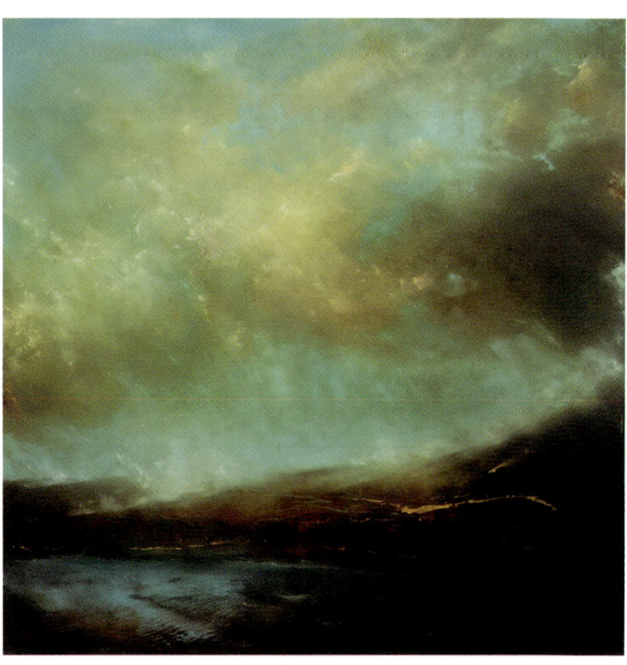

Drawn to Water, 90 × 90cm (35½ × 35½in), oils, cold wax, and gold leaf on board, features pathways scratched into the paint, to reveal the cerulean blue base layer beneath. This method not only creates intriguing textures, but is further enhanced by touches of gold leaf that infuses the painting with warmth and light.

Mark-making

Mark-making can be a powerful technique for suggesting scale and adding depth to your painting. Techniques such as scratching or sgraffito allow you to create fine details that help resolve your work, such as subtle patches of light in the sky or reflections on water, distant lights on the horizon, or a winding pathway through a landscape. Alternatively, using scrunched-up tissue can produce a crackle effect that reveals glimpses of colour from the underlying layers. The marks left behind can inspire more deliberate details, such as extending lines to create pathways or repeatedly dabbing with tissue in the foreground to suggest vegetation.

These marks also play a crucial role in conveying a sense of scale. Delicate, fine lines in the background, such as those indicating a distant path beneath a vast sky, contrast beautifully with bold, larger lines in the foreground that depict nearby elements such as vegetation. This interplay between light and dark, fine and bold, enhances the perception of depth within your painting.

In addition, marks that create leading lines can guide the viewer's eye, drawing them into the painting and immersing them in the landscape. By carefully considering the placement and scale of your marks, you can add both visual interest and a sense of narrative to your work, making it more engaging and dynamic.

Blending with brushes

The bulk of the blending will be with a squeegee, but as you move towards resolving the painting, the squeegee will no longer be the appropriate tool to use as it will blend and move paint around too much. There are likely to still be elements of your painting which need blending but on a more delicate, softer scale, which is where a fan brush will help to create finer tonal transitions in your work.

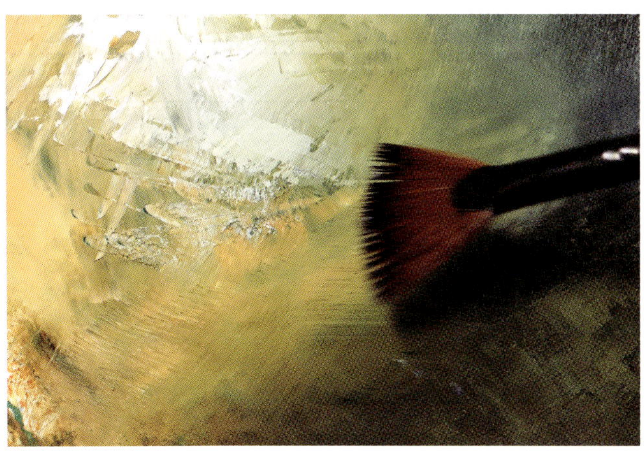

A soft synthetic fan brush is ideal for subtle blending and smoothing transitions between colours. Use a dry brush to gently sweep over the area in long, even strokes, followed by a crosshatching motion to achieve a softer, more seamless effect.

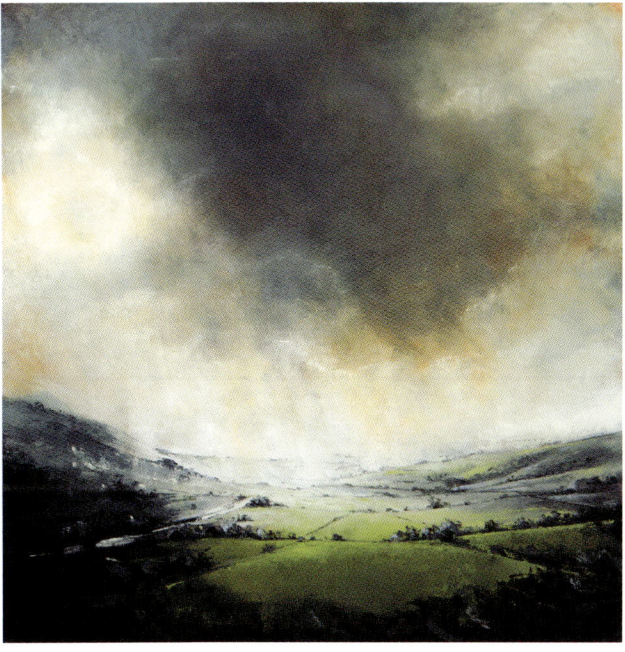

Bruised Sky, 100 × 100cm (39½ × 39½in), oils and cold wax on board. To achieve the shafts of light in this painting, I combined the use of a brayer and a fan brush to extend the lighter areas of the painting into the landscape. This technique enhances the sense of depth and atmosphere, evoking a dynamic interplay between light and land.

A soft synthetic fan brush allows you to gently blend paint, creating smoother tonal transitions. Start with a dry brush and lightly sweep across the area you want to blend, using long, even strokes. Repeat by brushing across your initial strokes in a crosshatching motion to achieve a softer, more natural blend. If the brush begins picking up too much paint, wipe it and then rinse in solvent and dry it thoroughly with a paper towel, as the wet bristles will separate and become less effective for blending. If the surface of your painting is touch-dry and a dry brush is not blending the paint effectively, try dipping the brush in solvent and removing any excess by drying it thoroughly. The small amount of residual solvent on the brush can help soften the surface just enough to allow for smooth and effective blending.

Blending with a fan brush may leave brush marks, which can add texture and interest to your painting. However, on darker areas, these marks may reflect light, making it harder to view the painting as a whole. If this is the case or if you prefer not to have texture in your painting, then carefully flatten out the brush marks with your squeegee by smoothing it over the painting. Do be very gentle with this, as your squeegee will want to move the paint.

You can also use a fan brush to disrupt and break up your horizon line, effectively creating shafts of light that pull lighter tints into the darker areas of your painting. When blending with a fan brush to achieve softer transitions between colours, apply a little more pressure as you drag your lighter colours into the darker hues. This technique not only blends the colours, but also creates a beautiful effect reminiscent of shafts of light filtering through the composition. For a more dramatic effect, consider using a brayer. In my painting *Bruised Sky*, I employed both a brayer and a fan brush to suggest light shafts in the sky. This approach effectively broke up the hard horizon line, resulting in a softer, more atmospheric quality that evokes a sense of distance in the composition.

Wet-on-dry brush work

Creating the base layers with tools such as a squeegee and a brayer involves mixing colours directly on the surface, allowing the painting to evolve intuitively. Once a direction begins to emerge, you may want to emphasise shapes, add highlights, and incorporate details using a range of brushes for wet-on-dry techniques. At this stage, it is important to shift colour mixing to your palette rather than the painting surface.

This is where understanding your colour palette and the range of mixes you can produce is important and doing that initial exercise in Chapter 4 will save you some time and frustration. Mixing the colours on your palette is important to ensure any colour you add relates to the rest of your painting. For instance, if you wanted to highlight or lighten up part of a cloud and used titanium white straight from the tube, the colour would be too stark and would not relate to the other colours in the painting. Attempting to blend it in on your surface using a squeegee would either be too disruptive and move colours, shapes, and values around, or in the case of a fan brush, would not be able to blend the white enough, leaving you with a lighter area of paint which does not link in with the rest of your painting.

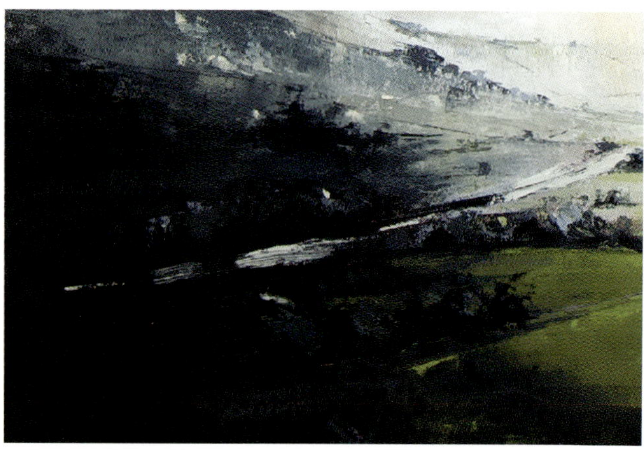

Close-up of brushwork in *Bruised Sky* (shown overleaf). A brush, heavily loaded with paint and applied wet-on-wet, sweeps across the surface to create the illusion of a wet road cutting through the landscape. Once dry, additional brushwork is used to extend and subtly break up shadows in the surrounding fields, adding depth and texture.

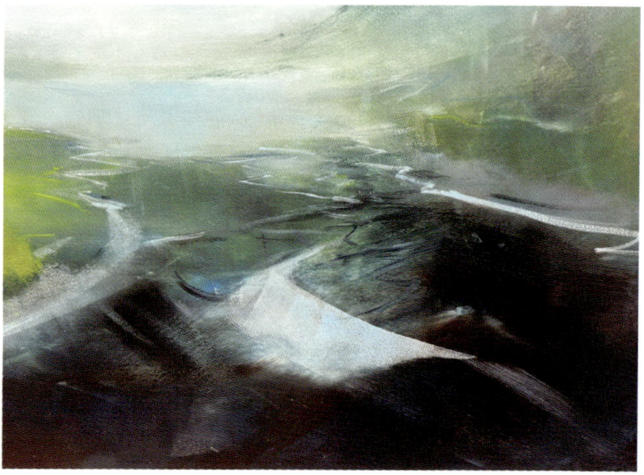

Close-up of brushwork in *Waterlines* (shown in Chapter 5). This section of the painting highlights a variety of lines that complement and extend the brayer marks. Fine, delicate lines made with a rigger brush contrast sharply with the bold, expressive strokes of the brayer and flat brush, adding depth and movement to the composition.

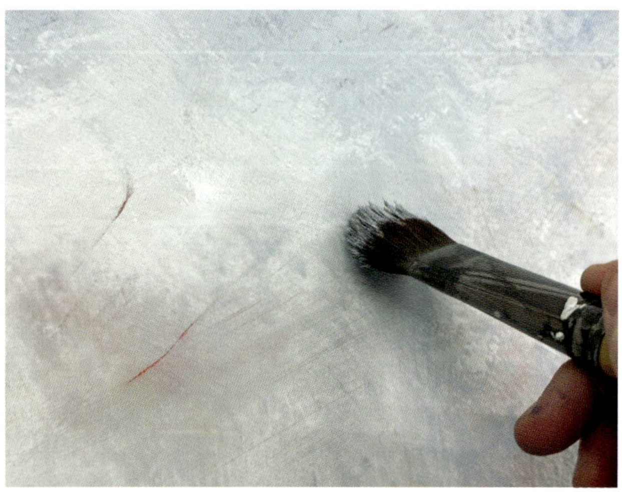

A round brush is ideal for creating flowing lines that bring movement and fluidity to your painting. Its versatility supports a range of techniques, from delicate details to broader strokes, even scumbling. For more dynamic marks, let the brush roll freely in your hand as you paint, releasing control over where marks are made on the surface of your painting.

Instead, mix tints on your palette to create highlights that harmonise with your painting. Begin with a darker tint and gradually work towards the desired lightness. Apply the highlight with a dry brush, using small amounts of paint. If needed, smudge the paint with your squeegee or fingers to emphasise the shape and achieve the desired effect. Some areas of your painting may require more paint to adjust tonal values; in such cases, a palette knife works well for spreading paint evenly, especially over larger areas that need covering or refinement.

This stage is often the most enjoyable, as your composition begins to take shape. Mixing colours on your palette ensures consistency across the painting and allows you to add dynamic brush marks that bring energy and interest to your work. These intentional marks can draw the viewer's eye and counteract any over-blending or loss of vibrancy that may have occurred earlier in the process. By combining careful blending with bold, expressive marks, you can strike a balance between precision and energy, creating a painting that feels alive and cohesive.

Drawing with paint

Drawing back into your painting once the surface is dry enough allows you to introduce bold, expressive marks that can enhance your work. Oil bars and Pigment Sticks® are excellent tools for this purpose. With thoughtful placement, these marks can inject energy into your painting, unify elements, or conceal areas you wish to downplay.

As Pigment Sticks® are softer, they are particularly versatile and allow you to easily target specific areas for adjustment, whether to unify or obscure, and their pigment can be smudged into the painting for a seamless integration. This flexibility makes them ideal for refining or adding dynamic elements to your composition.

To achieve fine lines with oil bars or Pigment Sticks®, the transfer technique provides an effective and precise method:

1. Rub the Pigment Sticks® or oil bar onto a piece of greaseproof paper.
2. Flip the paper face-down onto your painting, taking care not to press or rub too hard, as this will transfer more pigment than desired.
3. Use a fine pencil, barbecue stick, or even your fingertip to draw on the back of the greaseproof paper.
4. When you lift the paper, the pigment will have transferred onto your painting, leaving delicate lines.

This method allows for controlled mark-making, while preserving the spontaneity and energy of drawing, making it a valuable technique for adding detail and character to your work.

To incorporate fine drawn elements into your artwork using Pigment Sticks® or oil bars, start by applying the colour directly onto a piece of greaseproof paper.

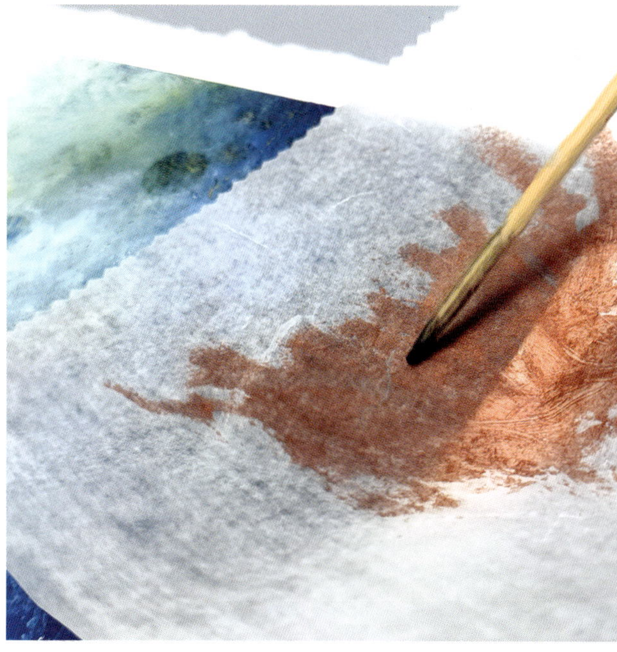

Flip the greaseproof paper over so that it is face-down on your painting. Using a pencil, a barbecue stick, or even your fingertip, gently draw on the back of the paper.

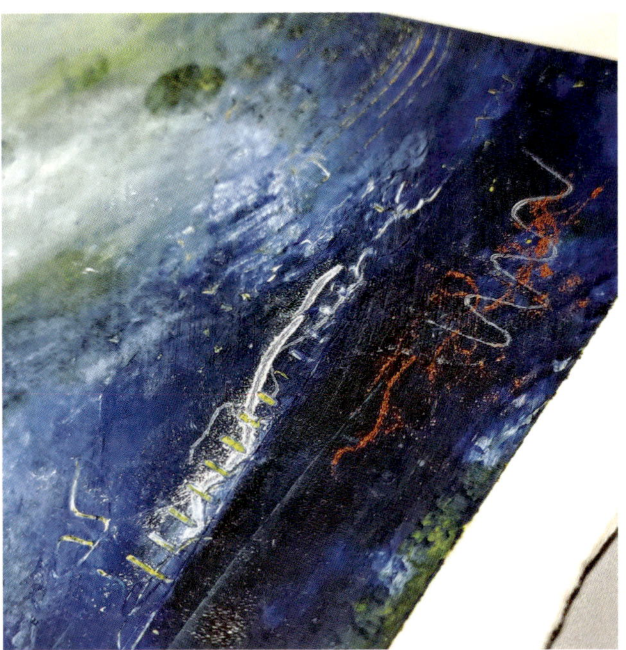

Experiment with different levels of pressure as you draw to produce a variety of line thicknesses and textures. Then, gently lift the greaseproof paper to reveal the transfer on your painting.

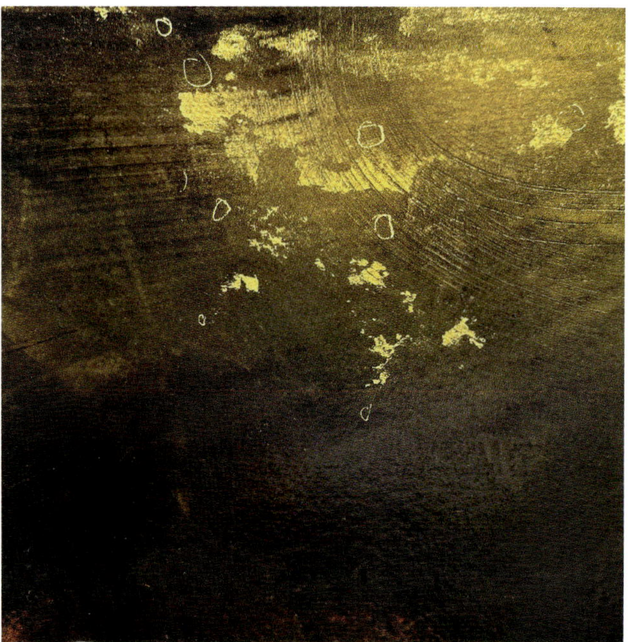

Detail of *Between the River and the Sea*. Metallic leaf is available as loose leaves or in books of transfers. The transfer leaves work in a similar way to drawing with paint and carbon papers; by drawing on the back, you can create intricate lines and shapes or transfer the entire leaf directly onto your work.

Embedding metal leaf

Cold wax is an excellent medium for embedding lightweight materials into paintings, and over the years, I have experimented with a variety of materials. Among these, the incorporation of metal leaf has become a staple in my work. Initially, I used metallic bronze powders to reflect light and add depth to the darker areas of my paintings. This technique evolved, and I began extending lines into my compositions, drawing viewers in with an array of metallic leaf options. I have explored silver, gold, and copper leaf, finding that the thickness of the copper leaf makes it more challenging to create fine lines, yet it lends itself beautifully to organic shapes.

I use two primary techniques for applying metal leaf, depending on the stage I am at with my painting. Both techniques are ideally suited when you are close to resolving your work as otherwise you end up wasting the metallic leaf by covering it up, or removing it if you are still moving paint around.

While the painting is still wet, I identify areas to apply the metal leaf. By placing the transfer paper down and drawing or rubbing on the back, I can effectively transfer the leaf onto the surface of the painting. Once the leaf is transferred, I gently brush over it with a soft mop brush to embed any loose pieces into the painting. I then use a squeegee or palette knife to shape the leaf as desired, or apply a transparent glaze over it with a squeegee. This technique allows me to push the metallic leaf back, creating a luminous glow and adding depth to my work.

For more precise application when the painting is dry to the touch, I use an oil size to mark exactly where I want the leaf to adhere. This method allows for greater precision; while carefully following the instructions for using the size, I can apply the metallic leaf directly with a mop brush. With this process there is more control, as you can use a fine brush to paint on the size or mask sections off with tape to create straight lines and blocks of metallic leaf.

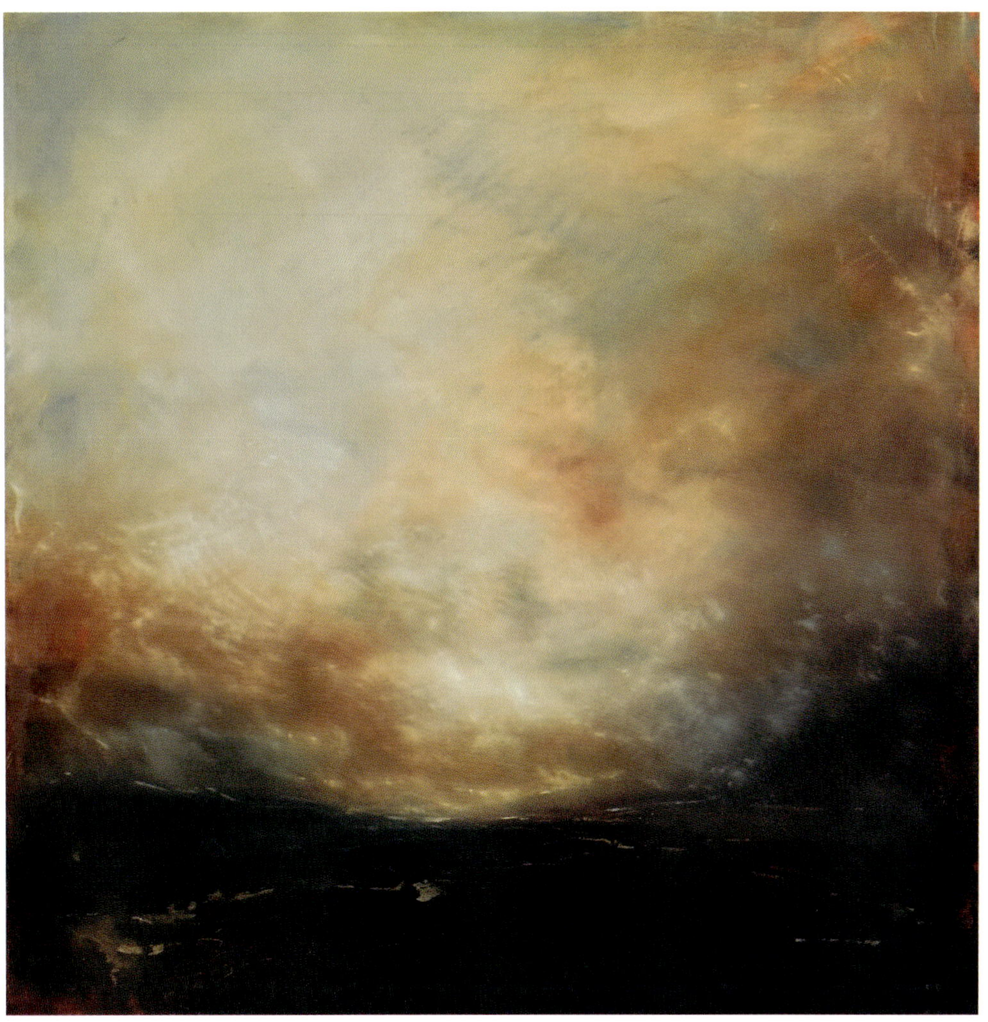

Lights Dance on the Horizon, 70 × 70cm (23½ × 23½in), oils, cold wax and gold leaf. Gold leaf has been applied to illustrate pathways extending towards the horizon, reflecting the shimmering highlights of the sky and enhancing the painting's sense of depth and movement.

Pigment splashes

Incorporating pigments can add a vibrant splash of colour and energy to your painting, but it requires thoughtful consideration. Since this process offers limited control, it is important to evaluate whether adding pigments will truly enhance your work, or if you are simply applying every technique in the hope of resolving the painting.

A more controlled approach is to transfer pigments using tissue (*see* Chapter 5). This method allows for precise placement, ensuring the pigment appears exactly where you intend. If the result does not work as envisioned, it is easy to paint over it and refine your composition without compromising the overall piece.

Drawing with pigment

If you want to create marks that you can make with pencils or pastels in your paintings, pigment carbon papers are an excellent option. While ready-made carbon papers are available in art shops, they typically offer limited colour choices and are generally not lightfast. By making your own carbon papers with the pigments

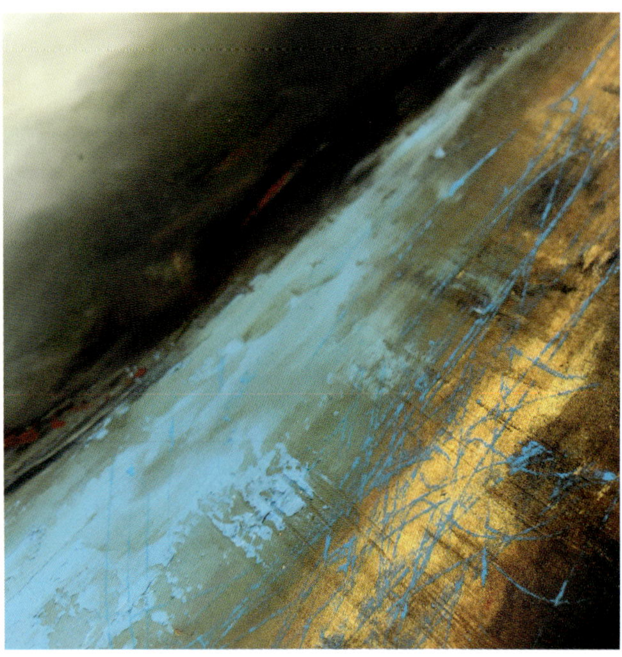

By drawing on the reverse side of carbon paper infused with turquoise pigment, dynamic, fine lines and vibrant pops of colour have been produced. These marks were made using black bamboo tools made by London-based artist Bina Shah.

used in your paints, you can ensure better lightfastness and have a broader palette that complements your work. Below, you will find instructions on how to create your own carbon papers.

Carbon papers are made by combining pure pigment with alcohol, which acts as a carrier. When the alcohol evaporates, it leaves behind the pigment, ready for use as transfer paper. Depending on the size of your carbon paper and the tools you use, you can create fine or bold expressive marks on your work. Similar to the oil bars and pigment sticks technique, place your carbon paper face-down on the painting and draw on the back. Be cautious not to rub too hard, as this can transfer more pigment than desired. Drawing on the back helps transfer the pigment and press it into your painting, but I also recommend varnishing your painting afterwards to protect the marks, as they can sometimes be smudged.

I am a big fan of carbon papers because they allow for additional contrasts in my work, creating beautiful pops of colour and delicate marks that complement bold, expressive strokes and blended areas.

Making carbon papers

Creating your own carbon papers is a straightforward process that requires only a few materials: methylated spirits, dry pigments, and waxed paper, such as greaseproof paper or deli wrap paper. It is crucial to work in a well-ventilated area, as methylated spirits have a strong odour and release harmful fumes. Consider wearing a protective mask if necessary, and limit your production to small batches to minimise exposure. Additionally, be aware that methylated spirits are highly flammable, so take appropriate precautions to manage any spills.

You will need the following:

- a small jar or container for mixing
- dry pigments of your choice – I have found that opaque colours produce the best results, as they create a solid colour when applied to the waxed paper.
- methylated spirits
- greaseproof paper or deli wrap paper (waxed on one side)
- a soft synthetic brush.

The alcohol should evaporate quickly, enabling you to create several sheets of carbon paper. I recommend making carbon papers in small batches and storing them in a plastic folder with sleeves. With the wide variety of pigments available, you can create a rainbow of coloured carbon papers.

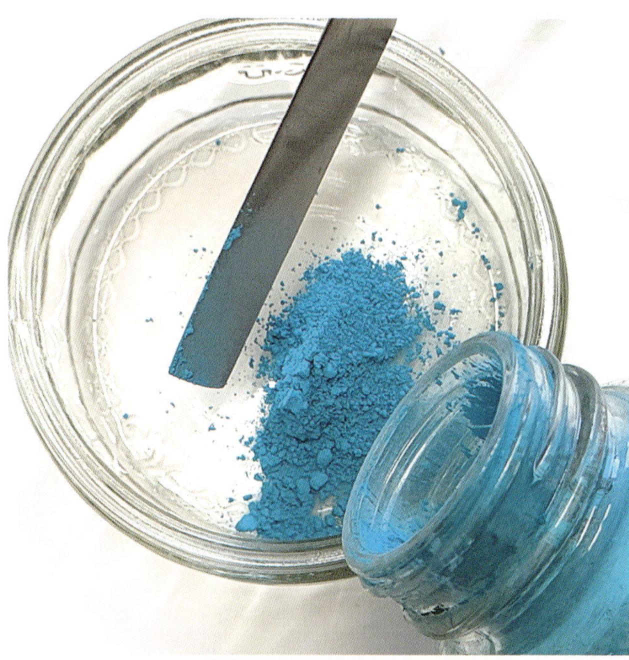

Carefully add a small amount of your chosen pigment to a dish or jam jar. We are aiming for a 50:50 ratio of pigment to methylated spirits.

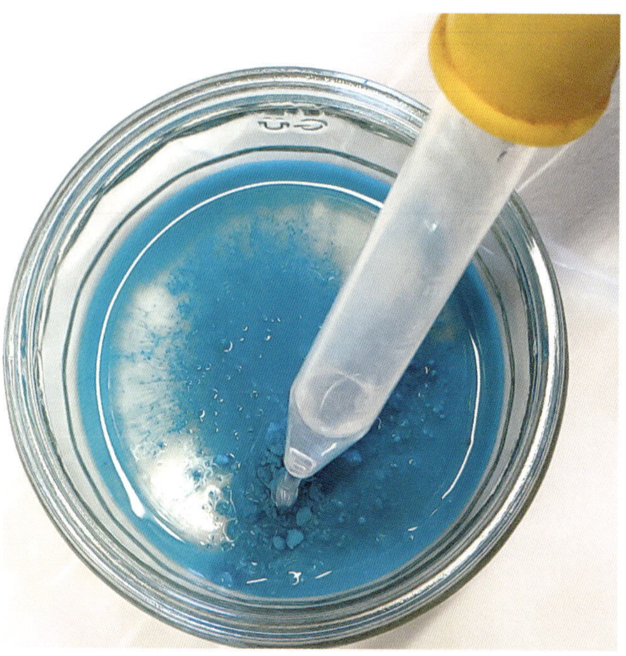

Use a dropper to add the methylated spirits gradually, allowing for better control over the consistency. Mix thoroughly with a soft synthetic brush, adding more methylated spirits if the mixture is too thick.

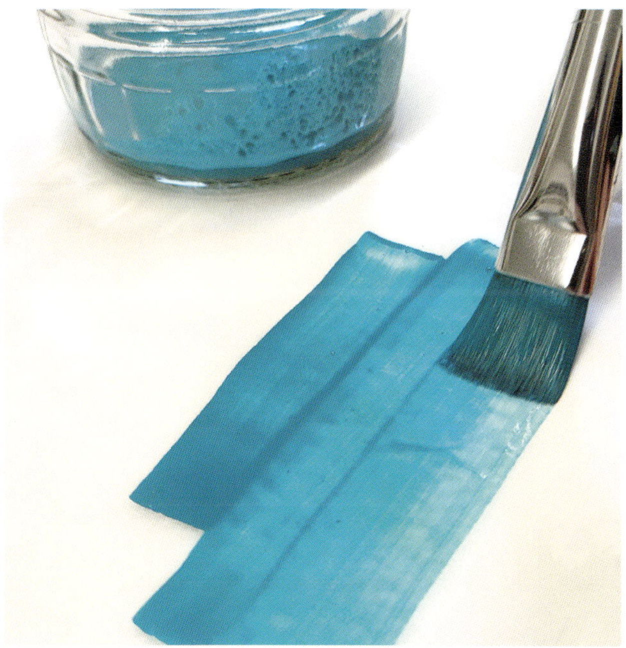

Prepare cut-up wax paper sheets (deli sheets work well) and apply a thin layer of the mixture to the waxed side using your brush. Allow the methylated spirits to fully evaporate.

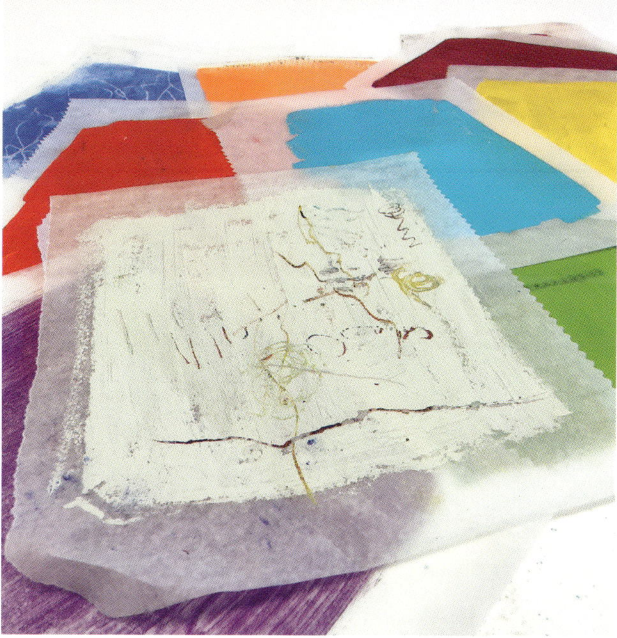

With just a small amount of pigment and methylated spirits, you can produce multiple carbon papers quickly. Store the finished sheets in a plastic sleeve to prevent the pigment from smudging.

LESS IS MORE

Effective composition is essential for creating artworks that resonate deeply with viewers, requiring a solid grasp of the various elements that contribute to visual harmony and impact. By thoughtfully considering aspects such as horizon lines, focal points, balance, contrasts, and cohesion, you can significantly enhance and strengthen your paintings.

While experimentation is important, it is often true that less is more. Although it may be tempting to fill a canvas with intricate details and techniques, embracing quiet spaces and reducing the number of elements can lead to a more powerful composition. Achieving a balance between complexity and simplicity can strengthen your message and enhance the impact of your artwork.

As you explore different techniques and materials, allow yourself the freedom to make mistakes and learn from them. Taking the time to step back from your work, evaluate its flow and balance, and make bold adjustments is an essential part of the process. Embrace the idea that a painting will evolve and transform through your choices and interventions.

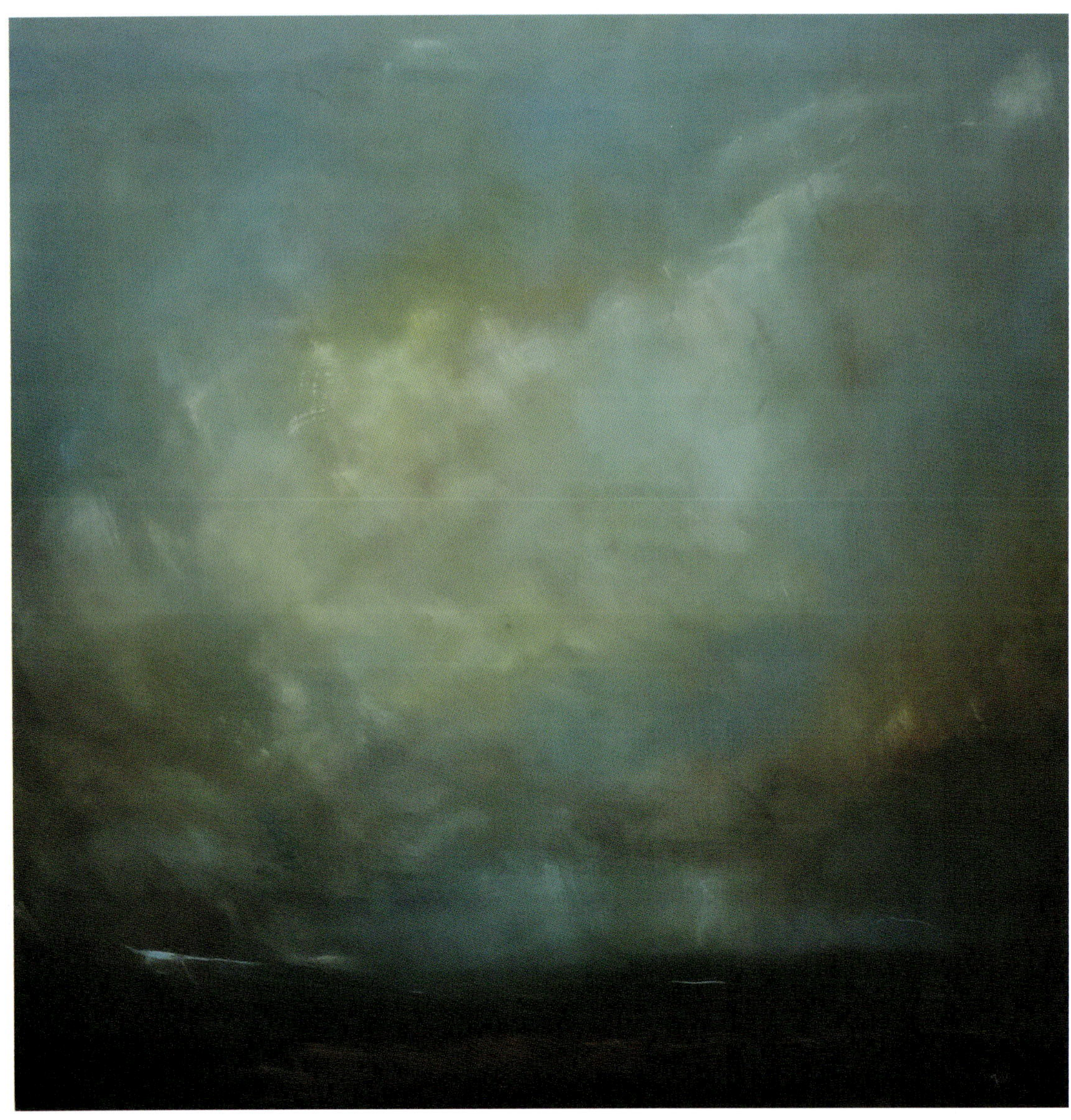

Crack of Light, 61 x 61cm, oils, cold wax and gold leaf on board.

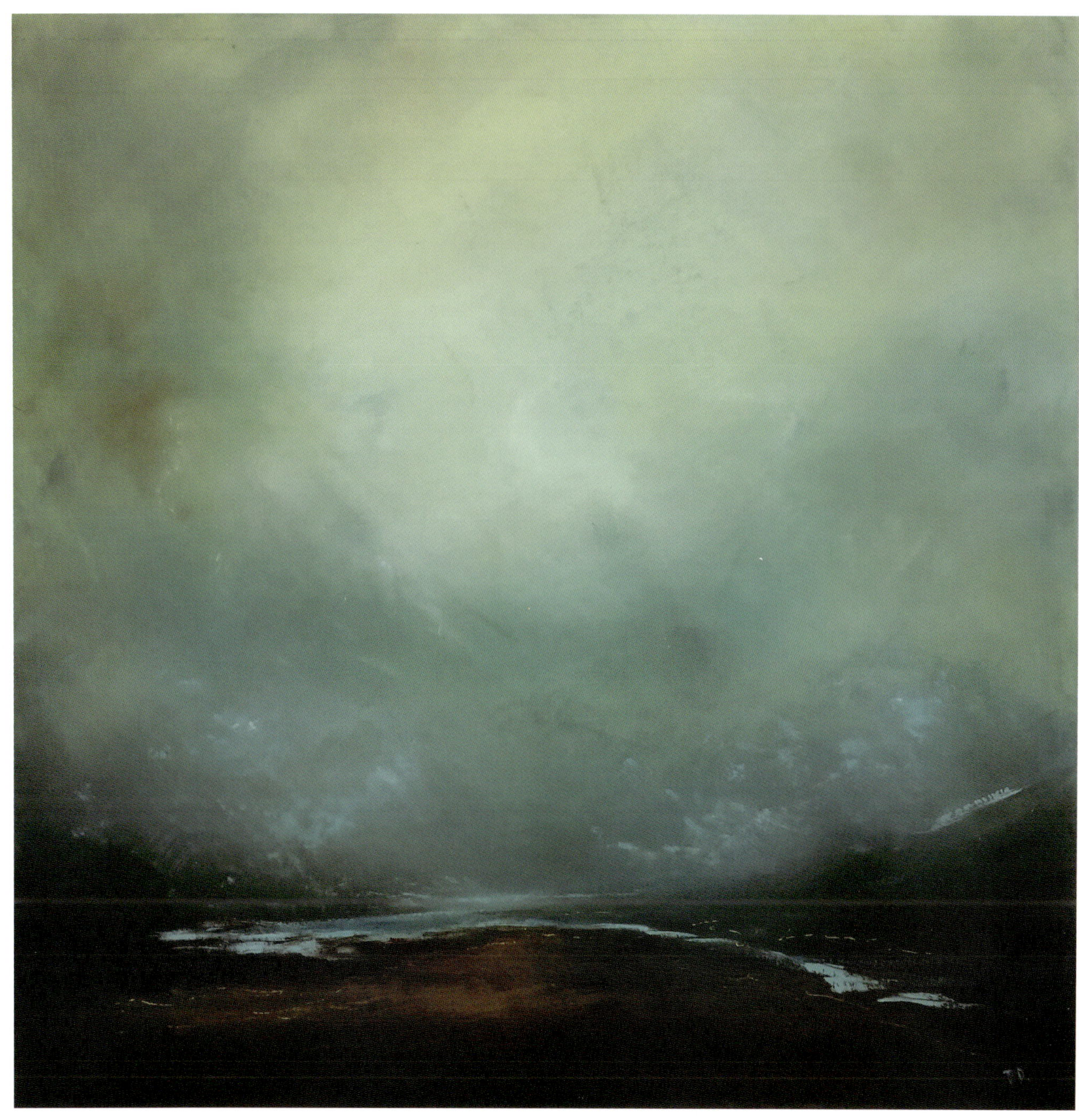

Aello (50 × 50cm/19¾ × 19¾in, oils, cold wax on a wooden panel) features a sweeping brushstroke of turquoise as its focal point, guiding the viewer's eye through the composition and towards the horizon. This vibrant turquoise contrasts strikingly with the rich browns and coppers of the foreground, creating depth and movement.

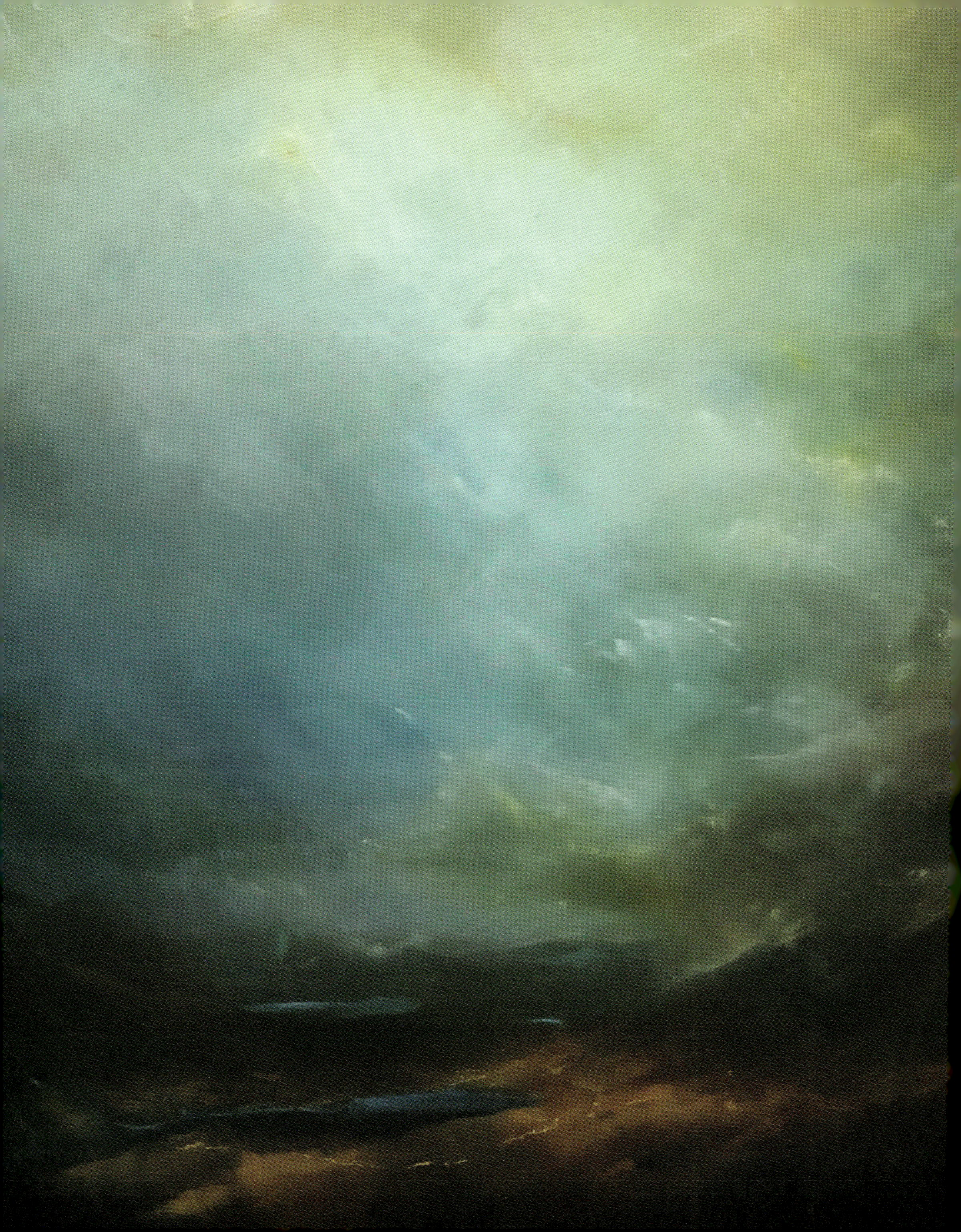

CHAPTER 8

SCALING UP

In this chapter, we explore the transformative process of scaling up your artwork, offering guidance on how sketches and warm-up exercises can serve as a foundation for larger works. It provides practical advice on scaling up mark-making, adapting painting techniques, and making necessary changes to your workspace for larger-scale projects. Additionally, it examines strategies for maintaining effective proportions and composition when transitioning to a larger scale.

Scaling up is an exciting step that can result in new creative opportunities. Working on a larger scale allows for broader gestures, more dynamic compositions, engaging your entire body in the process. Large-scale paintings demand attention and create striking visual experiences, inviting viewers to engage with them on multiple levels, both from a distance and up close – something smaller works may struggle to achieve. Scaling up challenges you to rethink composition and refine your techniques, while unlocking opportunities such as gallery exhibitions, public installations, and private commissions.

As we delve into the various aspects of scaling up, you will discover how to leverage the strengths of smaller works, while adapting your techniques and approaches to meet the challenges that larger formats present.

WHY SCALE UP?

Scaling up your work can be a powerful way to develop creatively and challenge the boundaries of your current practice. It requires you to reimagine composition, proportion, and techniques on a larger scale, pushing you to think beyond the confines of smaller works. It offers opportunities for experimenting with broader gestures, more dynamic forms, and layered complexities that may not be achievable in smaller formats. A larger surface invites greater expressive freedom, encouraging physical engagement and allowing you to involve your entire body in the process of painting.

Large-scale paintings command attention in ways smaller works often cannot. They have a striking presence that can fill a space, making a bold statement and inviting viewers to engage with the piece on multiple levels. From a distance, a cohesive image can emerge creating an immediate visual impact that will command attention and draw the viewer in. Up close, intricate details, textures, and subtle nuances come to life, creating an immersive experience.

Beyond their visual and emotional impact, large-scale works are particularly well suited for gallery exhibitions, public installations, and commissioned spaces, where their scale and presence can make a profound statement. They can demonstrate your ability to tackle ambitious projects, showcasing both your technical skill and creative vision. Including large-scale pieces in your portfolio demonstrates your versatility and can open doors to new audiences and markets, including collectors or curators looking for impactful statement pieces.

OPPOSITE: *Lakeland Fells* (91 × 122cm/36 × 48in, oils, cold wax and gold leaf) was painted on Arches Huile paper bonded to a deep cradle board. The scale and depth of the board eliminated the need for framing, as the deep cradle itself lent the piece a contemporary, gallery-style presentation.

TRANSITIONING YOUR IDEAS

Working on a small scale offers many advantages, as it provides a space to experiment with sketches, colour mixing, and testing out ideas before committing to a larger piece. These smaller studies allow you to explore concepts freely, without the pressure of creating polished, gallery-ready work. They are particularly practical for painting outdoors, where they can assist with capturing the essence of a place, the colours, or the shapes within a landscape to bring back to the studio for further exploration.

Smaller works are invaluable as warm-up exercises before starting to work on a larger piece. They help loosen you up, allowing you to be playful and experimental, preparing you both physically and mentally for the challenges of working on a larger scale. These studies enable you to test ideas, observe how colours blend and interact, and ensure the harmonies and tones align with your vision. By starting small, you can refine your ideas, make mistakes, and try again before moving to a larger canvas.

Small paintings will often evoke atmosphere and mystery with minimal marks, layers, and textures, offering subtle suggestions for viewers to interpret. However, translating this effect to a larger scale requires more than simply enlarging your mark-making; it demands thoughtful adjustments to complexity and detail. Scaling up necessitates layering, textures, and intricate elements to retain the depth and richness of smaller studies, while amplifying their presence on a larger surface. Without these considerations, larger pieces may feel sparse or even unresolved, making it essential to build on the strengths of your smaller works to achieve a comparable visual impact.

Increasing visual information

Moving from small-scale to large-scale painting is akin to enlarging a digital image: just as an image requires more pixels to maintain clarity and avoid pixelation, a large-scale painting demands greater detail, planning, and precision. The 'resolution' of your painting must increase

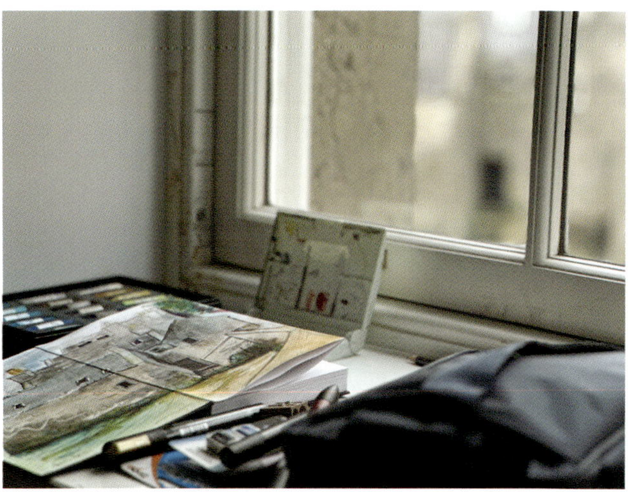

Sketching offers a versatile and enriching practice that serves multiple purposes. By experimenting with different materials and techniques in a dynamic environment, you can expand your mark-making repertoire, fostering creativity and allowing for more spontaneous, expressive pieces without the pressure of creating gallery-ready work.

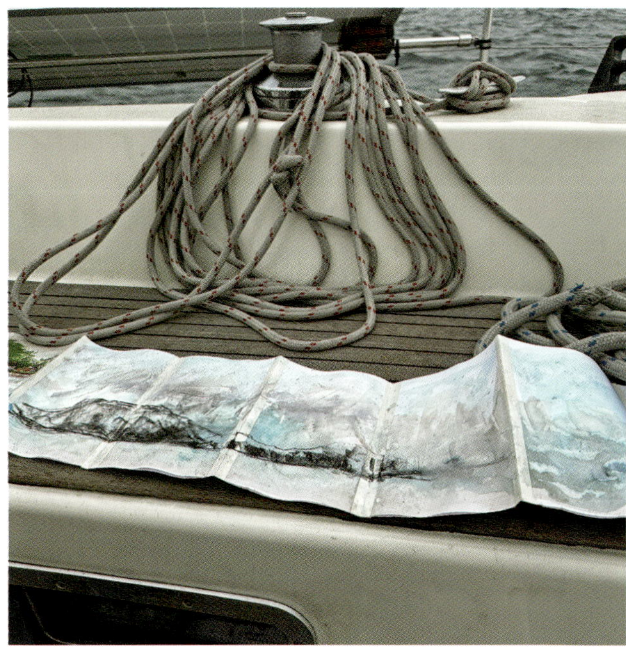

Painting and sketching outdoors further enhance this experience, immersing you in the essence of a location. You can capture vibrant colours, distinctive shapes, and forms found in the landscape, exploring your surroundings in ways that may inspire future projects. This process deepens your connection to the environment and provides a foundation for larger, more developed works.

Additionally, sketching acts as a visual journal, preserving fleeting ideas and impressions that can be revisited later. These quick studies and observations become invaluable tools for refining your vision and translating those initial sparks of inspiration into compelling, large-scale pieces in the studio.

proportionally with its size. Things you may wish to consider when scaling up include:

- Expanding your mark-making: Balance fine details with broader strokes to create a dynamic surface.
- Scaling composition thoughtfully: Ensure that all elements maintain their impact when viewed from different distances and are proportionate to the canvas scale.
- Enhancing visual depth: Use layers of colour, varied mark-making, and textures to add complexity.

Filling a larger canvas requires sufficient 'visual information' to ensure the piece holds up to being viewed close up or from a distance. Large-scale paintings have the potential to draw people in with their presence, but they need engaging details, interesting layers, and textures to captivate viewers.

Composition

Scaling up your artwork requires careful consideration around composition to maintain visual impact and effectively engage viewers. While small, detailed mark-making can create a rich surface, it is essential to encourage viewers to engage closely with your painting, rather than simply passing by. The composition principles discussed in Chapter 7 remain relevant, but when transitioning to a larger format, consider these specific strategies:

- Utilise the edges: Avoid confining your painting to the edges; let marks and shapes extend beyond the surface to create a sense of continuation and immersion.
- Create energy: Use diagonal marks and shapes to generate movement, guiding the viewer's eye through the composition.
- Encourage close viewing: Invite viewers to step closer and explore intricate details and textures.

By keeping these key points in mind, you can effectively scale up your compositions while maintaining their visual integrity and emotional impact. Increasing the level of detail and layering visual information will captivate and engage viewers, enhancing the overall presence of your large-scale painting.

Choosing your surfaces

When selecting surfaces for larger paintings, it is crucial to consider the size, weight, and how the painting will be framed or displayed. Larger works often require sturdier, more stable surfaces to prevent warping, so for my larger paintings, I will choose a cradled wooden panel which has either been pre-prepared with gesso or has paper bonded to it. Each surface has unique qualities that necessitate different approaches to painting, influenced by their texture and absorbency levels (see *Adapting your techniques* below).

Cradled wooden panels come in a variety of depths, impacting their weight, and potentially influencing your framing choices. A cradled panel is a practical option for scaling up, allowing you to hang the painting

When choosing the depth of your cradled board, consider the scale, weight, and presentation style of your work. Shallow (20–22mm/approximately 1in) and medium (25–32mm/1–1¼in) cradled boards are practical and lightweight, making them ideal for tray frames. In contrast, deeper boards (40–50mm/1½–2in or more) can create a striking visual effect, but may pose challenges in handling and framing.

vertically on the wall while you work, without requiring additional hanging hardware. The depth of the panel, along with its size, affects its weight, which is an important consideration if you anticipate needing to move your work around during the painting process. Cradled panels are available in a range of depths, from shallow options which may be braced on the back to limit movement, to deeper panels featuring a more solid cradle frame.

You can also scale up your work by creating a polyptych, which consists of artwork made up of more than one panel. This approach allows for a variety of arrangements and themes, depending on the number of panels involved. The most common arrangements are diptychs (two panels) and triptychs (three panels). Each individual painting can be a size that you are comfortable with, making it easier to work across two, three, or even four panels of the same size. This method significantly increases your overall scale in a way that feels more manageable than jumping directly to a large canvas. Additionally, for particularly large works, combining panels can be a more economical and practical approach for transport.

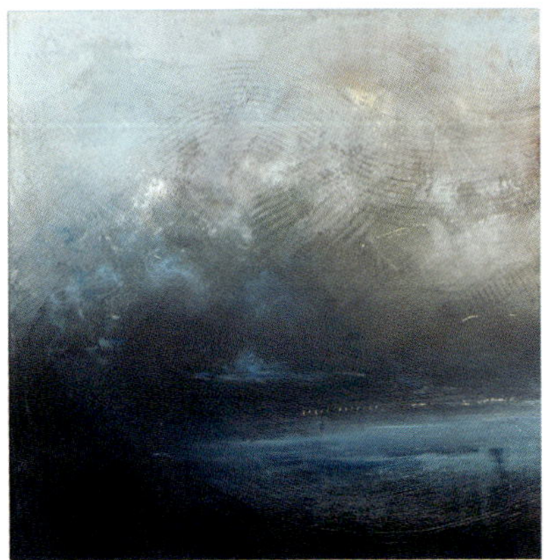
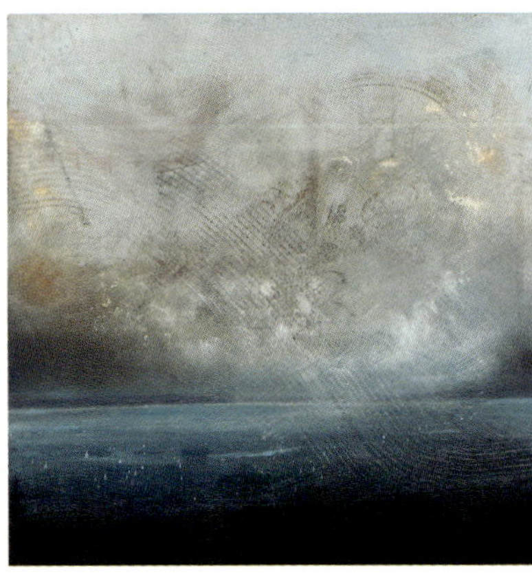
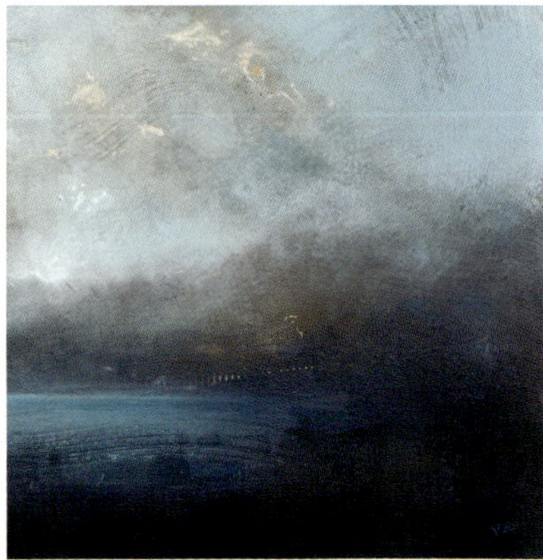

A Lightness of Air, 90 × 30cm (35½ × 12in), oils, cold wax and gold leaf on board. This triptych was created with three 30 × 30cm (12 × 12in) boards. While it represents a scale-up from smaller works, it still offers the opportunity to focus on each individual painting, ensuring that they are strong individually and as part of the triptych.

ADAPTING YOUR TECHNIQUES

The techniques and strategies you use for smaller works often need to be adapted when scaling up. For instance, blending wet-on-wet is simpler with smaller works, as they can typically be completed within a single day. In contrast, larger-scale paintings pose challenges in maintaining this approach if the blending process extends beyond a day, as the paint will begin to stiffen, making it challenging to move the paint around. Moreover, larger works require additional detail through mark-making and layering to ensure they remain engaging when viewed up close. For my larger-scale paintings, the blending process is merely the starting point for establishing colour, tonal range, and compositional balance.

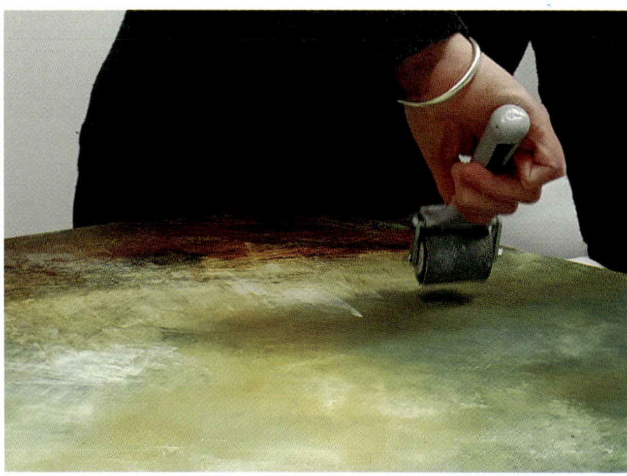

When working on a larger scale, I begin by applying the initial base layer with a squeegee, which helps achieve the most vibrant colour. As additional layers are built up and I move into the early stages of blending, I use a brayer to help create smooth, seamless transitions. The brayer is especially useful for larger works, allowing for efficient and controlled blending across areas.

Using different tools

While many artists scale up their tools for larger works, I generally stick to a 6-inch squeegee for blending, as it reduces hand strain compared to larger options. Achieving blends on a larger scale demands more energetic gestures and wider sweeps of the squeegee, making the process much more physical. Using the squeegee helps initially to cover the surface and to start blending colours together. However, as the oil and cold wax begins to stiffen, pulling paint across the surface becomes increasingly difficult, making blending more challenging.

For the initial layer of colour, I always opt for a squeegee, as it is perfect for pushing the pigment into the absorbent surface of Arches Huile paper. This tool is also highly effective at creating a thin, untextured base layer of colour that provides a solid foundation for subsequent layers. When it comes to blending additional colours, I find a soft brayer (4- or 6-inch) particularly effective for working on larger surfaces, as it allows for easier movement of the paint, especially as it starts to stiffen and becomes more difficult to manipulate.

A brayer creates a delicate layering effect by skimming over the surface, leaving behind subtle colour blends. However, it works best when the paint has started to stiffen rather than when it is very wet. If the paint is too wet, the brayer can lift off more paint than intended, causing over-blending and a muddy appearance. It is essential to retain the distinction between colours, as excessive blending can result in a flat, uniform surface.

When I am unable to achieve the desired colour blends before the paint starts to stiffen, I select a transparent colour from my palette and cover the entire surface with a thin layer of paint using my squeegee. This creates a fresh, wet base layer to restart the blending process.

Sectioning

If you are working on a large scale and anticipate challenges with completing the blending process before the paint stiffens, or if you feel overwhelmed by the size of the canvas, you may want to consider sectioning off your painting. This method breaks the composition into manageable areas, providing greater structure and alleviating the intimidation of tackling the entire canvas at once. You can start with a rough idea of how to divide your painting into sections, such as land, sea, and sky, and allow this division to develop and shift as your painting progresses. Sectioning enables intuitive work within each area without the pressure to complete the entire blending process in one go. This approach allows me to continue working wet-on-wet over several days and weeks without needing to add mediums to keep the paint fluid, which in turn can reduce the thickness of the oil and cold wax mixture, change its appearance and introduce variation to drying times.

After establishing an initial base layer of colour, I typically work from top to bottom, starting with the sky. This method allows me to work wet-on-wet, enabling smooth colour blends, transitions, and tones while the paint is still pliable. By working in this way, I can more easily integrate and adjust the various sections of the painting.

Sectioning off the canvas provides the flexibility to modify the composition, reposition the horizon line, refine focal points, and revisit different areas as needed. If a particular section is not working as intended, I can make changes without compromising the integrity of the entire piece. Overall, this structured approach to wet-on-wet blending effectively helps me manage the challenges of working on a larger scale.

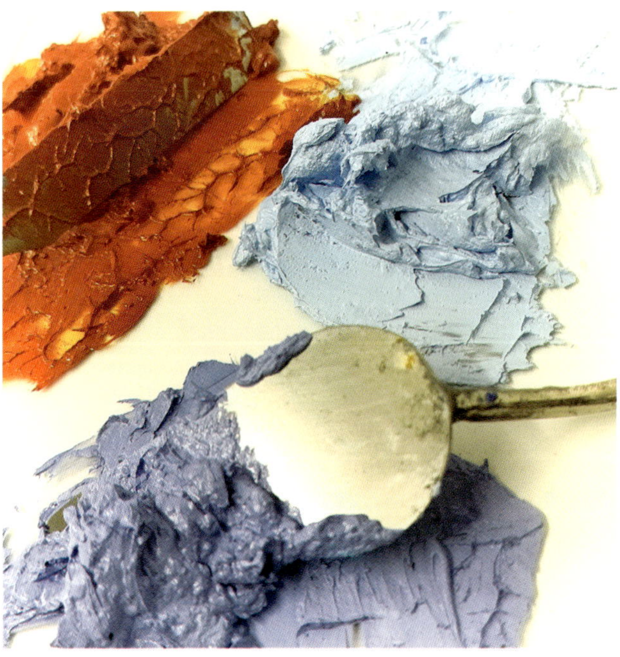

When working on a larger scale, it is essential to have a greater quantity of paint, especially if you mix your own colours instead of using pre-mixed options. Additionally, if you are using Arches Huile paper, its high absorbency necessitates more paint to achieve the desired coverage. This consideration is crucial for maintaining vibrant and consistent results in your artwork.

Mark-making

To create visual interest in your work, mark-making is essential not only for having a variety of marks, but also for ensuring that those marks are diverse. While small, intricate mark-making plays a vital role in larger paintings, complementing these with larger, broader, and more gestural marks that extend beyond the edges of your canvas can significantly enhance the energy of your composition. This approach not only fills the space, but also introduces a sense of movement and dynamism.

To achieve this, expand your range of mark-making tools to include options for creating bolder, more dynamic marks. For example, larger, fuller brushes can be used to create sweeping gestures that add a sense of movement and fluidity to your work. Pair these bold strokes with the delicate lines formed by a rigger brush to introduce intriguing contrasts and enhance visual interest. Additionally, incorporate intricate, fine lines scratched with a barbecue stick and juxtapose them against striking, bold marks revealed by scraping back to the base layers with a palette knife.

Common challenges such as maintaining coherence and managing proportions can arise when scaling up your mark-making. To overcome these issues, develop your own mark-making vocabulary and apply it consistently throughout your work. This consistency in mark types will help unify the composition. Additionally, making broader gestures will create more dynamic marks, fostering a cohesive yet lively visual experience. By thoughtfully incorporating both small and large marks, you can create a rich surface filled with texture and movement.

SCALING UP WITH SMALLER PAINTINGS

An effective way to start scaling up is by working across several small paintings. You can dive right in and start with a diptych or triptych, using a size of canvas you are already comfortable with. Alternatively, try dividing a sheet of Arches Huile paper into sections and working across the entire surface. This approach is an excellent step towards scaling up, as it encourages you to work beyond the edges of each individual painting while ensuring that each painting relates to one another through common marks, colours, and textures.

Step 1: Surface preparation

- Take a large sheet of Arches Huile paper (56 × 76cm/22 × 30in), fold it in half, and gently tear along the fold. You will use only one half of the sheet.
- Take one of the half sheets and fold it in half, then fold it in half again, and repeat until you have eight sections. Do not tear into eight individual sheets – we are using the creases as a guide.
- Securely tape along the creases starting from the centre outwards onto a piece of newsprint, ensuring all sections are firmly fixed.

Step 2: Establishing your base layer

- Make marks using oil bars, charcoal, and Pigment Sticks® across all eight sections, making sure you work across the edges and over the tape.
- Use a squeegee to apply oil colour mixed with cold wax over the surface of the paper, ensuring it is completely covered. You can choose to work with one colour or a range of bright colours to create a vibrant base layer to scratch back to.

Step 3: Developing complex colours

- Apply another layer of colour using your squeegee, focusing on creating thin, transparent layers. Experiment with colour combinations to explore their interactions.
- Use a large paintbrush to introduce a light opaque colour, such as white, and selectively cover sections of the previous layers. Apply only a small amount, focusing on enhancing the existing colours rather than covering the entire surface. Working wet-on-wet will allow the colours to blend and start to create complex colour mixes.
- Create some initial marks by scratching into the layers with various tools, such as sticks, palette knives, or your squeegee to produce interesting textures and to start to reveal some of the base layers.

Step 4: Blocking out sections

- Block out sections of your painting using torn newsprint or masking tape. These can be used to mask specific shapes or larger areas. For clean, straight lines, utilise the edges of the newsprint or masking tape.
- Mix a pale, neutral, opaque colour from your colour palette or take a light colour such as titanium white and spread a thin layer across your surface, covering the areas left exposed by the masks.
- Before removing your masks, consider adding extra marks or details to the exposed sections for added depth and interest.

Step 5: Unifying the surface

- Unify the surface with a transparent colour, choosing either a light colour such as lemon yellow or a dark colour such as alizarin crimson or ultramarine blue (as used in this example). Mixing one of your transparent colours with zinc white can create a lighter version of these darks, while retaining transparency.
- The transparent colour will push back the pale opaque colours applied in the previous step.
- At this stage, the painting may seem chaotic, but this is perfectly fine. Focus on having a diverse array of rich colours, shapes, and marks to work with, as they will provide a solid foundation for further development.

Step 6: Adding texture through scratching

- Create marks by scratching into the surface with various tools, such as sticks, palette knives, or a brush comb, to produce interesting textures. Aim for

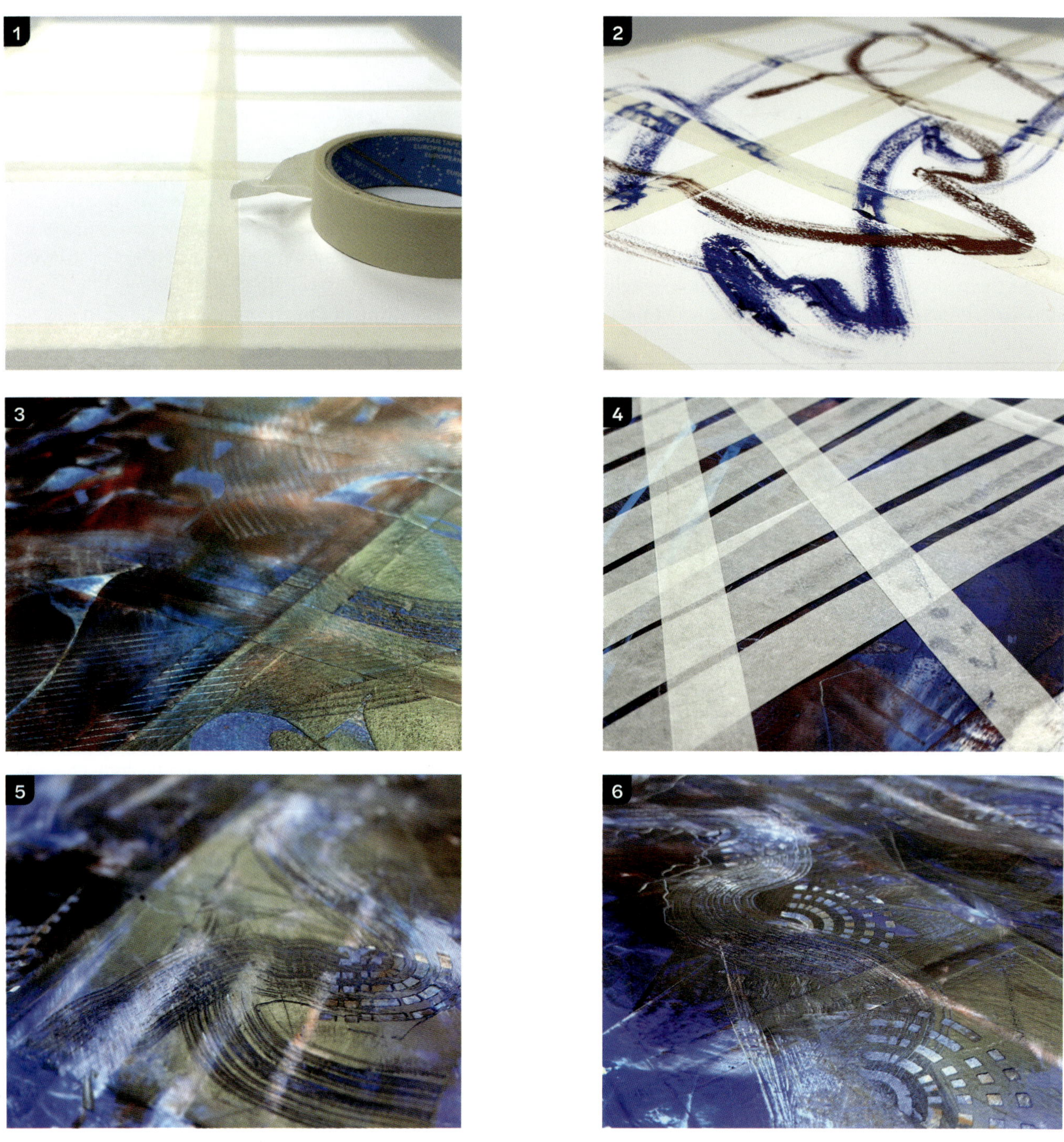
1
2
3
4
5
6

a variety of marks, balancing delicate and bold, with expressive and controlled.
- It is important for the next step that you have a good range of marks on your surface.
- Leave your painting to rest overnight to allow it to firm up. It does not need to be completely dry, but if it is too wet, continuing to work on it may result in over-blending your colours and losing all your marks.

Step 7: Applying a film of colour

- Returning to your work, check that the painting is not too wet; you should only get a faint print of paint on your fingers when touching it. It is crucial not to work on it before it has dried sufficiently, otherwise in the next step the brayer will lift the paint.
- Mix some titanium white or an opaque tint of your choice with cold wax. Load your brayer with paint, ensuring an even spread. If there are peaks of paint on your roller, then remove the excess paint by rolling it onto some print paper.
- Roll a thin film of the paint mix across the surface of your painting. This layer should be thin enough to enable you to see the textured marks you made in the previous step, while still unifying the surface.

Step 8: Exploring solvent reduction

- Drip solvent onto your painting using a brush, a dropper, or apply it with a brush stroke. Wipe the solvent off with a gentle pull of your squeegee across the surface. This should leave you with a range of organic marks, revealing the layers underneath. Repeat as necessary.
- Once the solvent has evaporated, use a transparent colour across the surface to push everything back, diminishing the intensity of the underlying colours and marks revealed by the solvent. This technique adds depth and allows previous layers to recede slightly, with the transparent colour acting as a unifying layer.

Step 9: Iterating the process

- Repeat the process of using solvent drops to create additional organic marks. Introduce further texture using lace, bubble wrap, and scrunched-up tissue to create imprints.
- Continue alternating between adding transparent layers, blocking out sections of your work, solvent reduction, and mark-making until you see a potential direction in which to develop your painting.

Step 10: Framing your perspective

- Examine each individual painting using a frame view. You can create a frame using a mount board cut to the size of your individual paintings, which will help to visualise their edges, and where the tape will come off.
- Alternatively, take some masking tape and gently place it around the border of each of your individual paintings. Do not stick the tape down – you are just using the tape as a guide to help you frame your work and see where it could be improved.
- Assess whether each painting works on its own. Check for good tonal value (lights and darks), colour contrast (warm, cool and complementary), and for varied marks and shapes.

Step 11: Finalising your composition

- If you are ready to focus on your composition, consider whether incorporating collage would enhance it. If you choose to use collage, be mindful of the tape's location to avoid placing materials over it, as removing the tape could pull up your embedded elements.
- Embed dry pigments or use carbon paper to add a pop of colour. You can paint details with a brush, squeegee, or your fingers, or scratch in to extend lines or reveal colours. Consider each addition carefully to ensure it contributes to the overall piece.

Step 12: Reveal your work

- Once you are satisfied with how each individual painting works and how the entire series works together, carefully begin to remove the tape.
- Individual paintings can be displayed on their own or, for a more striking effect, frame them as a series, either mounted on a wooden panel or framed behind glass.

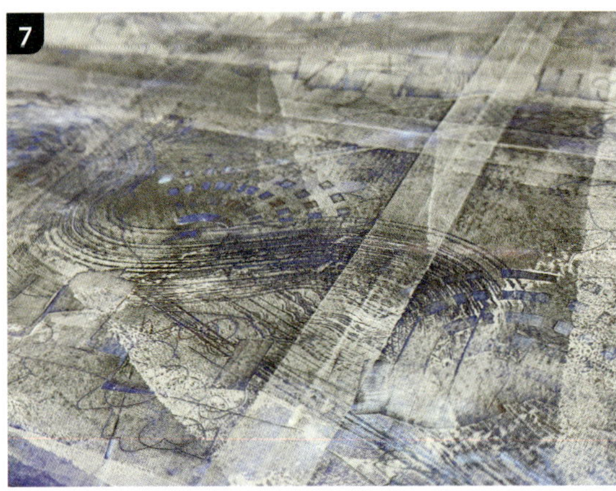

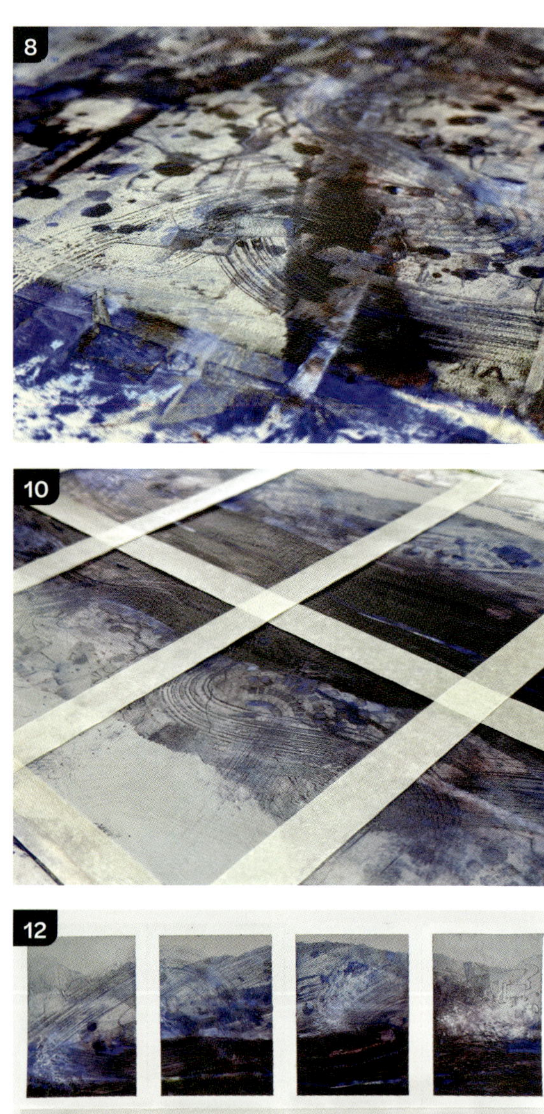

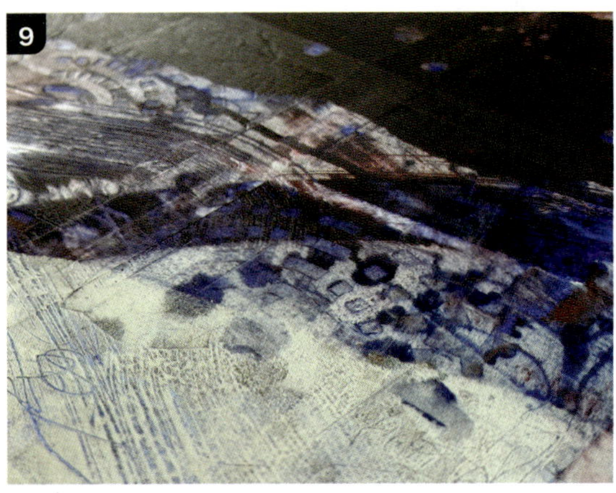

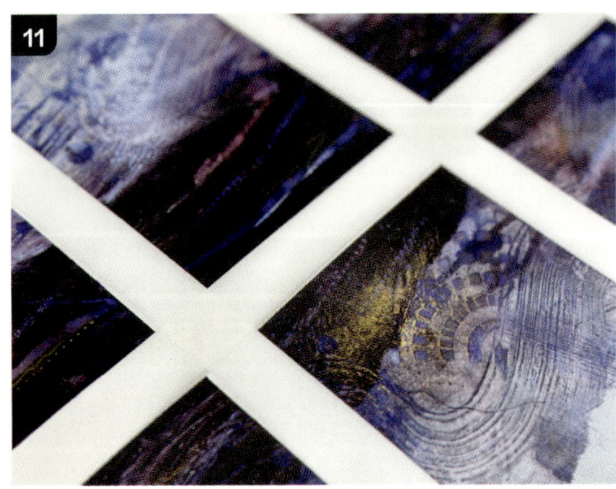

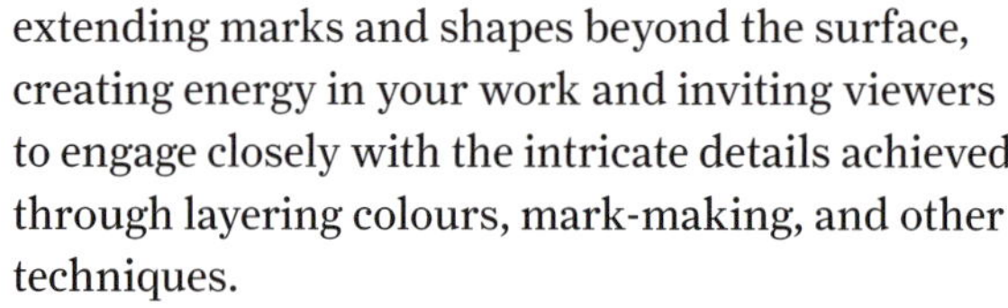

Scaling up your work through a series of smaller paintings allows you to break down a larger surface into manageable sections, while fostering a cohesive relationship among the individual pieces within the series. This approach enables you to experiment with extending marks and shapes beyond the surface, creating energy in your work and inviting viewers to engage closely with the intricate details achieved through layering colours, mark-making, and other techniques.

ADAPTING YOUR WORKSPACE

Working vertically is crucial when scaling up a painting, as the perspective changes significantly when a larger piece is laid horizontally. Since your work will ultimately be hung on a wall, it is essential to assess how your shapes, lines, colours, and textures interact in the viewer's intended perspective. While some techniques, such as solvent reduction, may necessitate a horizontal approach, it is important to return the painting to a vertical position at the height at which it will generally be viewed. This allows for a more accurate assessment of perspective, colour, and texture, as these elements can appear quite different when viewed from a horizontal angle, or while leaning against a wall at floor level.

As paintings increase in size, especially on wooden panels, they become more cumbersome and heavier. Therefore, it is essential to set up your workspace to facilitate the easy movement of your painting, whether that means raising, lowering, or even flipping it upside down when necessary. Having a vertical space to work on your paintings allows for easy height adjustments and helps make it easier to reach all areas of the painting without having to lean over or crouch down, which can help reduce physical strain. If you are limited on space, an easel can be a practical solution for manoeuvring your work. Additionally, having a vertical wall space, such as a grid system, allows your paintings to rest or dry safely while you focus on other pieces.

THE POWER OF SCALING UP

Scaling up your artwork is more than just increasing size, it is about embracing the challenges and possibilities of creating on a larger scale. From adapting techniques and materials to rethinking composition and layering, working on large surfaces requires bold experimentation. Whether you are using a diptych or triptych to step into larger formats or diving straight into expansive canvases, scaling up offers an opportunity to make a stronger visual impact. With careful consideration of composition, mark-making, and substrate choices, your work has the potential to resonate deeply with audiences and captivate viewers both up close and at a distance. Ultimately, scaling up allows you to bring your artistic vision to life on a larger scale, showcasing your ability to innovate and inspire through your practice.

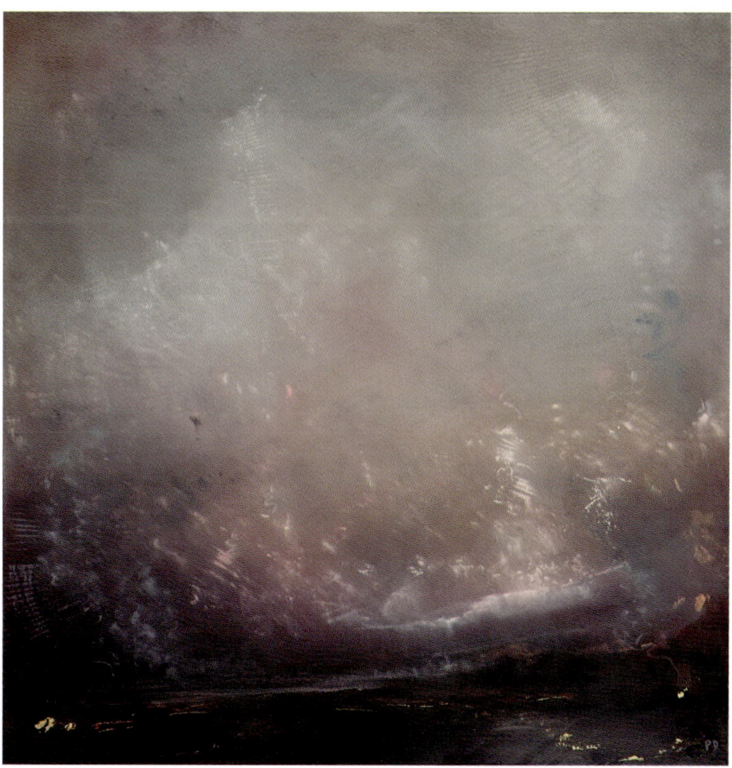

Autumn's Mist (50 × 50cm/19¾ × 19¾in, oils and cold wax on a wooden panel) highlights wet-on-wet blending techniques to create soft colour and tonal transitions. The initial layers were refined with brushwork, incorporating repeated adjustments to tonal values. This process enhanced the composition's subtle gradations, atmospheric depth, and interplay of light and shadow.

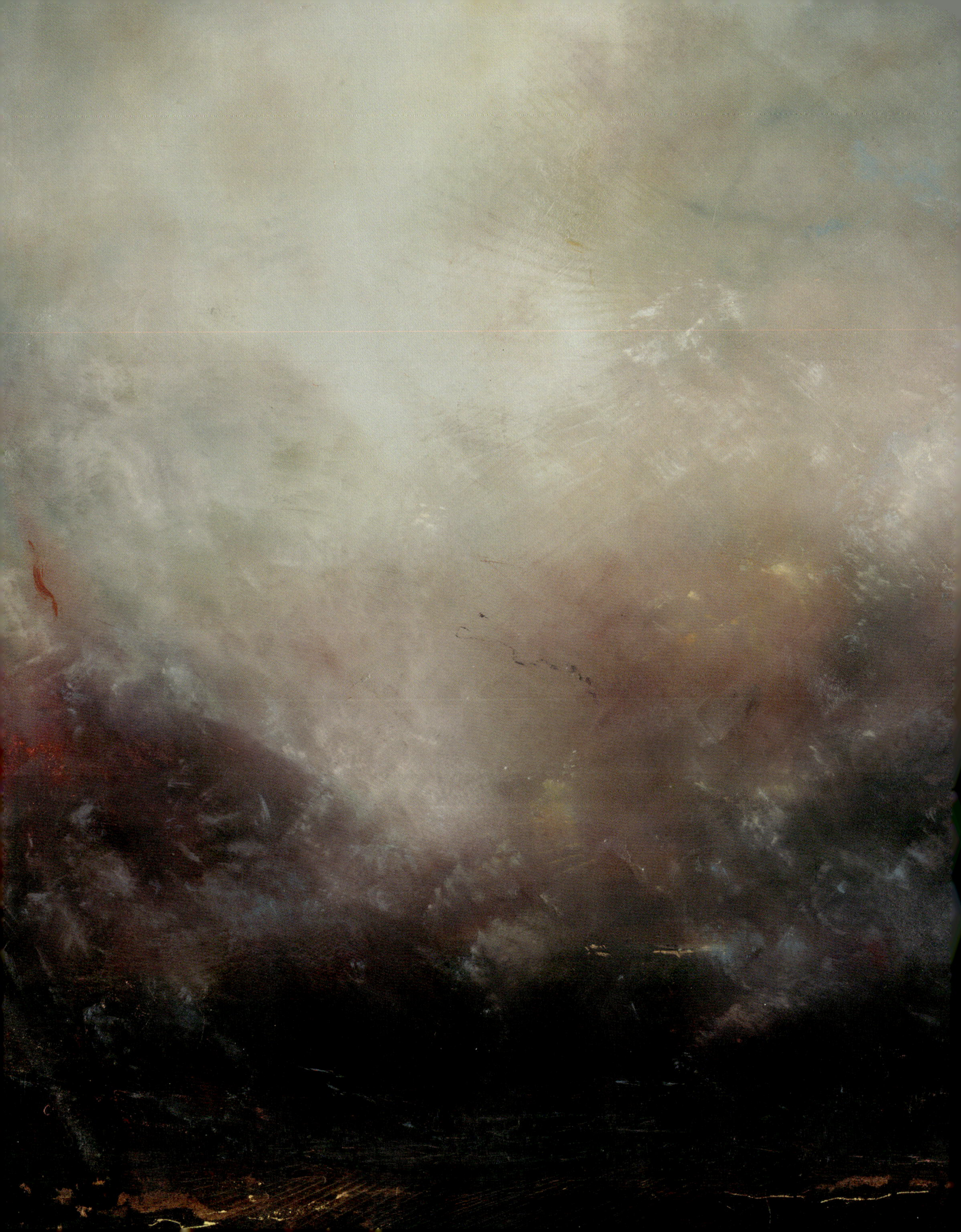

CHAPTER 9

INSPIRATION AND THE CREATIVE PROCESS

'The world is very, very beautiful if you look at it, but most people don't look very much.'

David Hockney

In this chapter we explore the sources of my inspiration and examine how these elements shape my creative process, influencing my approach to creating meaningful work. Each piece begins as a seed of inspiration, evolving through exploration, mistakes, and the iterative process of trying again. My approach to painting embraces experimentation and discovery, allowing the act of painting to guide the outcome rather than focusing solely on the final image. I engage with both familiar and new techniques, exploring 'what if' scenarios and embracing the unpredictable to continually find innovative paths. By taking inspiration from my surroundings and experiences, I transform these initial sparks into tangible expressions of creativity, weaving together various influences to create work that is both personal and resonant.

Inspiration serves as the starting point of my creative process, arising from my connection to the land, the colours I encounter, and collaborative dialogues with other creatives. This initial moment compels me to explore and create, providing the motivation to innovate. Observation is a critical component of this process. By closely observing my surroundings I gather insights that inform my work, encouraging me to delve deeper into my subjects. This exploration of details and nuances generates ideas that resonate with my experiences, leading to further exploration of themes in my paintings.

Sometimes an idea is sparked and begins to take shape and I realise that I need to carry out further research and investigation, to develop the idea and realise its fullest potential. This seamless integration of observation and ideation fosters a dynamic creative process, where the insights gathered inspire experimentation and exploration. Observation, whether through sketching, photography, or simply walking, becomes a rich source of inspiration that fuels the exploration and experimentation needed to realise my creative ideas.

The insights gathered through observation become the foundation for experimentation in my studio. Each observation holds the potential to spark a new idea or technique, shaping the direction of my work. As inspiration sparks the creative process, innovation transforms these initial ideas into tangible outcomes, allowing me to explore new techniques and approaches that ensures my work evolves.

Innovation manifests itself through experimentation, exploration, and creative problem-solving. It involves refining, testing, and trying out new techniques and materials, pushing boundaries to discover new possibilities that help develop my artistic voice and style. Reflection plays a crucial role in this cyclical process, enabling me to learn from my experiments and refine my practice. It informs future inspiration and innovation by allowing me to think critically about the choices I make and how they align with both the initial idea and the final result. This cycle of inspiration, observation, innovation, and reflection forms the foundation of my work, keeping me engaged and constantly seeking ways to create new and compelling art.

OPPOSITE: *Burn Back* (detail) features layers of gold leaf which have been covered with a translucent glaze, pushing it backwards and enhancing the depth and richness of the painting. Fine lines and shapes were then added with gold leaf to complement the brushwork and emphasise the movement and energy within the painting.

INSPIRED BY

The natural world

Inspiration serves as the spark that fuels creativity, providing the mental stimulation needed to breathe life into new ideas. It opens the door to new perspectives and for me can be drawn from an array of sources: the surrounding landscapes, the shifting moods of weather, light, and seasons, the vivid colours evoked by memories of my walks, and the dynamic energy of collaboration with others. Rather than seeking to create literal representations, I strive to capture the essence of memory, the shifts of light, and the atmosphere of each scene.

An increasing awareness of environmental concerns has become a significant influence on my practice. Immersion in nature deepens my sensitivity to the impact of human activity on these spaces, shaping my themes and encouraging a more profound engagement with issues of conservation. These diverse influences come together to enrich my creative process, broadening my understanding and enabling me to weave layered, nuanced narratives into my work.

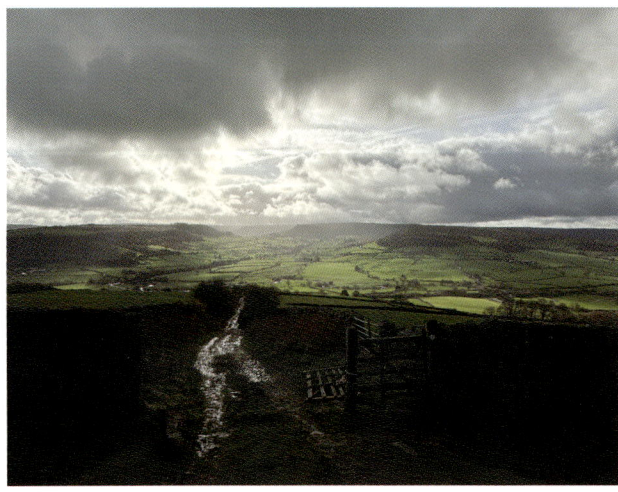

While photographs instantly capture a place and serve as valuable memory aids, they offer only a single perspective. To truly capture a landscape's essence, I need to be there, walking its paths, experiencing its shifting moods, and immersing myself in its changing light and textures. Observing its hidden details deepens my connection and fuels my creativity.

My paintings are deeply rooted in the landscapes that I explore, where the weather and the shifting light play central roles. Walking is integral to this connection, enabling me to experience smells, textures, colours, and shapes: details often overlooked when our focus is elsewhere. These walks foster a sense of place, which forms the foundation for my paintings.

The ever-changing weather and interplay of light are central to everything I do, artistically, shaping my choice of colours, compositions, and the mood of each painting. A burst of sunlight breaking through storm clouds might inspire a dramatic, bold composition, while the soft, diffused light of a misty day invites a muted palette and a more abstract approach, seamlessly blending the boundaries between sky and land.

These elements infuse the landscape with emotion, creating dynamic moods that enhance the visual interest and drama in my work. Light interacts with the landscape to create captivating effects, such as wet roads shimmering like rivers or shafts of light illuminating parts of the landscape, each offering inspiration to capture in a painting. This dynamic interplay of light, weather, and movement energises the scene, influencing my techniques, colour choices, and the overall direction of each piece.

Different weather conditions provide the opportunity to create unique atmospheres that can add depth to my work. Capturing these elements enables me to convey specific moods and themes: the misty embrace of fog evokes mystery and quietness, while a snow-covered landscape suggests a calm stillness. The weather and seasonal changes significantly influence the landscape, which can be transformed by effects such as fluctuating water levels or the die-back of foliage, revealing the hidden contours of the land. The landscape can be reshaped in a moment: shifting light, the shadows cast by the movement of clouds, plunge previously visible landforms into darkness, and simultaneously illuminate other areas with a burst of sunlight. Observing the world around me during various weather conditions

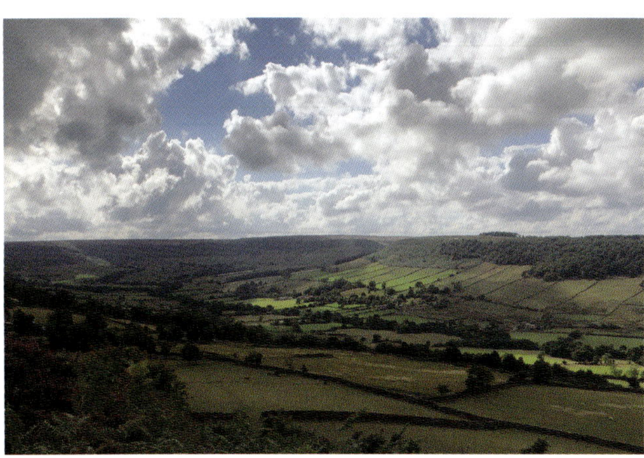

Exploring the land is essential for seeing it from different angles and perspectives, observing how light and weather shape the landscape. It allows me to understand the scale of its elements and discover how to translate them into a two-dimensional painting, creating depth and atmosphere that will immerse the viewer into the scene.

and seasons invites me to explore further, revealing new layers and opportunities within each scene.

We easily overlook everyday moments as we rush to our destinations, but I have learned to slow down and observe my surroundings. My daily walks to the studio through woodlands, beside rivers, and over moorland helps me tune in to seasonal transitions and the constant movement of wildlife. By revisiting the same routes throughout the year, I can witness these shifts and observe how the weather and seasons transform the atmosphere of each location. These quiet moments of observation allow me to process ideas and develop concepts, while fostering a growing sense of responsibility towards the natural world.

Exploring and wandering without time constraints is essential to me, as it provides the freedom to immerse myself in my surroundings and satisfy my curiosity. Although I often find myself getting lost along the way (and usually very muddy), these meanderings frequently lead me back to the studio with discovered (discarded) objects in my pockets, fresh ideas, and a desire to learn and understand more.

The joy of colour

While the landscape, weather, light, and atmosphere are significant influences in my work, I approach each painting without a fixed idea of what the final piece will look like. Instead, I let the process unfold naturally, guided by intuition and inspiration rather than a predetermined plan. This approach encourages exploration and experimentation, allowing me to uncover new ideas and directions as I work, driven by an initial attraction to a specific colour or colour palette and a desire to evoke a particular atmosphere.

Colour is at the heart of my creative process, with hues encountered during my walks often reappearing in my work long after I first observed them. My attraction to specific colours frequently emerges from subconscious memories, such as the vibrant yellow of gorse flowers seen on a clifftop walk, the way light cascades over a hillside to illuminate the bracken, or the familiar hues of everyday objects. Rather than aiming to replicate a specific scene, I explore the emotional resonance of colour as it connects to memories and experiences, as well as the atmospheres they evoke. For instance, the vibrant green of moss in a shaded hollow or the golden glow of sunlight on a hillside may not immediately inspire a painting, yet they eventually resurface, shaping my palette in unexpected and captivating ways.

I am entranced by the interplay of colours and how the weather can both enliven and mute them, adding depth that draws the observer in. Certain hues evoke specific landscapes, such as the stunning rich turquoises of the coast or the sweet pea greens of a springtime valley, while others exude a delicious vibrancy, reminiscent of juicy oranges and crisp greens. Colour invigorates and inspires me; even the most subdued tones ignite my imagination and encourage experimentation, allowing me to explore the diverse atmospheres they can help me create.

From the moment I select my colours, I aim to establish a dynamic dialogue between them, balancing

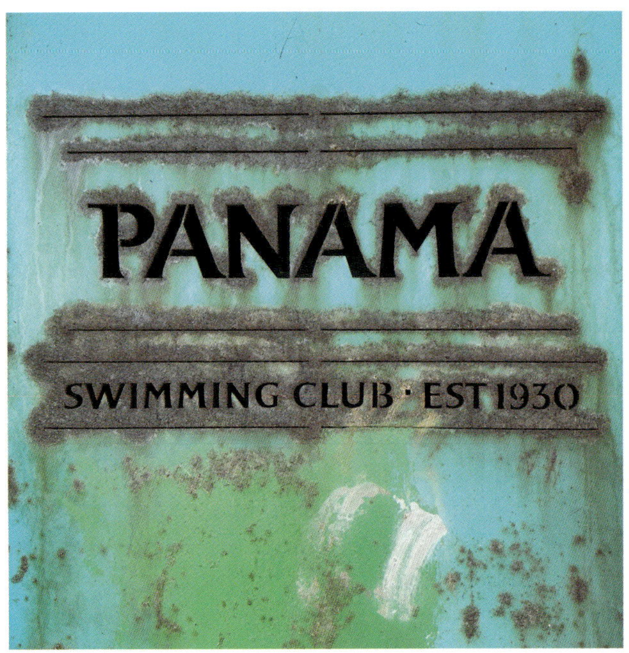

Colour excites me and fuels my desire to paint. A photograph captures its intensity, while a simple sign anchors the memory to its coastal setting. These subtle details often shape a painting in unexpected ways.

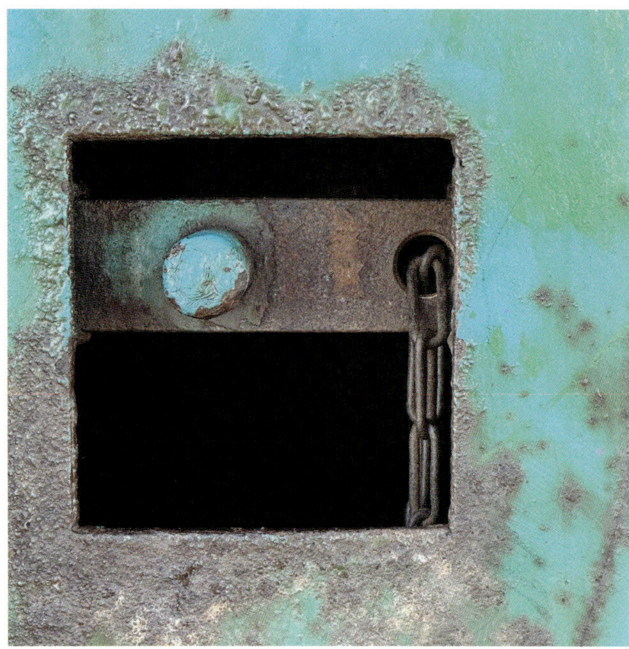

I am drawn to the contrast between the vibrant colour of the paint and the texture of the weathered post. These images linger in my mind until I return to the studio where I instinctively reach for my paints.

their intensity and exploring their relationships. This process involves experimenting with transitions, harmonising tones, adjusting contrasts, and ensuring that the chosen dominant colour stands out without overwhelming the composition, ultimately creating the depth and atmosphere I seek to achieve in my work.

When a painting feels stagnant, it often indicates a lack of harmony with the colours, suggesting that my focus on colour may be misaligned. Since colour is the driving force behind my work, getting my palette right from the outset is crucial. When a painting stalls and loses its flow, it typically stems from the colours not working together effectively. In these moments, I may remix the palette, apply a new transparent layer over the surface, or even start anew by scraping off the paint, and allowing the fundamental act of painting guide me forward.

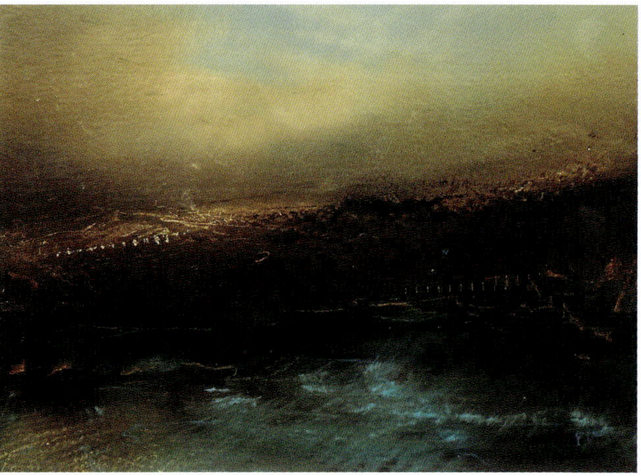

Swimming in Turquoise (20 × 25cm/(8 × 10in), oil, cold wax, and gold leaf) inspired by the luminous Scottish waters or the corroded beauty of a metal sign on a cold winter's morning along England's northeast coast.

Working with others

Collaboration brings new perspectives to my work. By engaging with writers, conservationists, curators, and fellow artists, I can deepen the narratives I explore and expand the themes within my art. These collaborations often begin as moments of inspiration, evolving into larger projects that may span years. The goal is not only to represent, but also to tell a story that resonates with viewers and invites them to engage with broader issues.

Working on a project with conservation teams at a national park has been particularly valuable for me. It has deepened my understanding of land management efforts on the moors and enabled me to respond meaningfully to my observations. The natural forces, such as weather, erosion, and rivers, alongside human activities such as cultivation and infrastructure, all leave lasting marks, shapes, and patterns on the landscape. This mark-making fascinates me and has become a central focus of my work on this project as I explore how these elements intersect and evolve over time. This collaboration allows my art to respond to the conservation teams' efforts while celebrating the beauty of the landscape, enabling us to collectively tell a more comprehensive story.

Collaborating with writers on joint publications, working alongside other artists on collaborative pieces, and engaging a community in co-creating work allows me to explore new themes and develop fresh perspectives. These partnerships enable me to incorporate diverse voices into my art, enriching the stories I aim to tell and revealing deeper layers of meaning. Collaboration often leads to unexpected breakthroughs, inspiring me to experiment with new techniques, ideas, and even mediums.

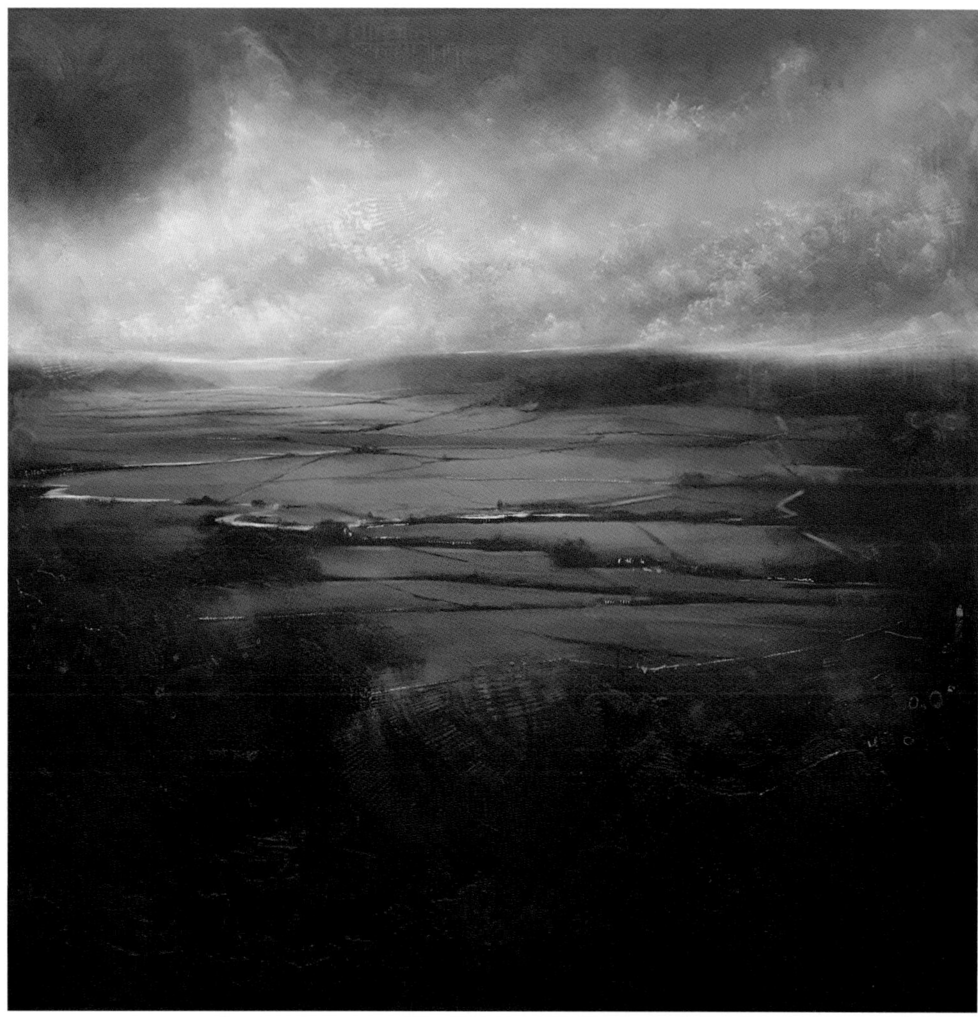

During a site visit to the North Yorkshire Moors, I was captivated by the sight of rainwater running off the recently burned moorland into the dales. This experience inspired me to adopt a purple and blue theme for my painting, reflecting the issues of flooding and the decline of biodiversity on the moorland, rather than merely replicating the colours of the Yorkshire landscape before me.

WORKING TOWARDS INSPIRATION

Inspiration can be unpredictable, manifesting suddenly or developing over time. Waiting for it can result in inertia and an overwhelming pressure to create the 'perfect' painting.

Many creatives, myself included, find that inspiration often emerges through the act of doing. Initiating the work signals to your mind that you are ready to create, and the act of creating frequently brings ideas to the surface. Action primes the mind for creativity, creating a feedback loop where effort sparks ideas, which in turn fuels further effort. Taking those first steps helps push past procrastination or self-doubt, ultimately leading to progress.

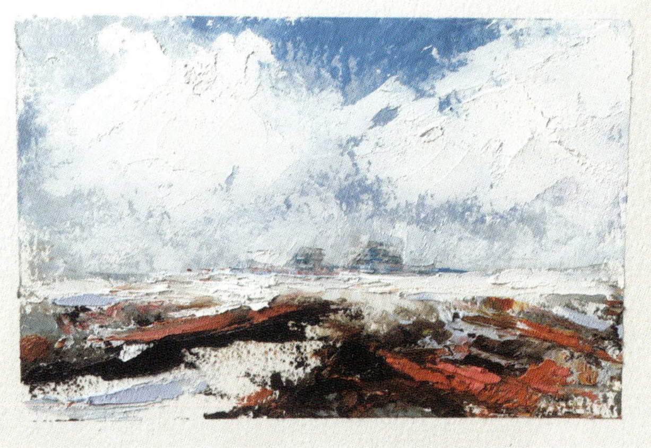

Generating momentum can be a challenge, especially when working on a larger scale and stepping out of your comfort zone. The key is to dive in and start creating to get the energy and ideas flowing. Consider sketching or producing smaller pieces within a set time frame, as these exercises can help spark inspiration.

> *'Inspiration exists but it has to find you working.'*
>
> Pablo Picasso

Action generates momentum, and as you continue working, the progress you make can motivate you to keep going. This momentum can lead to a state of flow, where time seems to disappear, and you become fully absorbed in your task.

Staying focused is crucial, especially when the work becomes challenging. For me, the most difficult stage often occurs midway through a painting, when I transition from the meditative flow of moving paint across the surface to the intense focus required for resolving a composition. This stage demands problem-solving and concentration, making it easy to succumb to distractions and the urge to switch to something new creeps in.

Establishing discipline in your studio practice is essential. While inspiration may fluctuate, deadlines for projects and exhibitions remain constant. A structured routine can be immensely beneficial; for me, my daily walk to the studio sets a positive tone for the day, while the return journey allows for reflection and processing. This rhythm helps ideas surface from my subconscious, creating momentum in my creative process. By establishing a rhythm, whether through my walk to the studio or dedicated time for experimentation, I create a foundation where the freedom to explore can thrive. The interplay between structure and freedom energises my practice, as structure provides the environment for creative expression to flourish, opening the door to new ideas and opportunities.

OBSERVATION

Observation provides the essential raw materials, colours, shapes, and atmosphere, which fuel my ideas and anchor them in reality and help to deepen my understanding of the subject. For me, it is often the memory of a place, rather than the place itself, that informs my work. The colours, textures, and emotions associated with specific moments in time serve as starting points for my paintings, enabling me to translate personal experiences into intuitive and emotional expressions. Memory filters and transforms the raw material of observation, shaping the palette, mood, and atmosphere of each piece and creating a deeper, more personal connection to the work.

Documenting my experiences is important, especially for projects that unfold over months or even years.

Sketchbooks, photographs, found objects and written notes act as visual anchors, capturing the essence of the places I have wandered and explored. These tools help me refine ideas and preserve moments that might otherwise fade from memory.

To truly understand a landscape, however, I will immerse myself in it. I walk the land, observing it from different viewpoints, watch how the light shifts across its surface and how the weather shapes my perception of its character. This 360-degree perspective allows me to connect deeply with the environment, ensuring my work reflects what I find unique and captivating about this place. By immersing myself in the process of observing and connecting with the natural world, I create paintings that not only capture the essence of a location, but also convey the emotions and memories tied to it. Observation is not just a tool for recording the world; it is the starting point for innovation, enabling me to transform inspiration into meaningful and evocative art.

Capturing the essence of place

Sketching and drawing on-site are not intended as direct references for finished works, but help cement a landscape in my mind, the light falling across the land, the interplay of weather, and the movement of clouds, while also sharpening my observational and drawing skills. This practice also provides the freedom to experiment with materials I might not use in painting, releasing the pressure of creating a finished piece. Through this playful exploration, I test how materials behave, experiment with techniques, and uncover new approaches. By documenting these experiments, I build a library of ideas to revisit, whether immediately or years later. I explore the effects and relationships of colours, using this time to consider how they might influence future paintings. Sketching becomes both a method of recording and a tool for innovation, serving as a process of discovery that directly informs my creative practice.

Documenting my ideas, thoughts, and experiments with materials, along with capturing the essence of a place in my sketchbook, are all essential parts of my practice. The physical act of sitting, observing, and sketching a landscape helps embed its shapes and atmosphere in my mind, allowing me to recall them later when back in the studio.

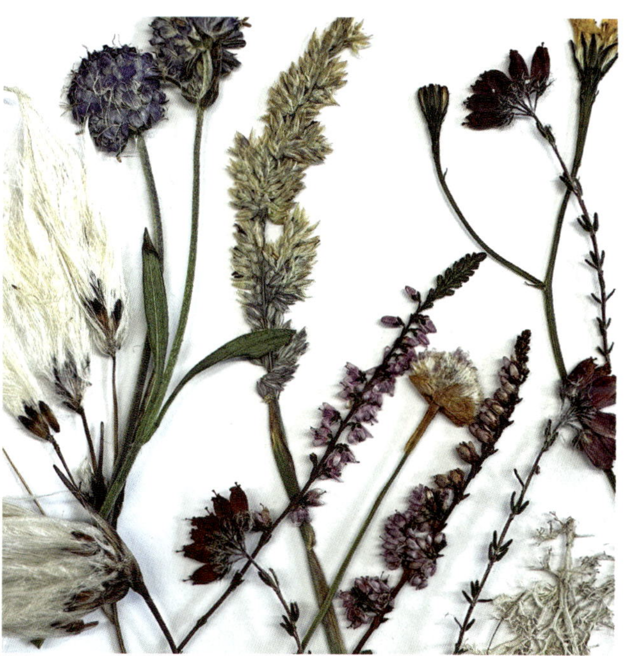

I collect found objects such as shells, stones, and feathers, for their textures, and their colours act as reminders of places I have visited. Recently, I have expanded to pressed flowers, wool, and even old gun cartridges. Cataloguing them helps me recall landscapes, and whether they become part of my work or inspire a story, they deepen my connection to these places.

Photography also plays a significant role in capturing fleeting moments and ideas. While some photographs are printed and added to my sketchbooks as references, I rarely work from photographs alone. For me, a photograph is often just a starting point, a way to trigger memories and refine my understanding of a place.

During site visits, I gather objects: flowers, moss, and leaves to press and preserve; feathers, wool, and fur caught in fences; and pebbles, sand, seashells, and seaweed. These collected treasures are kernels of inspiration, waiting to take root and flourish, perhaps days, months, or years later. Together, these elements weave a narrative that documents and also informs my creative process, shaping the stories behind each project.

Perspective is equally important. I strive to immerse the viewer in the landscape by exploring unconventional vantage points, looking down from a height, emphasising vast expanses, or scaling up elements such as mountains or sky. This approach invites the viewer to experience the landscape through my eyes, to feel it as I do, and to hopefully build a sense of connection, of presence with the scene they are looking at. Ultimately, this connection with the land influences every aspect of my painting, from the scale and orientation (portrait, landscape, or square) to the techniques I employ and whether the piece evokes energy or stillness.

INNOVATION THROUGH EXPLORATION

An artist is not just someone who produces finished pieces; they are innovators who constantly test techniques, mediums, and materials while discovering new ideas. Perhaps sometimes artists show us new ways to look at and appreciate landscapes and environments we had previously believed we 'knew' and had allowed to become stale. The creative process is fluid and deeply personal, driven by flexibility, intuition, and discovery. Experimentation and pushing boundaries are vital for growth and originality, as being an artist is inherently tied to exploration, making mistakes, learning from them, and trying again. Embracing this process with curiosity and openness fosters artistic growth. Whether through playful experimentation, process-driven creation, or pushing the limits of traditional materials, this approach keeps your practice evolving and reflective of your experiences.

Experimentation and discovery

Every artist's process is individual and singular, shaped by their experiences, materials, techniques, and inspirations. While learning from others can refine your skills, true growth comes from integrating these lessons into your own work, allowing your style to evolve naturally. Experimentation and embracing mistakes are essential to this process. Mistakes are not just inevitable; they are opportunities, chances to discover something unexpected, push beyond the familiar, and uncover new possibilities. For me, trial and error have been pivotal in refining and growing my practice

Through exploring different materials, themes, and concepts, I moved from working with textiles and threads,

BALANCING CONTROL AND CHAOS

And the Wetlands Shall Rise Again was an experimental painting developed over several months with the goal of creating a large statement piece for an exhibition. I aimed to create a painting that connected with a particular landscape, while maintaining the atmospheric quality that defines my work.

Unusually for me, I began with reference material while also experimenting with new techniques, such as incorporating metallic leaf. This proved challenging, as I navigated both the scale of the work and unfamiliar techniques. At times, relying too heavily on the reference material caused the painting to tighten up more than I intended. To counteract this, I dribbled and flicked paint over the surface to introduce more dynamic marks and a more abstract feel. While I loved the effects, I sacrificed much of the detail I had worked on.

The experimenting at times made it difficult to find the right direction for the painting. It became a process of pushing and pulling over the course of several months – experimenting, trying new things, making mistakes – until, finally, the painting began to resolve itself.

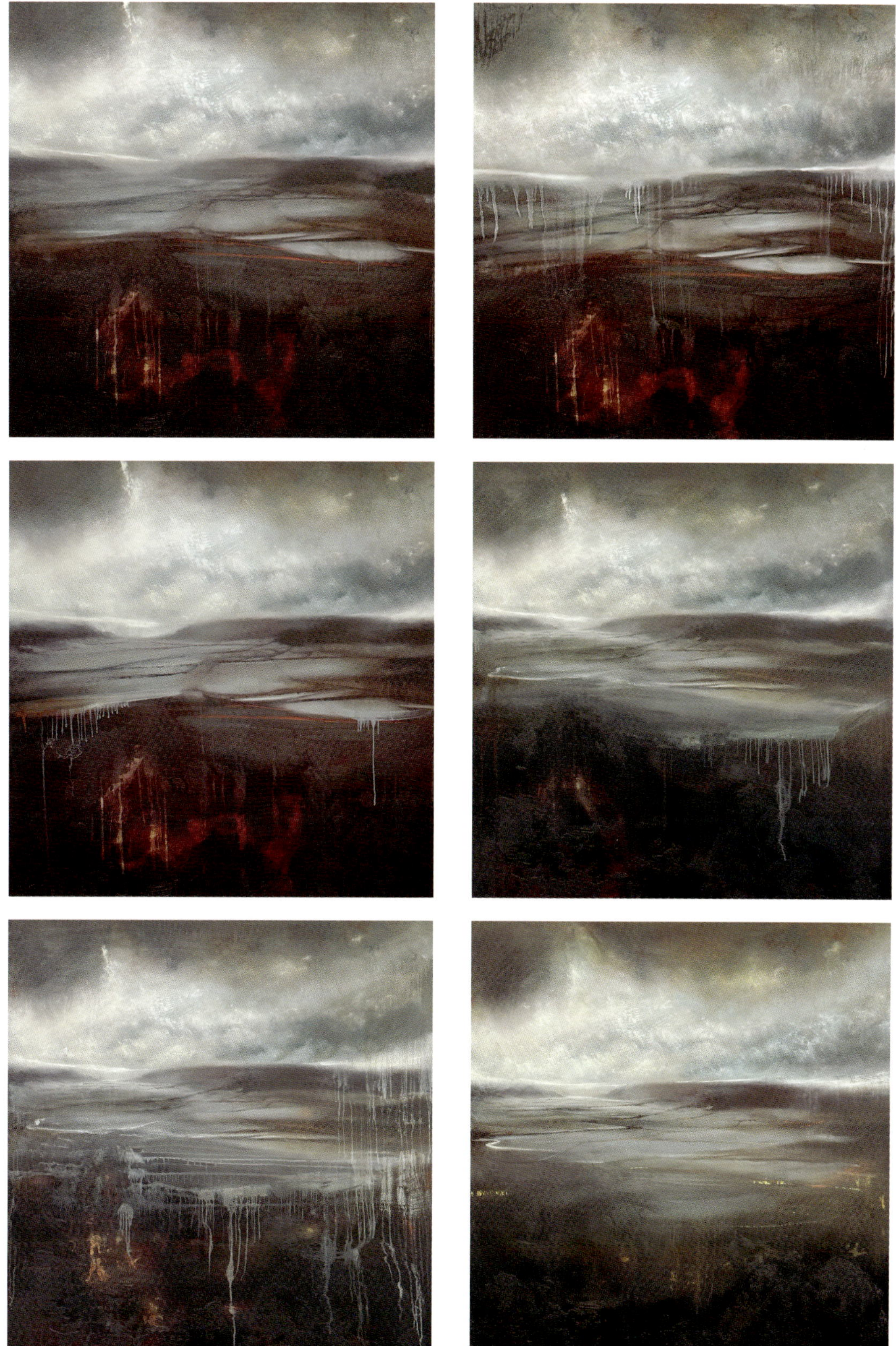

The Wetlands Shall Rise Again – a work in progress, captured through images that illustrate the experimental journey. Trying new techniques, exploring possibilities – until, at last, the painting began to resolve itself.

having been drawn to their rich colours and tactile surfaces, to experimenting with oil paints, which allowed for faster, more dynamic creations while still achieving depth and texture. My early paintings focused on large representational landscapes, utilising impasto techniques and palette knives to build layers that reflected the terrain I was trying to capture. I relied heavily on sketches and photographs before committing paint to canvas.

Over time, I have developed my style as I embraced a more intuitive and experimental approach, moving toward abstraction while still retaining recognisable elements of a landscape. My work will continue to develop as I deepen my understanding of landscapes and colour, incorporating new techniques and materials while exploring opportunities for larger-scale, more abstract, or even installation-based projects.

Developing confidence in your work is a gradual process that requires study, practice, and growth. Over time, you learn how to respond to mistakes and adapt creatively, turning challenges into opportunities for innovation, all the while ensuring your practice remains dynamic and personal.

The power of play

For many artists, innovation is deeply connected to the act of creation. The process of making art becomes an exploration, where mistakes and so-called 'failures' are embraced as catalysts for growth. There is a liberating power in play: experimenting with materials, breaking rules, and releasing the pressure to achieve a specific outcome.

Play does not need a defined purpose; it is about freedom, the freedom to take risks, make mistakes, and explore new possibilities. This mindset encourages me to step beyond my comfort zone and venture into unchartered territories, where experimentation leads to discovery and growth.

My approach to painting is intuitive and experimental, grounded in the interplay of colour, layering, and mark-making. Working with mediums such as cold wax has unlocked exciting opportunities for innovation, encouraging me to be more playful and open in my process. This method allows for spontaneity, enabling me to embrace the unexpected and accidental as integral parts of my work.

I rarely approach a painting with a fixed plan. Instead, I begin by experimenting with familiar techniques, while remaining open to new ideas. I allow the process to guide me, letting the unknown shape the final outcome. As the painting evolves, I follow its suggestions, but resolving a piece often requires adaptability. Sometimes, this means radically shifting direction to strengthen the work.

Maintaining an open mind is essential, even when it is challenging to paint over areas with beautiful colours, textures, or depth. Letting go of these elements can be difficult, but it often results in a stronger, more cohesive painting. This willingness to adapt ensures my creative decisions prioritise the integrity of the whole piece rather than preserving any one part.

Experimenting with unconventional materials also broadens the scope of my practice. Cold wax, for instance, has allowed me to build rich layers of colour, while incorporating materials such as pigments, ash, marble dust, and metallic leaf to add depth and dimension. By pushing boundaries and experimenting in unexpected ways, I continuously discover new avenues for innovation and personal expression.

Finding inspiration through experimentation

Sometimes, the most inspiring moments can occur when I stop trying to control the outcome. By following my intuition and allowing the brush to move freely, I trust that the work will resolve itself. I have learned over the years that it is not necessary to plan every step; rather, it is about creating space for the subconscious to guide the process.

Inspiration often does not present itself fully formed. As I engage with my materials, a dialogue emerges, and the process begins to shape the piece. What starts as an initial idea often evolves in unexpected ways, often beyond my initial intentions, and it is this evolution that excites me.

Experimentation is a powerful catalyst for inspiration. For many artists, inspiration arises not from observation or contemplation, but from the simple act of experimenting with materials, techniques, and new approaches. The process of encountering failure, making mistakes, or experiencing unexpected outcomes can lead to new pathways and insights, especially when your practice is rooted in trial and error.

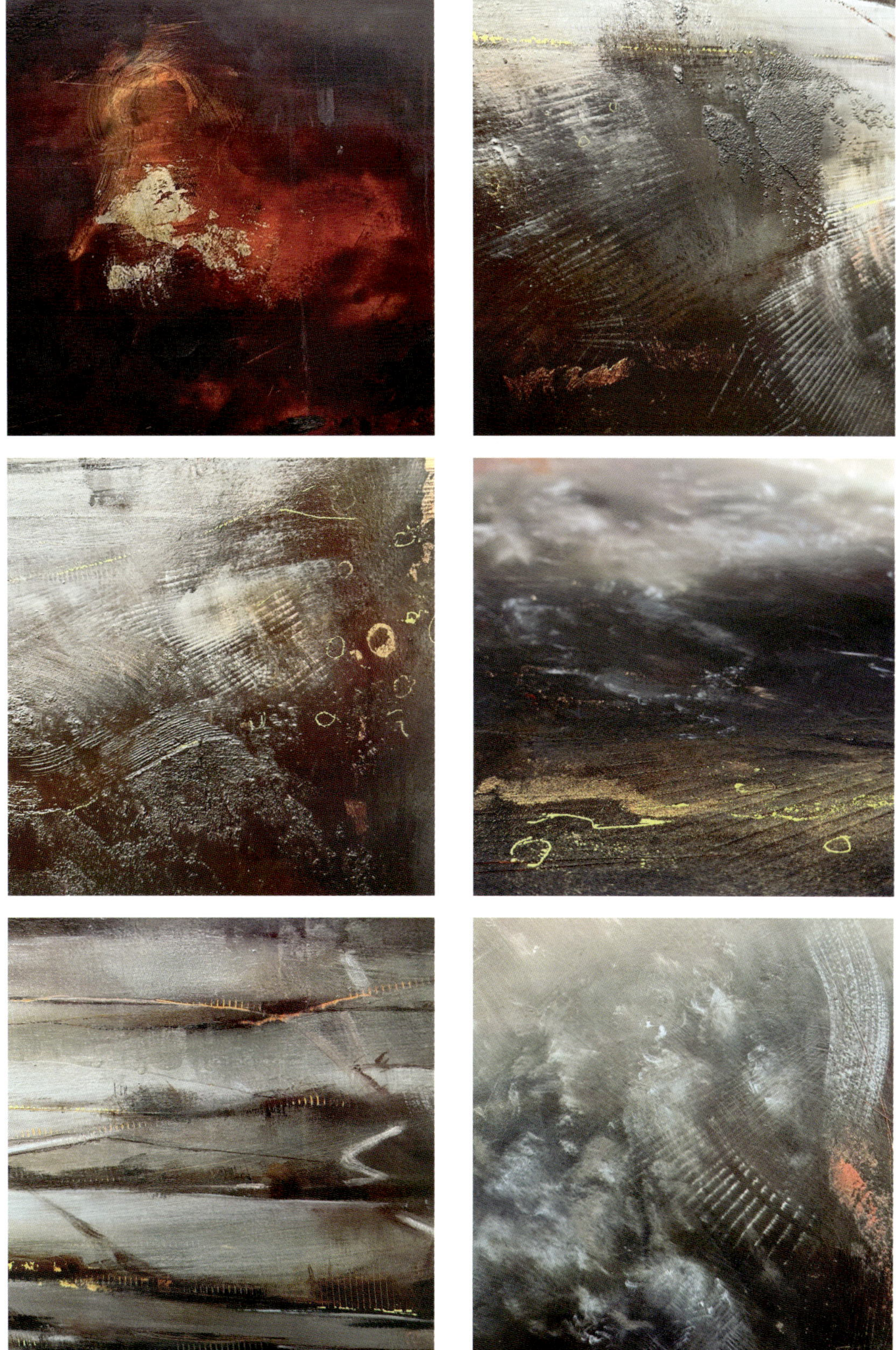

Inspiration through experimentation — exploring a variety of materials, from gold leaf to marble dust, and testing different tools for mark-making to embed new textures and energy into the work.

I cannot always wait for inspiration to strike; instead, I create the conditions for it through experimentation. I will try a previously untried method. Sometimes, the piece does not unfold as expected, but more often than not, those so-called 'mistakes' open up new directions I had not previously considered.

By embracing the unpredictability of experimentation, I open myself to a world of possibilities. Each stroke of the brush and each unexpected outcome becomes a stepping stone in the process, guiding me toward new ideas and innovations. The process of experimentation transforms my artistic practice into a dynamic dialogue, where inspiration is constantly evolving and reshaping itself.

REFLECTION

Taking time to reflect is a crucial part of my artistic journey. Each day, as I leave the studio after a day of painting, I use my walk home to clear my mind. Often, this quiet time leads to breakthroughs, sudden ideas for resolving challenges with a painting: the subconscious is always working, we just have to give it time. However, some issues take longer to unravel, requiring days or even weeks of contemplation. For larger, experimental projects, I may need months to let ideas percolate before a clear direction emerges.

Realisations can also occur in various settings, such as visiting exhibitions or exploring a new landscape, conversations with other artists, and writers. These experiences often spark new ideas that connect with found objects or concepts documented in my sketchbooks. The notion that inspiration just happens and can be switched on when needed is a myth: instead, I constantly juggle numerous project ideas in my mind, many of which I set aside due to time constraints. Most remain parked, waiting for that moment of clarity to join the dots and unlock their potential. This process of reflection is essential for nurturing inspiration, allowing it to grow into fully realised ideas that push my practice forward and foster innovation.

DISCOVERING WHAT MATTERS

Ultimately, what is important to you is what gets you up in the morning and into the studio. Identifying these passions can be challenging; they often become clear only when faced with projects that are difficult to engage with or find motivation in. This struggle can arise when you are asked to step outside your comfort zone, which can be a double-edged sword. While pushing boundaries can serve as a positive challenge, it may also lead to moments of resistance.

Have you ever grappled with a piece of work, not because it stretches your creative muscles, but because you simply cannot connect with it? It may be a subject that does not resonate with you, or a collaboration with an organisation that misaligns with your values. When confronted with such circumstances, it becomes crucial to evaluate whether you can truly produce your best work. Does a project or commission provide the freedom necessary for you to create at your best?

Understanding your values is essential; they form the foundation of what you create and serve as the primary motivation behind your artistic practice. Collaborating with others who share your interests can enrich this experience, allowing you to collectively tell a story that resonates more deeply. For me, my passion for landscape and wildlife informs not only the projects I pursue, but also the creatives and organisations I choose to work with.

While my work may not be overtly narrative, I actively seek collaborations that allow us to weave together narratives reflecting our shared interests. These partnerships foster a stronger narrative, guiding me into new territories that lead to a richer and more profound body of work. The exploration and learning that comes from collaboration ultimately results in a more engaging artistic experience.

While anyone can create a visually appealing piece, the true connection often lies in the story behind it, whether it is the narrative of how the artwork was conceived, insights into your creative process, or the themes you aim to explore. These stories deepen the artwork, inviting viewers into a more meaningful dialogue and enriching their experience.

Having a compelling story to tell ignites inspiration and drives you to create a cohesive body of work. It encourages innovative approaches to your practice, expanding your portfolio, enhancing your skills, and introducing you to new mediums. By aligning your creative endeavours with what is genuinely important to you, you can create work that deeply resonates and endures.

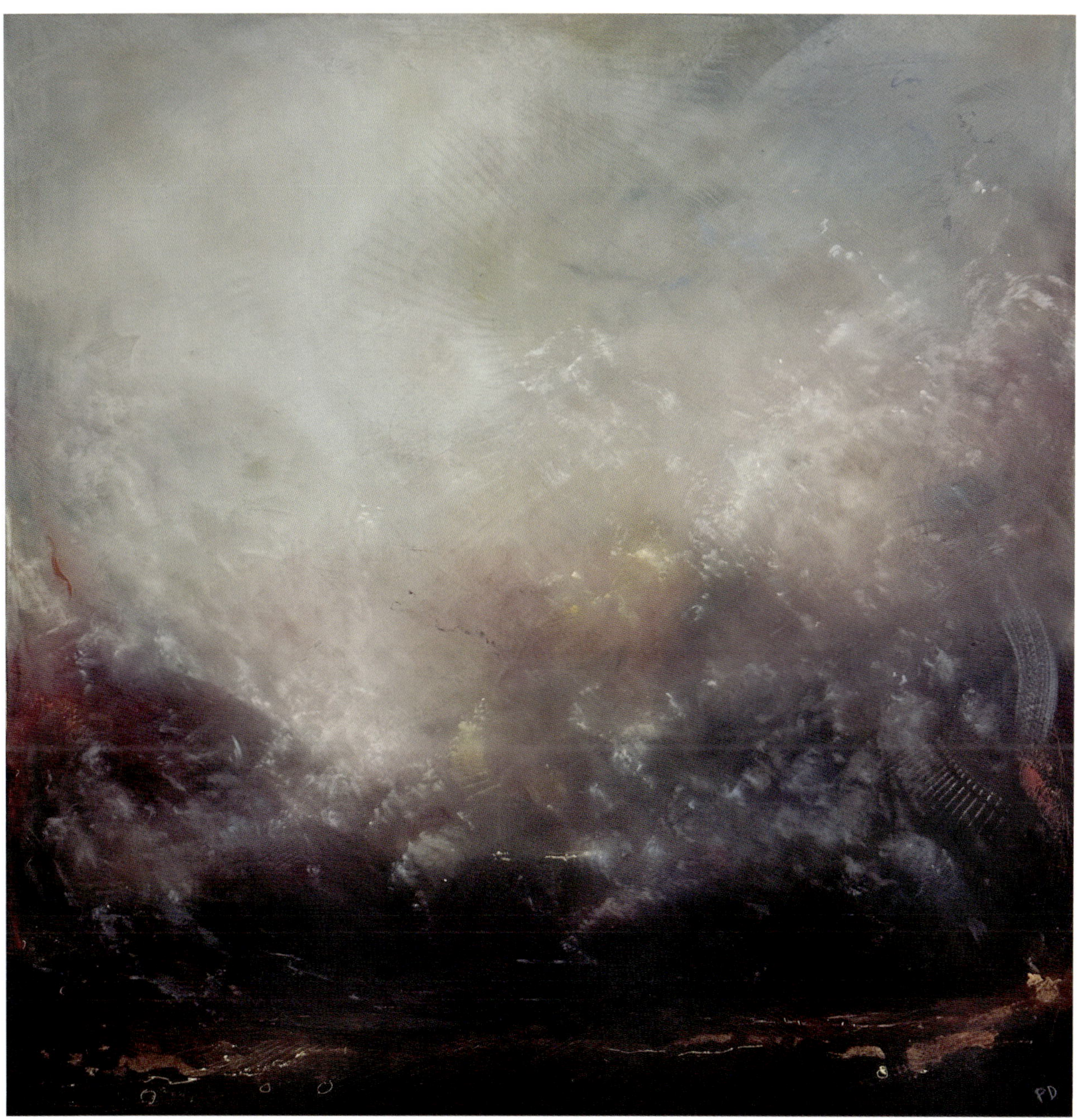

Burn Back (60 × 60cm/23½ × 23½in, oils, cold wax and gold leaf on Arches Huile paper bonded to a wooden panel). With its delicate shades of greys, pinks, yellows, and blues seamlessly blending, this painting evokes the ethereal sense of smoke drifting across the moorland. While it exudes a serene atmosphere, it draws inspiration from a darker narrative, reflecting the complexities and challenges that impact this landscape.

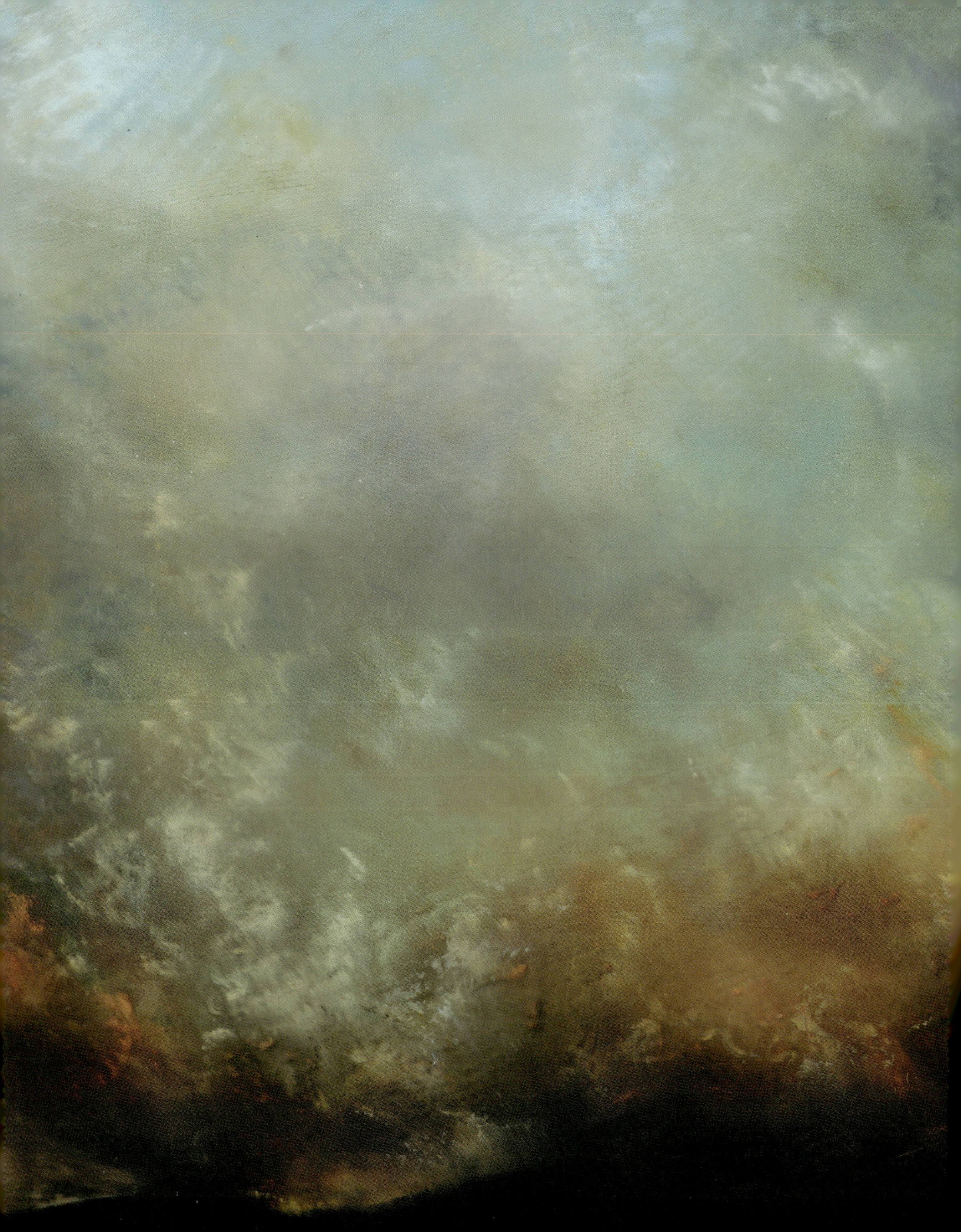

CHAPTER 10

FINISHING YOUR WORK

'A work is never completed, but merely abandoned'
Paul Valéry

In the final chapter, we explore the essential steps for finishing your paintings and ensuring they are exhibition ready. We cover topics such as drying times and varnishing techniques to protect your work. You will find a step-by-step guide for bonding paintings on paper to wooden panels, along with valuable suggestions for mounting and framing that enhances the presentation of your artwork, as well as offering a level of protection to it. Additionally, we discuss the importance of proper storage, packing, and transportation methods.

WHEN IS A PAINTING FINISHED?

This is a question I am often asked, and I am not sure I have a definitive answer. I usually rely on my gut feeling to determine when a painting is complete. There is a sense of excitement as I begin to resolve a painting, adding finishing touches, defining pathways and areas of interest in the work. However, that excitement can sometimes be tempered when I revisit the painting with fresh eyes and realise there is still more to do.

Generally, a painting feels finished to me when all the elements are in place; the composition is visually balanced; when no areas feel empty or overly cluttered; colours and textures work cohesively; and I am satisfied with the level of detail and refinement. It is important that the painting does not feel overworked – knowing when to stop is critical, as adding more can sometimes detract from the overall effect. Ultimately, a painting is finished when you decide it is.

DRYING TIMES

Using cold wax can speed up the drying times of your oil paintings, but factors such as your working environment and the colours you use also play a significant role. Drying times vary depending on room temperature, airflow, and the surfaces you are painting on. While each painting is unique, understanding the factors that affect drying times can help you gain greater control over the process.

Warmer temperatures generally dry paintings faster than those in cooler environments. While increasing the room temperature may slightly accelerate the process, the effect is minimal and unlikely to significantly impact drying times. Using direct heat, such as a hairdryer (as is common practice with water-based paints), is not effective and can warm the cold wax, potentially releasing excess solvent fumes that may be hazardous to your health. To speed up drying, focus instead on improving airflow.

The pigments (colour) in your oil paints also influence drying times, as some contain properties that accelerate this process, while others may slow it down. As a rule, paints with higher oil content take longer to dry. Any oil

OPPOSITE: *Tumultuous (cropped)*, measuring 60 × 60cm (23½ × 23½in), combines oils and cold wax on a cradled wooden panel. Soft colour and tonal transitions are achieved, allowing hues to intermingle harmoniously while preserving their individual identities, creating a dynamic yet balanced composition.

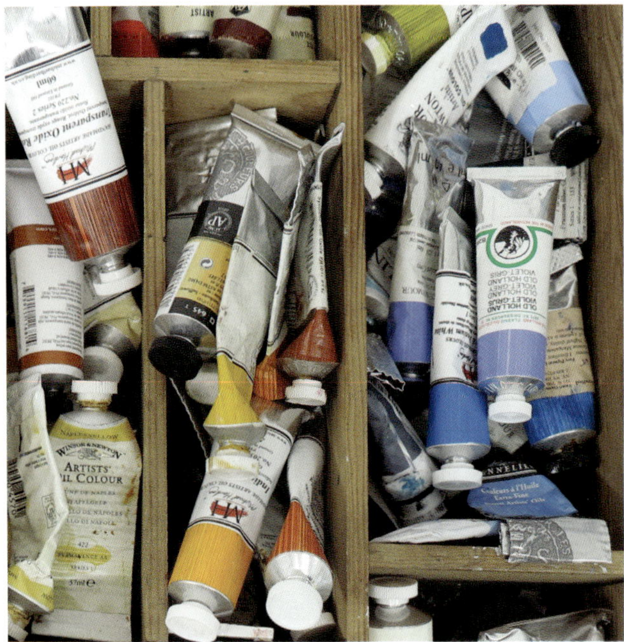

Fast-drying colours include burnt umber, cobalt blue, raw sienna, and burnt sienna. In contrast, slower-drying paints include vibrant reds such as cadmium red and alizarin crimson, yellows such as cadmium yellow and Naples yellow, blacks such as mars black, lamp black, and ivory black, as well as whites such as titanium white.

paint that is transparent, a cadmium or a hue contains lots of oil and therefore will have a longer drying time. Pigments such as earth tones dry faster than others because they have a higher oil absorption rate, which speeds up the drying process, whereas organic pigments such as alizarin crimson tend to dry slower due to their lower oil absorption rate. Additionally, the type of oil used as a binder will affect the drying speed, for example, linseed oil dries faster than walnut oil or safflower oil (Casey, 2022)

Other factors that influence drying times include:

- Humidity: Low humidity allows paintings to dry faster than high humidity.
- Surfaces: Absorbent surfaces, such as Arches Huile paper, speed up the drying process by soaking up the paint.

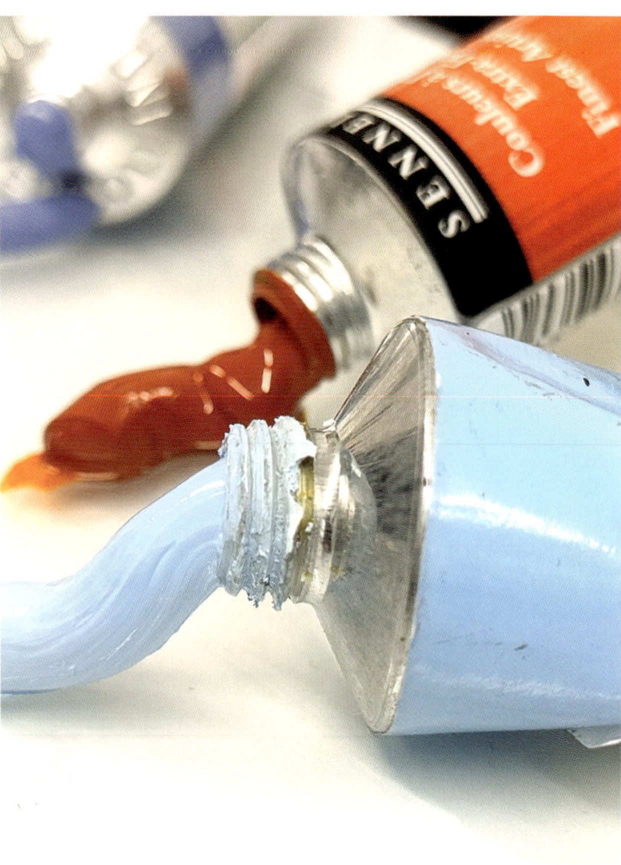

Paints are classified by their drying speed into four distinct categories: Very Slow, Slow, Medium, and Fast. You can find this valuable information on the paint label or online product information sheets.

- Dry materials: Pigments, marble dust, sand, and so on, incorporated into your painting (*see* Chapter 5) will absorb the oil.
- Paint thickness: Thicker layers of paint will take longer to dry.

If you want to test whether your painting is dry, gently touch a small, inconspicuous area of the paint surface with the back of your finger. If it feels tacky or sticky, the paint is still drying. If it feels dry and smooth, it has likely reached the touch-dry stage. Always perform these tests carefully to avoid damaging your painting.

MOUNTING YOUR WORK

In Chapter 2, we covered how to bond paper to a wooden panel before painting. However, some artists prefer to complete their painting on paper first and then bond it to a panel afterwards. This method offers greater freedom for creating expressive marks that extend beyond the painting's edges and allows for cropping to achieve a stronger composition. Unless you plan to crop the painting before mounting, I recommend purchasing your panel in advance of painting and cutting your paper slightly larger. This approach ensures you can use a standard panel, avoiding the higher cost of ordering a custom-sized one.

What you will need:

- a wooden panel, or cradled panel approximately 1–2cm (½–¾in) smaller than your finished painting. Ensure the surface is not primed, as this will prevent proper adhesion.
- tissue paper to protect your painting
- a sharp craft knife
- PVA or heavy/extra heavy gel medium (it is best to use pH-neutral glue so that it does not discolour or become brittle)
- a squeegee or roller
- a palette knife
- fine or extra fine grade sandpaper and sanding block.

Step 1: Prepare your painting
On a clean, flat surface, lay down some tissue paper, then place your dry painting face-down. This will protect it from picking up any debris from the surface and being damaged. Ensure your painting is dry before you attempt this.

Step 2: Apply adhesive
Take the pH-neutral PVA or heavy/extra heavy gel medium and generously coat the front of your panel, paying particular attention to the edges and corners. Spread the adhesive evenly using a palette knife, a squeegee, or a roller for larger surfaces.

Step 3: Position the panel
Carefully position the panel face-down on the back of your painting. You may find it helpful to hold the painting and panel up to a light source to ensure they are properly aligned and that the panel does not overlap the border of the painting.

Step 4: Bond the surfaces
Flip your panel so that your painting is now face-up. Keeping the tissue on the surface of your painting, gently smooth out the surface with your hands, noting any lumps or unevenness. Start from the centre of the panel and work your way outwards, smoothing any lumps of adhesive toward the edges of the panel. In this example I am using a baren to help smooth out the surface.

Step 5: Leave to dry
Once you are satisfied that your painting is adhered to the panel, including the edges and corners, place more tissue on top along with some heavy weights such as books or other panels to help the surfaces bond. For my smaller pieces I use an old book press to help bond the surfaces, but this is not essential as a heavy weight works just as well. Leave overnight to dry fully.

Step 6: Paint the edges
After the adhesive has dried, flip your panel so the painting is face-down on your work surface, using tissue to protect it. Before trimming the painting, you may want to paint the edges and the back of the panel as this is a quicker way to do so and minimises the risk of splashing paint onto your painting. I recommend using white acrylic gesso to quickly apply a couple of coats to the bare wood.

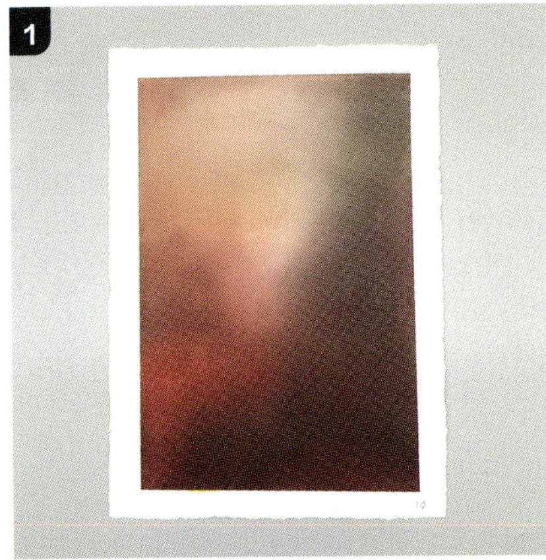

Place the painting face-down on a surface.

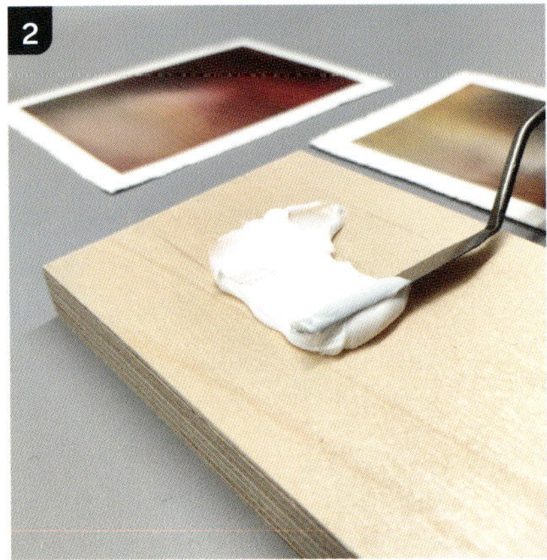

Apply adhesive.

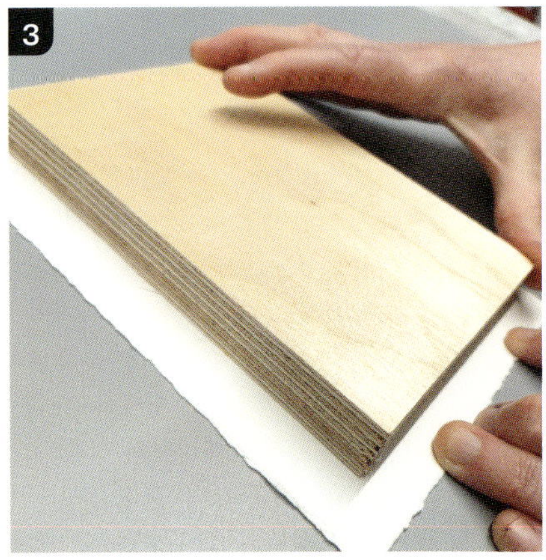

Hold the painting up to the light.

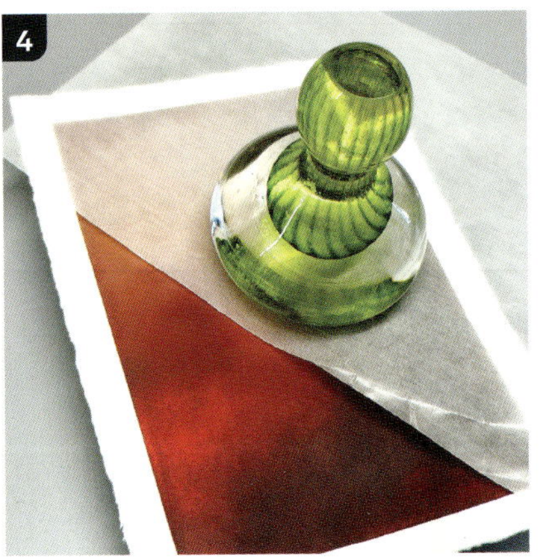

Smooth down the surface.

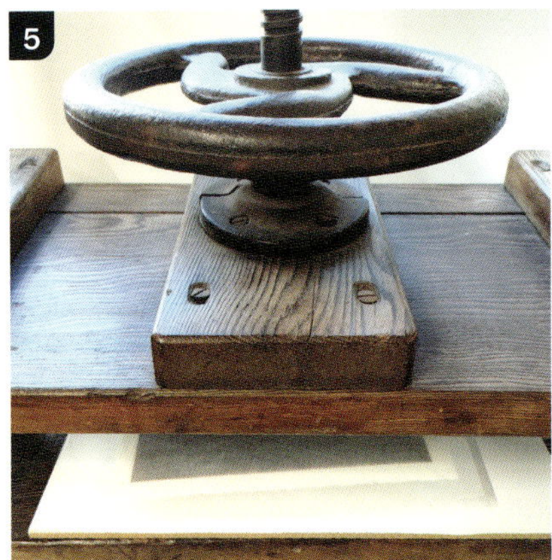

Place weights on to the painting.

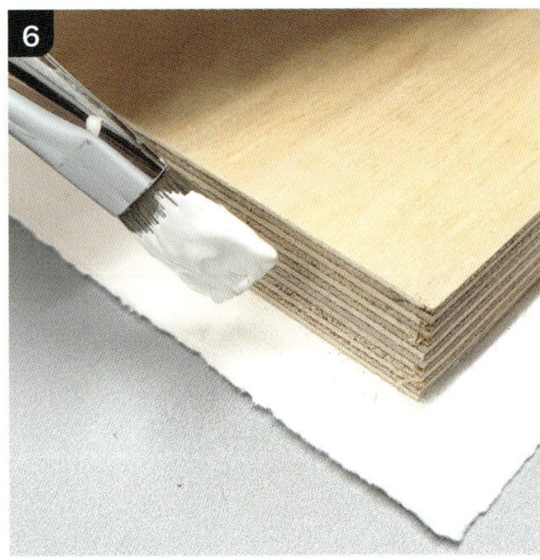

Paint the edges.

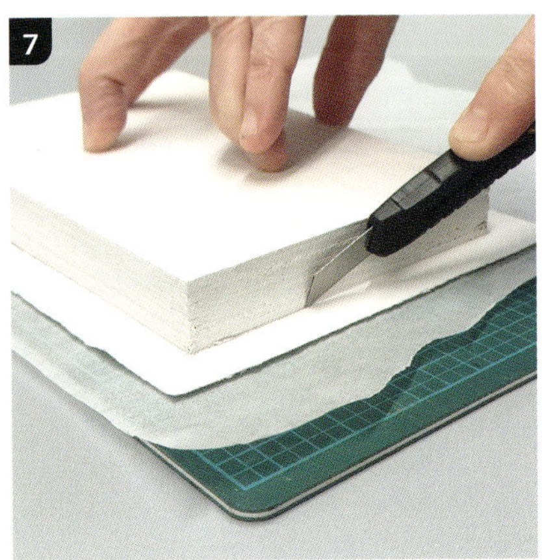

Trim the edges.

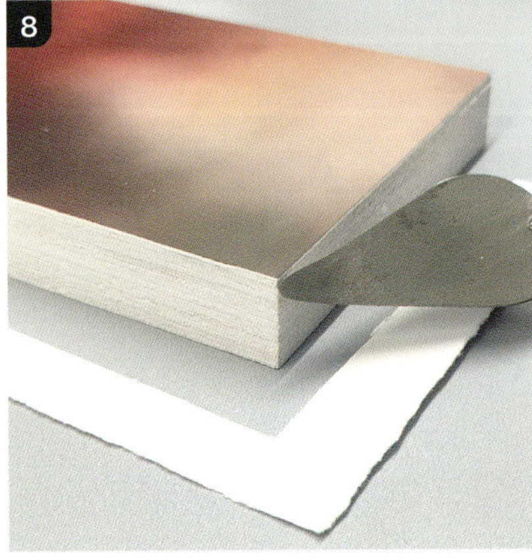

Check the edges.

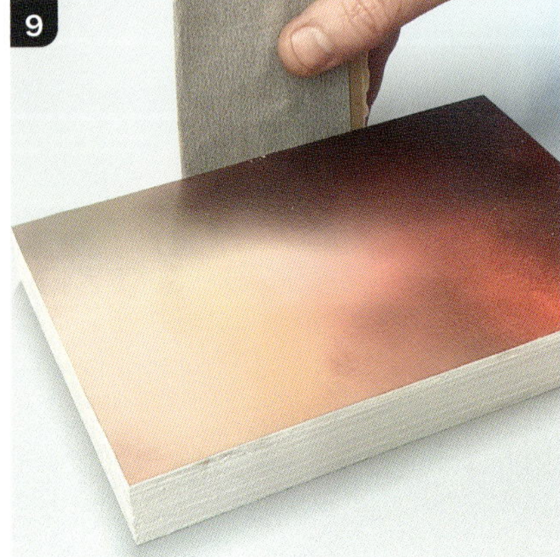

Sand the edges.

Step 7: Trim the edges
Once the paint on the edges and back of your panel has dried, use a sharp craft knife to carefully trim the painting border, using the panel edges as a guide. A sharp knife is essential, as the thick Arches Huile paper makes it challenging to achieve a clean cut without a sharp blade.

Step 8: Check edges and corners
After trimming, inspect the edges and corners of your panel to ensure the painting is securely fixed. If the paper lifts, use a palette knife to apply adhesive into the gaps, wiping off any excess and smoothing the surface with your hands. Avoid getting adhesive on the painting, and repeat as needed until securely fixed, then allow to dry.

Step 9: Finish the edges
Once the adhesive is dry, use fine grade sandpaper wrapped around a block and gently sand the edges of your panel, removing any dried adhesive and smoothing any ragged edges of your painting. Be very careful during this step to avoid damaging your painting. Your painting is now ready to varnish and frame.

VARNISHING YOUR WORK

If your painting is not going to be protected by glass, varnishing is an important step to consider. It provides a protective surface that helps prevent scratching, guards against UV damage, and protects the painting from dirt and dust that can accumulate over time. Varnishing also enhances the vibrancy and depth of the colours in your painting, drawing attention to detail, emphasising textures, and unifying the surface.

There are several varnishing options for oil paintings, each creating a different effect. You can choose from gloss, satin, or matt finishes to suit the aesthetic of your piece. For oil and cold wax paintings, a varnish can help restore a gloss or satin sheen to an otherwise matt surface.

Traditional varnishes

Damar varnish is a traditional option for oil paintings, as it allows the oil paint to breathe while still curing and is made from plant-based resin. Gamblin's Gamvar is another well-known varnish that works similarly, permitting the painting to breathe during curing. However, it is made from synthetic resin, dries faster, and is less likely to yellow over time. Whichever varnish you choose, they should only be applied when the painting is touch-dry, ensuring the surface is clean. Use brushes to apply thin layers and avoid pooling the varnish, as this can create an uneven surface.

When varnishing an oil and cold wax painting, it is important to test the varnish on a discrete area first to ensure it does not react with the painting. Cold wax can be more sensitive to solvents and varnishes, especially when applied thickly or when not fully dry. When using a high concentration of cold wax in your painting as I do, there is a risk that applying varnish too soon can lead to smudging, streaking, or softening of the paint or cold wax. The drying time of your cold wax painting is crucial; be sure to allow the wax medium to fully cure and dry, which can take anywhere from six weeks to six months, depending on the thickness of the paint, the colours used and the environment.

Smearing and smudging of paint and cold wax when varnishing is something I have experienced. After several years of experimenting with different varnishes, my preferred method of finishing a painting is to apply thin layers of cold wax. While this method does not offer the same UV protection or long-term durability as traditional varnishes such as Damar and Gamvar, it allows me to maintain consistency in my work by utilising a medium already present in the painting.

Application of cold wax as a varnish

When applying cold wax as a varnish, it is important to ensure the surface is clean and free of dust or anything that could interfere with the finish. To apply I recommend using a squeegee, as it allows for a thin, even spread across the painting, helping to avoid streaks or patches. When you first apply the cold wax, you will notice that the colours in your painting appear deeper and more vibrant. However, once it dries overnight, the surface will return to a matt finish. At this point, you can take a clean paper towel and gently buff the surface to achieve a satin look or continue buffing for a high gloss finish. If the initial layer does not create a consistent

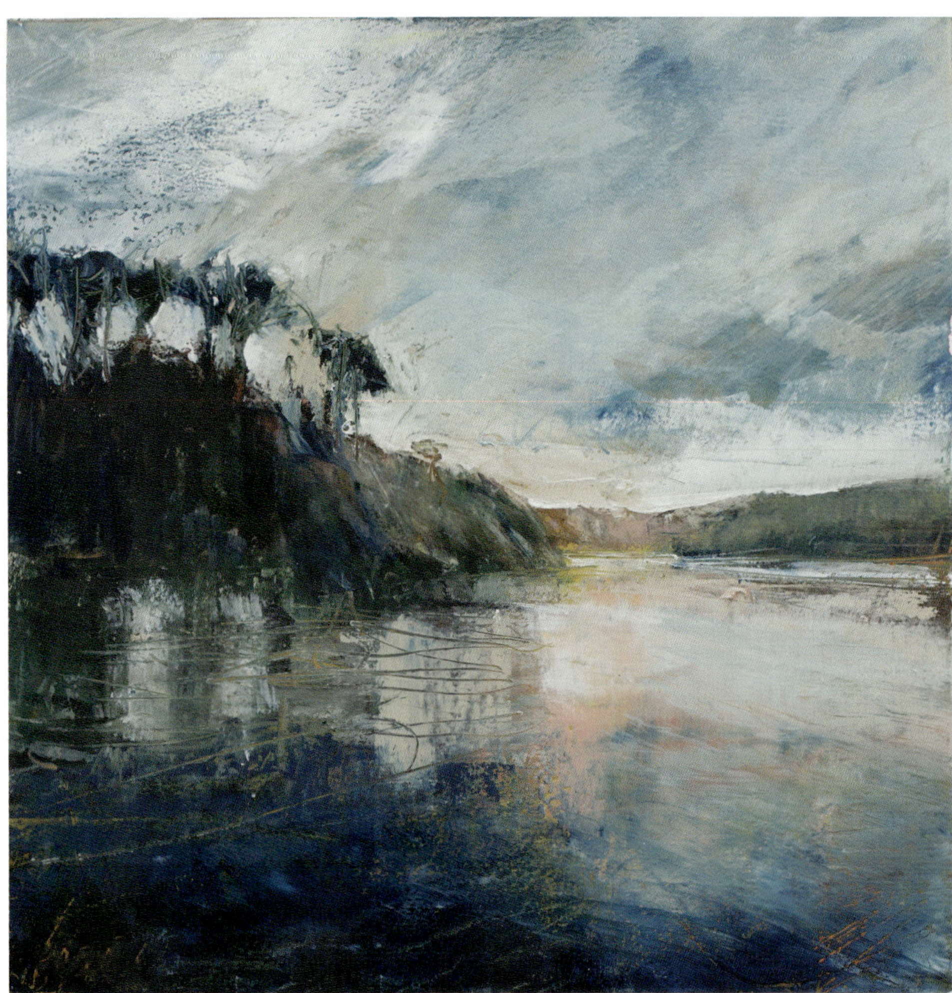

Frenchman's Creek Dusk, 35 × 35cm (13¾ × 13¾in), by Sophie Velzian is an oil and cold wax painting on Arches Huile paper, varnished with three coats of cold wax and buffed to a soft sheen. This sheen beautifully complements the gentle colours of the piece, ensuring that the varnish enhances rather than detracts from the softness of the painting.

sheen, you can repeat the process by applying another thin layer of cold wax, allowing it to dry, and then buffing it again. Keep repeating until you achieve your desired level of finish.

Occasionally, you may find that a section of the painting has a textured, bobbly finish, which remains matt even after buffing. This can happen when the cold wax has not been applied thinly enough. The best way to remove this is to gently dab it with a small amount of solvent on a paper towel. After allowing the solvent to evaporate and ensuring the paint has not been softened, you can apply a thin layer of cold wax and repeat the varnishing process.

For textured areas, such as those with marble dust or heavy impasto, applying cold wax with a squeegee can be tricky. You can gently warm the cold wax by placing it on a warm surface (such as a radiator or windowsill) in a well-ventilated space. Aim to soften the cold wax rather than completely melt it; avoid putting it on a heat ring and do not heat it over an open flame. The softened wax is easier to apply, allowing you to brush it into the textured areas. Apply the cold wax as thinly as possible; otherwise, it will not dry transparently and may create a frosted effect on the surface. If you want to create a soft sheen or gloss finish, which is particularly effective at highlighting textured surfaces, use a clean, dry, stiff shoe polish brush to buff the surface. Gently work the brush across the textured area, taking care not to leave any brush hairs behind.

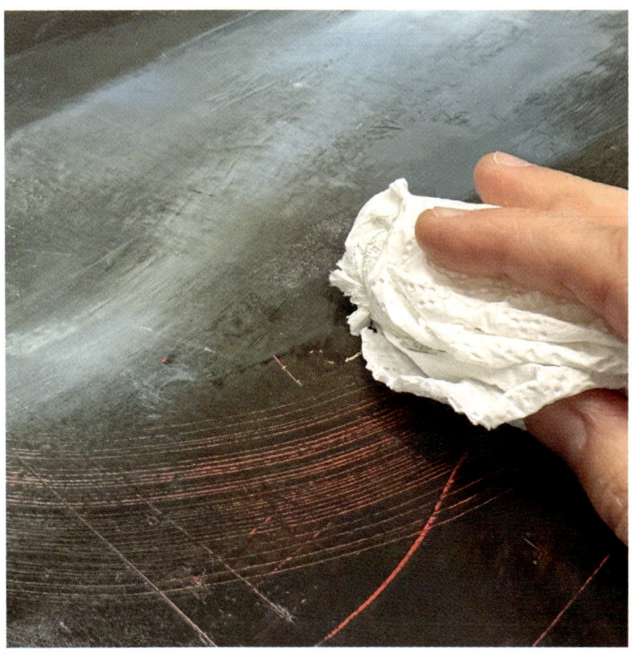

Ensure your painting is dry before varnishing. If the paint is not fully dry, you risk lifting the paint or damaging the surface, which can be very difficult to fix. Patience is key when applying cold wax or any varnish to an oil painting; take your time to allow each layer to dry fully to achieve the desired finish.

FRAMING YOUR WORK

Framing can be used to protect your work, but it can also enhance your painting by giving it space to breathe, drawing attention to specific elements of the painting as well as creating a visual edge to the work. A frame can help integrate a painting into its surroundings and can also give the perception of adding more value to a painting, especially when framed using quality, museum-standard materials. Framing is an artform and identifying and working with a skilled craftsperson can help create the best option for your artwork, utilise new technologies and products as well as providing solutions for framing and displaying more complex projects.

Framing for protection

A frame serves multiple protective functions for a painting, particularly for delicate artwork. If a piece is likely to be displayed, framing it behind glass provides an additional layer of protection against dirt and humidity changes, even if the work has already been varnished. Frames also make paintings easier to handle and hang without direct contact with the painted surface, reducing the risk of damage from touch. They offer protection during transit and though frames themselves may occasionally get damaged, replacing a frame is far easier than repairing a painting.

When displaying works on paper with unpainted or unvarnished borders, it is best to frame them behind glass to shield the exposed paper from environmental changes. A mount (or matt board) ensures that the glass does not touch the surface of the artwork, minimising the risk of the painting sticking to the glass. It is crucial to choose materials classified as fine art or museum quality, as cheaper mount boards often contain acids that can damage your artwork over time. For larger paintings on paper, specialised glazing, such as anti-reflective or museum-grade glass, reduces reflections and shields the

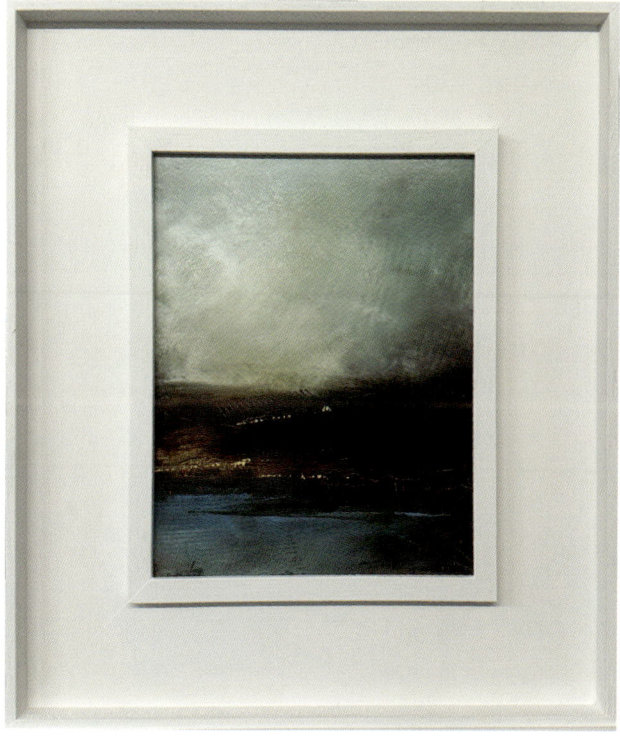

Safe Harbour, 20 × 25cm (8 × 10in), oil, cold wax, and gold leaf, demonstrates how a well-chosen frame can enhance a smaller painting. By adding scale, it draws the viewer in and gives the artwork room to breathe. This approach is especially effective with St Ives-style frames, which create a sense of space without overwhelming or diminishing the artwork.

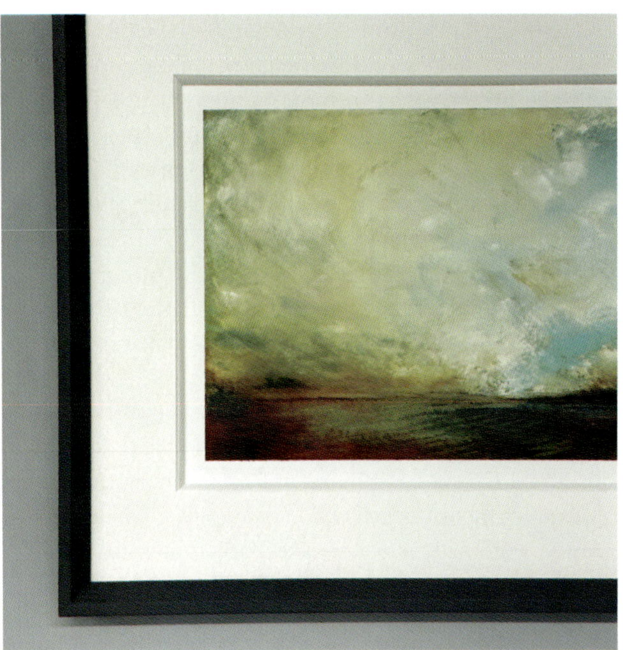

Mount board or matt board creates a gap to prevent the glass from touching your painting. Additionally, mounts can enhance your framing. In this example, a deep bevel mount has been used to create a distinctive finish, adding depth and interest to the overall presentation, while ensuring the artwork remains protected from direct contact with the glass.

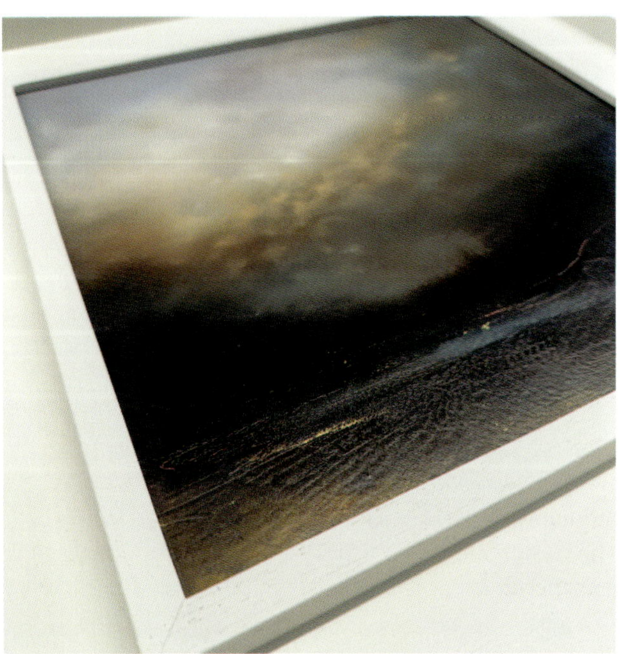

Soft Autumnal Glow, 30 × 30cm (12 × 12in), oil and cold wax, and finished with gold leaf. This piece is framed with a hand-painted St Ives style frame, featuring a traditional rebate that the painting sits within, partially covering the surface and offering protection to the edges.

artwork from harmful UV rays that can cause colours to fade over time.

Paintings on wooden panels and canvas can be framed without glass (including paintings on paper mounted to wooden panel) and can be protected from environmental changes if varnished (see section above). However, the edges of paintings are often vulnerable to bumps, scratches, and abrasions during transportation or hanging. A frame provides a level of protection, especially if it has a rebate, which completely encloses the edges of the painting. Rebate frames are a traditional way to frame paintings, offering both effective protection and a solution for concealing untidy edges. Alternatively, frames without a rebate, such as tray frames, can also offer protection if the frame has a lip that is slightly higher than the artwork itself.

Enhancing your work with framing

A frame can significantly complement and enhance the visual impact of your painting. A simple frame provides a visual boundary, giving the artwork breathing space between it and the surface it hangs on. This allows the painting to shine in, rather than compete with, its surroundings. Framing can have a similar effect to removing the tape from a small painting on paper. Have you noticed how a painting can suddenly come into its own once the crisp white border is revealed? A simple frame can achieve the same effect for paintings on panels or canvas, further enhancing their visual impact.

Equally important is choosing a frame that highlights key aspects of the painting, such as colours, textures, and themes. This can help draw the viewer's eye into and around the artwork. For example, selecting the right colour for the inner or outer part of a slip frame can draw attention to specific colours within the painting, guiding the viewer's focus. Framing your artwork requires some important decisions to make and can leave you feeling a little unsure and anxious as to whether you have made the right decision. Sometimes it is difficult to know until you see the finished piece whether your decision is the correct one.

When framing, it is important to strike a balance, ensuring that the frame gives your painting the breathing space it deserves. With smaller paintings, there is often a tendency to choose a small frame, or a small mount,

The style of a frame can dramatically affect the overall look and feel of your artwork. Ornate frames, often associated with classical works, may not be the best choice for contemporary paintings, where a simpler, more minimalist frame could be a better fit.

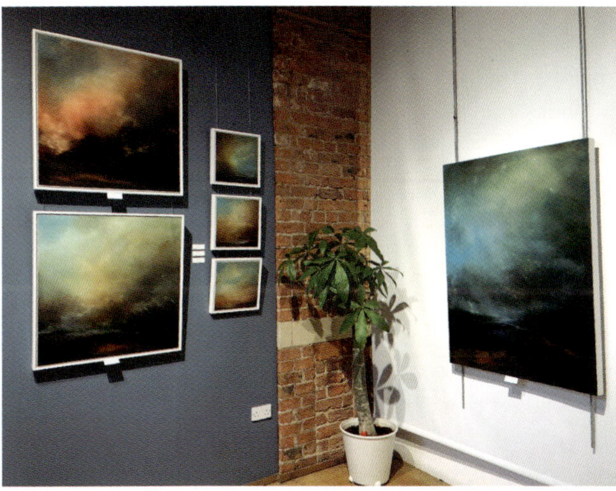

In this collection, the large painting on a deep cradle board was left unframed, as the cradle served as a built-in frame. Paintings on shallower cradles were finished with simple tray frames for added protection and presentation. The smaller works were similarly framed, ensuring a cohesive and unified appearance across the entire collection.

to avoid overwhelming the artwork. However, this can result in the painting feeling cramped. A small painting can benefit from a simple frame with a large border or 'moat', which adds scale and draws the viewer in, allowing the painting to breathe. This approach works particularly well with St Ives-style frames for smaller pieces, as they provide space without making the artwork feel 'lost' or swamped by its surroundings. Just as you create quiet spaces in your painting, the frame can offer the same sense of space and room for the painting to breathe.

For larger-scale works, the presence of the painting itself is often enough, and adding a bulky frame can make the artwork feel cumbersome, drawing attention to the frame rather than the painting. The size of the frame should not only be considered for aesthetic balance but also for practical reasons, such as weight. For example, a large painting on a deep cradle wooden panel may not need a frame at all, as the cradle itself can serve as a built-in frame, giving the piece a contemporary feel. A shallower cradle, however, may benefit from a tray frame, which offers protection while elevating the painting's presence.

The style of the frame is also crucial, as it can dramatically affect the overall look and feel of your artwork. Ornate frames, often associated with classical works, may not be the best choice for contemporary paintings, where a simpler, more minimalist frame could be a better fit.

When choosing a frame, it is also important to consider where the paintings will be displayed and whether they will be hung together. While this may be outside your control, when preparing a new collection for an exhibition or gallery, I always ensure that the frames complement each other. This creates a cohesive experience for the viewer. There is nothing more challenging for a curator than working with a collection of paintings framed in a variety of styles that lack harmony. A mismatched selection of frames can distract the viewer and detract from the artwork itself rather than enhance it.

A CURATOR'S PERSPECTIVE ON FRAMING

Courtney Spencer (aka Court) is a curator, collaborator, and artist who specialises in curating exhibitions in both gallery and non-traditional spaces. She also sources artworks for collectors and commissions pieces for public and private settings. Her collaborations include projects with The British Library, the National Trust, Leeds Playhouse, and The Mercer Art Gallery in Harrogate. In 2022, she founded The Art Court to support artists and collectors. She shares her professional insights and perspectives on framing artwork.

Framing is far more than a protective or decorative element – it is an essential aspect of how an artwork is perceived and experienced. As a curator, I view framing as a critical tool that elevates a piece, enhances its perceived value, reinforces the narrative, and provides subtle insights into the artist's values and intentions. A well-considered frame can significantly influence how a painting or artwork resonates with its audience.

When making framing decisions, it's important to think beyond the individual artwork and consider the broader context. For solo exhibitions, framing choices should work harmoniously across the entire body of work. Consistency can create a sense of cohesion, but a thoughtful variety of framing approaches might also serve to emphasise distinct aspects of different pieces. These decisions depend on the exhibition's goals and the story the artist or curator seeks to tell.

I often gravitate towards fairly neutral frames, though some works call for bolder, more unconventional choices. Ultimately, the responsibility of framing falls to the artist, who must present their work in a way that feels true to their intentions and enhances the overall impact of the piece. While curators can sometimes collaborate with artists on framing decisions, in most cases, artists must consider framing without knowing the context in which the work will be displayed. This uncertainty highlights the importance of well-thought-out framing choices that are adaptable and allow for reframing if required.

Framing in group exhibitions

In group exhibitions, the curator's role is to consider the context and curate a cohesive experience for the viewer. Framing becomes part of the visual language of the exhibition, helping to establish a rhythm or dialogue among the works. Uniform framing can create a sense of unity, guiding viewers through the space, while deliberately varied framing can add dynamism, particularly if the diversity aligns with the exhibition's conceptual themes. Striking the right balance requires careful attention to how frames interact with one another, the artwork, and the gallery environment.

Practical considerations are equally important. For example, non-reflective glass can improve the visibility of artworks under gallery lighting and is essential for capturing clear photographs of the exhibition. Museum glass is another option that offers a UV filter to protect work that is susceptible to sun damage.

Additionally, ornate or elaborate frames that might suit a domestic or private collection could appear overwhelming or out of place in a minimalist gallery setting. It is useful to know the context, as framing should harmonise with the exhibition venue's aesthetic and the expectations of its audience.

Narrative and conceptual framing

In thematic exhibitions, framing can be used to reinforce the curatorial concept. For instance, in a show exploring sustainability, frames made from recycled or ethically sourced materials can support the overarching message. These decisions are often the result of collaboration between the artist, curator, and framer, ensuring that framing choices enhance the narrative without overshadowing the artworks themselves.

Practical and logistical considerations

Beyond aesthetics, framing plays a crucial role in the safe transport and preservation of artworks. Works on paper, for instance, benefit from archival-grade materials to protect against environmental damage. Frames for touring exhibitions must be durable, designed to withstand repeated handling and packing, and equipped with appropriate fixings for secure installation.

Attention to logistical details is essential for a smooth exhibition process. Before installation, it's important to clarify the technical requirements of the frames, including specific fixings and if there is a limit on the size and weight. For example, the choice of frame materials and hardware may be influenced by how the artwork will be displayed, whether it's wall-mounted, suspended, or integrated into a larger installation. Similarly, transportation considerations should inform framing decisions to ensure the artwork remains secure from studio to gallery and beyond.

Conclusion

Framing is more than a finishing touch, it is an integral part of the art itself, shaping how it is seen, understood, and appreciated. By carefully considering both the artistic and practical aspects of framing, artists and curators can elevate the presentation of an artwork and create meaningful connections between the piece, its audience, and its environment.

STORING AND TRANSPORTING YOUR WORK

Whether you are working in the studio, painting en plein air or delivering your work to a gallery, ensuring your artwork is safely stored and transported is essential. Both wet and finished paintings require careful handling, especially when travelling long distances or working outside your usual environment.

While your work is wet

Transporting wet oil paintings can be challenging, although for works on paper, the process is relatively simple. Wrap your paintings loosely in greaseproof paper or tissue to protect the surface and keep them flat to prevent smudging. Depending on how wet the paintings are, the protective paper may stick to the surface. As soon as you get the work back to the studio, carefully unwrap them and make any necessary adjustments if the protective wrap has lifted any paint. Then leave your paintings to dry naturally.

For larger works on canvas or wooden panels, the process is more complex. The safest option is to place your artwork in a crate, ensuring it is laid flat. Crates provide the best protection against accidental bumps or shifts during transportation, minimising the risk of damage to the wet surface. They also allow you to stack paintings on top of each other. While crates are an investment, they are reusable and worthwhile if you frequently transport pieces of similar sizes. A cheaper alternative is a slightly oversized cardboard box laid flat. This can mimic the function of a crate but may not be strong enough to support stacking multiple paintings.

Transporting finished work

When transporting finished work, there are several important considerations to ensure your paintings arrive safely at their destination, whether that is a gallery or a collector's home. Before wrapping your painting in bubble-wrap, place a layer of glassine, wax paper, or tissue paper over the surface. Even if the painting is dry and varnished, materials such as bubble wrap can leave imprints on the surface of your work. While these marks can often be buffed out with a paper towel, they are not something you want your gallery or collector to encounter. Bubble wrap is an excellent protective material, but its plastic surface can cling to the painting. To prevent this, always place a barrier between the bubble wrap and the artwork.

After adding the protective layer of glassine, place a sheet of cardboard, cut to the size of the painting, over the front of the artwork to shield it from sharp objects that could penetrate the packaging material. If your work is glazed, adding foam protection to the glass to act as a buffer can help safeguard it against impact damage. Secure protective foam or cardboard corners to the painting, then wrap the entire piece in bubble wrap.

If your work is being transported by a courier, a final step is to wrap your painting in a double-wall cardboard box. The box should be large enough to fit the painting snugly, but not so large that it allows movement. For larger works being shipped overseas, or for glazed pieces, consider using a wooden crate. While this requires additional effort, preparation, and cost, it offers greater assurance that your painting will remain safe during transit or storage. For larger paintings, it is best to use a specialised courier who has experience of handling artworks. Many courier services offer insurance for valuable pieces, which is especially important when transporting across long distances.

Storing your work

There will be times when you need to store your artwork before sending it out to a gallery or to its new home. Proper storage can make all the difference in keeping your work in pristine condition.

For works on paper, store them flat, preferably without stacking them on top of each other. If stacking is unavoidable, place a layer of glassine paper between each piece to protect the painted surfaces from direct contact. Always ensure there is enough space for your pieces to breathe, especially during curing periods.

For artwork on cradled wooden panels, canvases, and framed pieces, using purpose-built shelving is a space-saving and protective option. Shelving ensures that artworks are not stacked directly on top of each other, which, for larger and heavier works, could lead to warping or damage. When storing paintings this way,

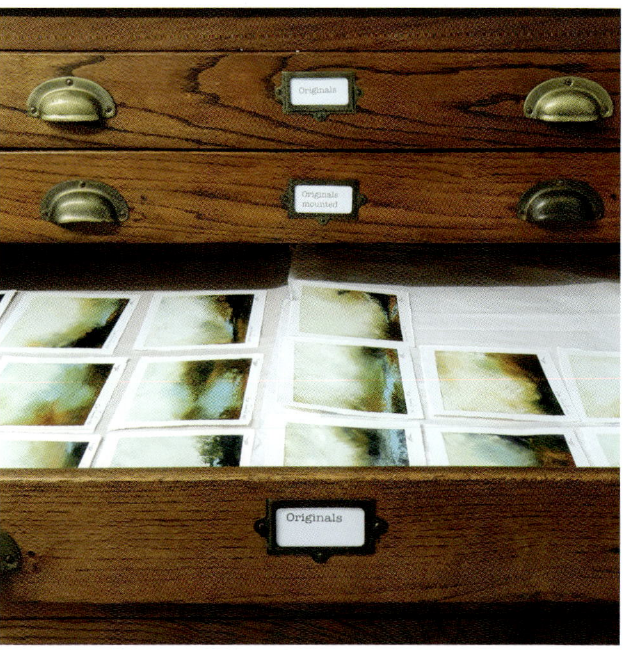

An old architect's plan chest is perfect for storing and stacking unframed works on paper. Its flat, spacious drawers provide ample room to keep artwork safe and organised, preventing bending or creasing. This type of storage not only protects your pieces from dust and damage, but also makes it easy to access and view your work.

wrap them carefully paying particular attention to the corners and surface, to protect them from contact with other pieces. This will also help to avoid scuffing of edges when removing larger works from the shelves. For a sustainable option for storing your larger work consider investing in a purpose made art bag.

If your artwork is framed or includes frame hanging hardware, stack pieces face-to-face to avoid damage. Hanging hardware can scratch painting surfaces or, more commonly, the front of frames when works are stacked incorrectly. For efficiency and ease of identification, label your wrapped artworks so you can quickly find specific pieces without needing to unwrap them.

Storing and transporting your artwork requires careful attention to detail but with the right precautions, you can ensure your paintings remain in excellent condition. Whether you are working on a wet piece or preparing to ship a finished work, the key is to provide adequate protection, use proper materials, and select experienced couriers when necessary.

THE LIGHT OF 100 DAYS

In 2021, during a challenging period marked by widespread COVID restrictions, I decided to participate in the Instagram 100-day project to bring focus to my painting. Typically, I plan my year around exhibitions, so committing to this three-month project was an unusual choice. However, it provided structure, opened new opportunities, and resulted in the creation of a substantial body of work. The concept was simple: to create a small 10 × 10cm painting each day, reflecting the weather and creating a diary of the changing seasons.

The project expanded in scope when I decided that all 100 paintings should be exhibited together as an installation, allowing visitors to fully appreciate its scale. This decision introduced challenges: how to achieve this without exceeding my budget and within limited space and time. Given the size of each painting, it was also crucial that the frames did not cover any part of the artwork as a rebate frame would.

My framers devised an innovative and budget-friendly solution that allowed me to handle much of the final framing process myself. This involved bonding each painting to wooden panels, varnishing them, and placing them into pre-made frames. To meet the unique requirements of the project, the framers adapted a frame moulding by flipping it side-on to create shallow tray frames, perfectly suited to hold the individual paintings. Their innovative approach not only solved practical challenges, but also underscored the invaluable role that professional framers play in helping artists realise their creative ideas.

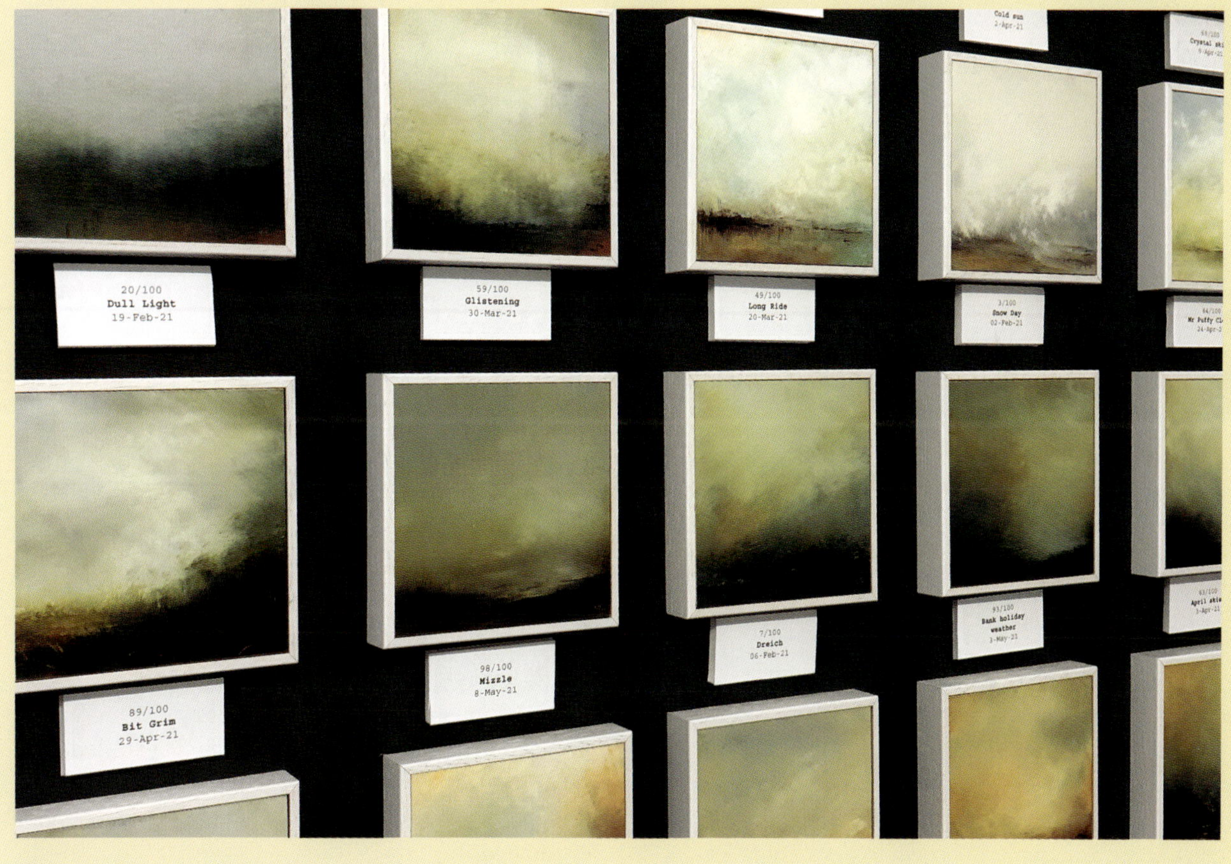

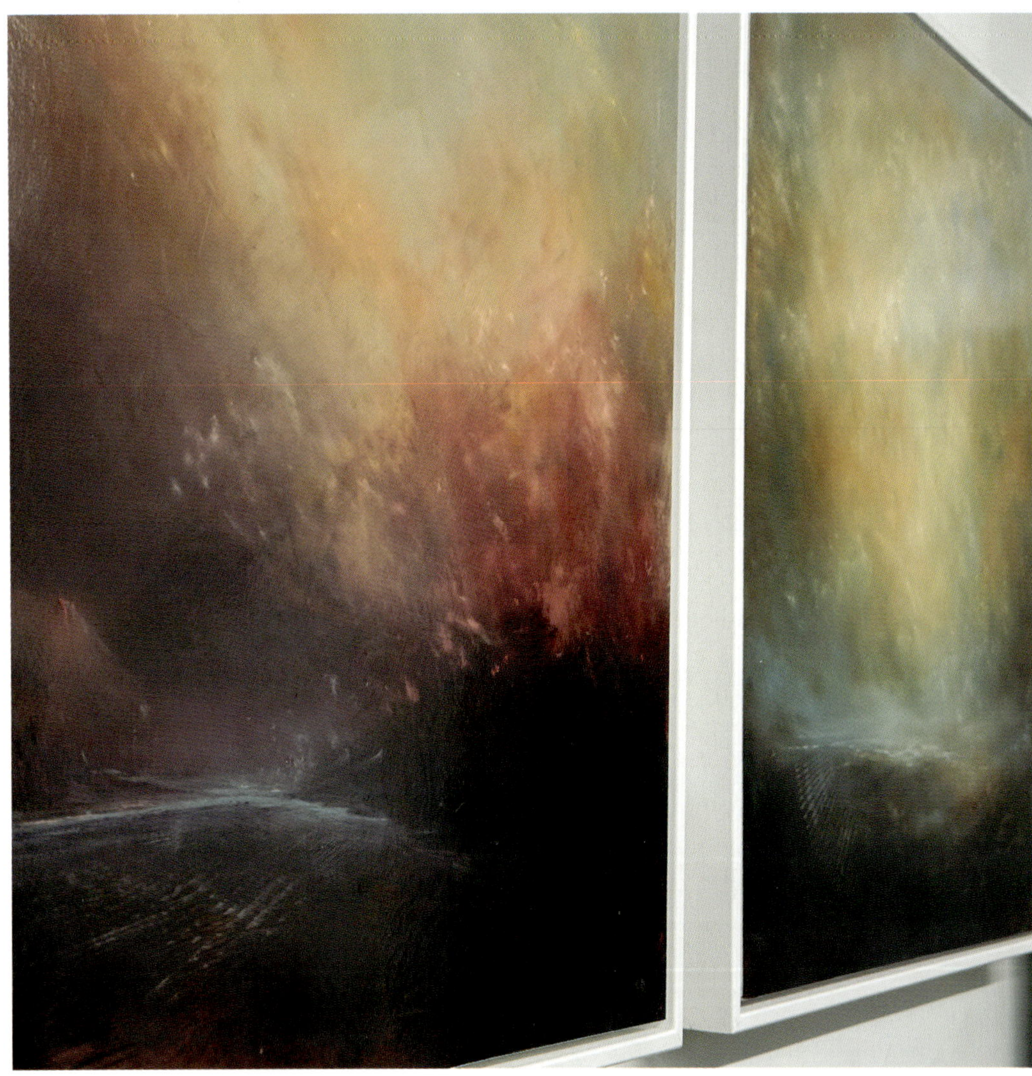

Audra and *Carried on the Wind*, two large paintings on cradled panels, were completed with simple white wooden tray frames, enhancing both their protection and presentation. The clean framing complements the work without distraction, allowing the textures and colours to take centre stage, while providing a polished, gallery-ready finish.

CONCLUSION

Working with cold wax has opened exciting avenues for innovation in my art and encouraged me to embrace spontaneity. Throughout this book, I have shared my techniques and experiences to inspire you to do the same: to find joy in creative exploration.

It may be an odd thing to say as the conclusion to a book such as this, but in truth, the best way I have found of developing my talent as a practising artist is to play, to experiment and to take risks, which does include allowing myself to fail. Things do not always have to go to plan – the mistake or digression may lead you somewhere wonderful, somewhere you would never have otherwise thought of going.

So be bold; you won't always get it right, but if you're paying attention, you will learn. And hopefully you will have some fun along the way.

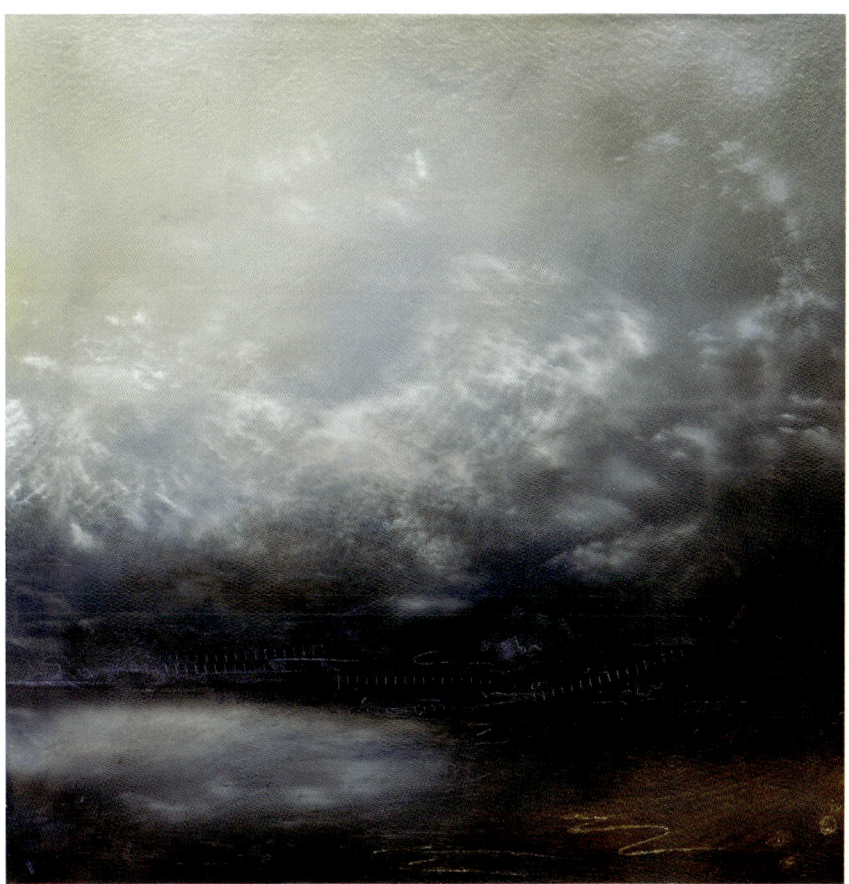

Autumn's arrival, 30 x 30 cm, oil, cold wax and gold leaf on board.

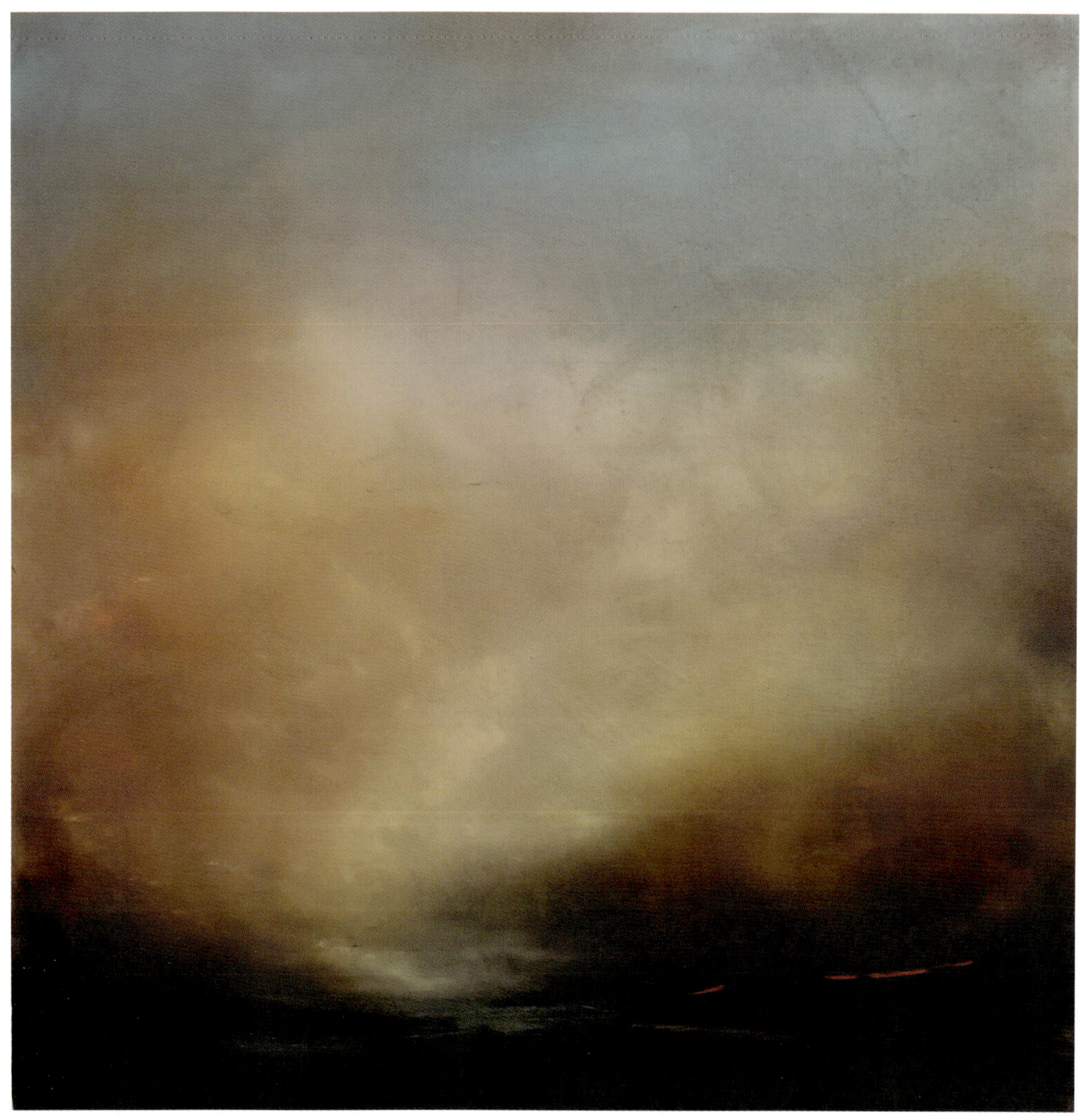

Blush, 30 x 30 cm, oil and cold wax on board.

SUPPLIERS

UK & EUROPE

Artpakk sustainable art bags - https://www.artpakk.com/
Bina Shah's bamboo tools - https://www.binashah.co.uk/
Jackson's art supplies – www.jacksonsart.com
L. Cornelissen & Son art supplies - https://www.cornelissen.com/
Messermeister silicon tools - https://messermeister-europe.com/
The Art Works Framing - https://artworksframing.co.uk/
Thomas Petit glass barens - https://thomaspetitglass.com/
Wallace Seymour art supplies - https://www.wallaceseymour.co.uk/

USA

Blick art materials - https://www.dickblick.com/
Cold wax academy - https://coldwaxacademy.com/shop/
Messermeister silicon tools - https://messermeister.com/

CANADA

Gwartzman's art supplies - https://gwartzmans.com/

AUSTRALIA

The Sydney art store - https://thesydneyartstore.com.au/

BIBLIOGRAPHY

Albers, J. *Interaction of Color, 50th anniversary edition* (Yale University, 2013)

Casey, TM. *The Oil Painters Color Handbook: A Contemporary Guide to Color Mixing, Pigments, Palettes and Harmony* (Monacelli Studio, 2022)

Coles, D, *Chromatopia: An Illustrated History of Colour* (Thames Hudson, 2018)

Crowell,R & McLaughlin, J. *Cold wax medium: Techniques, Concepts & Conversations* (Squeegee Press, 2016)

Doerner, M. *The Materials of the Artist and their use in Painting* (translated edition) (Harcourt, Brace & Company, 1921).

Hornung, D. *Colour: A Workshop for Artists and Designers* (Laurence King, 2012)

Jackson's Art Supplies. *Paper guide* (Jackson's Art Supplies, 2021)

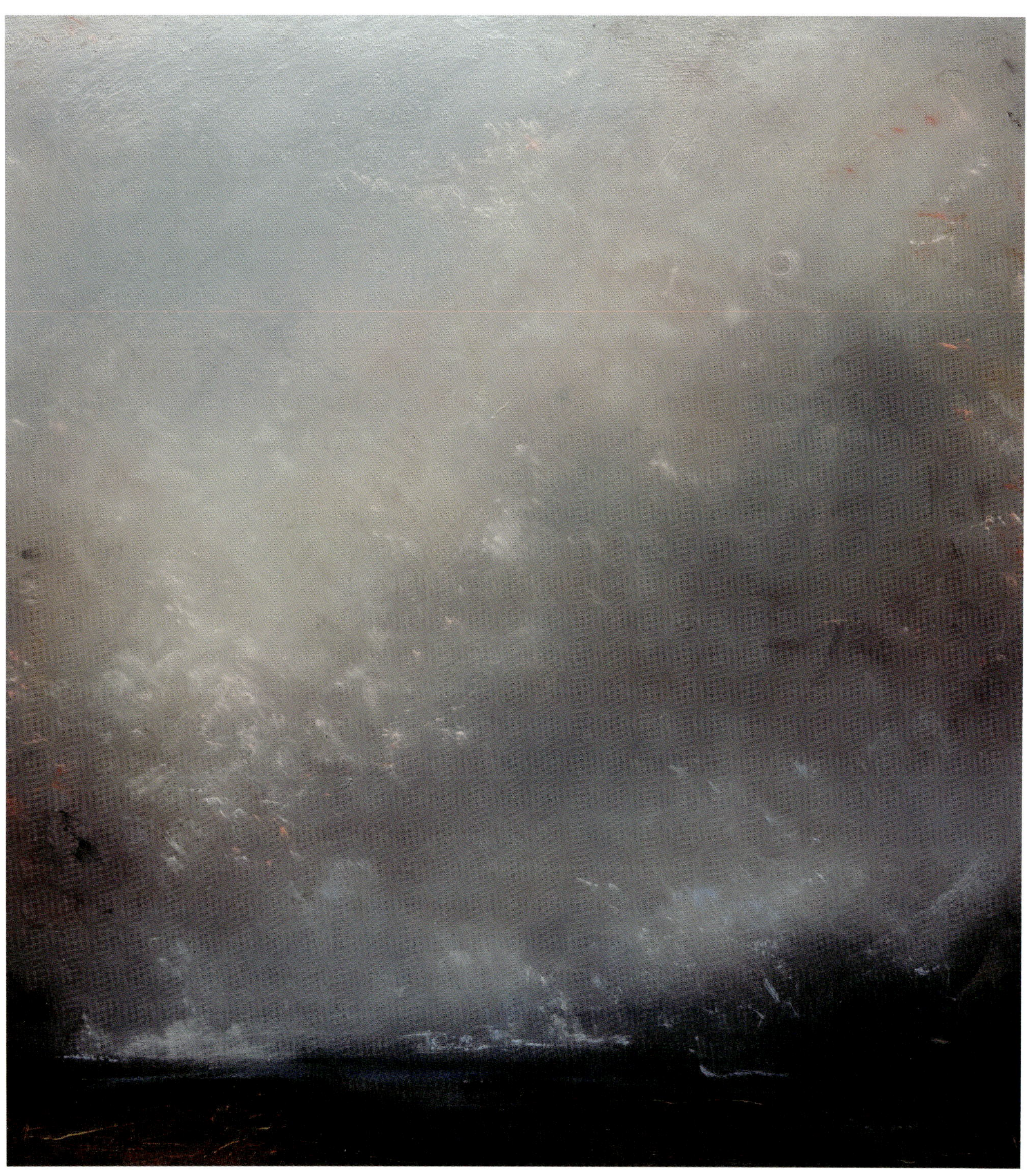

Soft wind, 50 x 50 cm, oil, cold wax and gold leaf on board.

CONTRIBUTORS

Paula Dunn (Author)
Instagram: @pauladunnartist
Website: https://pauladunnartist.com/

Caroline Mackintosh ASWA
Instagram: @caromackintosh_art
Website: https://carolinemackintosh.co.uk/

Bina Shah
Instagram: @Bina5hah
Website: https://www.binashah.co.uk/

Court Spencer
Instagram: @court_spencer
Website: https://www.courtspencer.com/

Sophie Velzian
Instagram: @sophievelzian
Website: https://sophievelzian.co.uk/

Photographers

Ian Burdall
Instagram: @ianburdall

Simon Hylton
Website: https://www.hyltonphotography.co.uk/

Jonathon Smith
Website: https://square-studios.co.uk/

Index

First published in 2025 by
The Crowood Press Ltd
Ramsbury, Marlborough
Wiltshire SN8 2HR

enquiries@crowood.com
www.crowood.com

This impression 2026

British Library Cataloguing-in-Publication Data
A catalogue record for this book is available from the British Library.

For product safety-related questions, contact:
productsafety@crowood.com

ISBN 978 0 7198 4551 2

Typeset by Envisage IT
Cover design by Sergey Tsvetkov
Printed and bound in India by Nutech Print Services Pvt. Ltd.

ACKNOWLEDGEMENTS
This book is dedicated with much love to Nick. Thank you for helping me articulate my ideas, for not laughing *too much* at my clunky grammar, and for your unwavering love, encouragement, and patience.

To Rebecca Crowell – your knowledge, generosity, and teaching have guided me on this path with oils and cold wax, reigniting my joy for painting. My deepest thanks also to Sophie Velzian, Caroline Mackintosh ASWA, Bina Shah, and Court Spencer for their invaluable contributions and incredible patience with my last-minute requests.

To Martin at The Art Works – your extensive knowledge of framing and creative solutions for my random projects have been invaluable – thank you. And to Ian Burdall, for your time, patience, friendship, and expertise and for ensuring the photographs in this book are the best they can be.

Finally, a heartfelt thank you to The Crowood Press for reaching out to me and giving me the opportunity to write this book. Your support and encouragement throughout this process has been invaluable.